THE MIRAGE OF CHINA

Culture and Politics / Politics and Culture

General Editors:
Laura Nader, *University of California, Berkeley*
Rik Pinxten, *Ghent University, Belgium*
Ellen Preckler, *Ghent University, Belgium*

Cultural Identity, whether real or imagined, has become an important marker of societal differentiation. This series focuses on the interplay of politics and culture and offers a forum for analysis and discussion of such key issues as multiculturalism, racism, and human rights.

Volume 1
Europe's New Racism: Causes, Manifestations and Solutions
Edited by **The Evens Foundation**

Volume 2
Culture and Politics: Identity and Conflict in a Multicultural World
Edited by **Rik Pinxten, Ghislain Verstraete,** and **Chia Longman**

Volume 3
Racism in Metropolitan Areas
Edited by **Rik Pinxten** and **Ellen Preckler**

Volume 4
When God Comes to Town: Religious Traditions in Urban Contexts
Edited by **Rik Pinxten** and **Lisa Dikomitis**

THE MIRAGE OF CHINA

Xin Liu

Berghahn Books
NEW YORK • OXFORD

Published in 2009 by
Berghahn Books

www.berghahnbooks.com

Library of Congress Cataloging-in-Publication Data

Liu, Xin, 1957–

The mirage of China / Xin Liu.
    p. cm.
Includes bibliographical references and indexes.
ISBN 978-1-84545-545-3 (hbk.) -- ISBN 978-0-85745-611-3 (pbk.)
    1. Capitalism—China. 2. Capitalism—Social aspects—China. 3. Globalization—
Social aspects—China. 4. Globalization—Economic aspects—China. 5. China—
Economic conditions—2000–. 6. Social change—China. I. Title.
HC427.95.L588 2009
330.951—dc22

                                                                2008053755

British Library Cataloguing in Publication Data

A catalogue record for this book is available from
the British Library.

Printed in the United States on acid-free paper

ISBN: 978-0-85745-611-3 (paperback)   ISBN: 978-0-85745-612-0 (ebook)

If one may say of the revolutionary period that it runs wild, one would have to say of the present age that it runs badly.

— Søren Kierkegaard, *The Present Age*

It seemed to me that one could set two intellectual projects in opposition. The first rightfully appears to have been a dead end: the project of metaphysics of the present or of an epochal thinking. The second, I believe, is endowed with a more solid philosophical basis and a clearer signification: the project of an anthropology of modernity.

— Vincent Descombes, *The Barometer of Modern Reason*

Contents

Preface

The mirage of China, as both local metaphor and global reality, is a mirror image in and for the contemporary world. As I shall argue, the world of China, contrary to the common or journalistic view, is not the Chinese world; it is a symptomatic moment of our world at the present time.[1] Globalization as both a discursive and a material force is historically produced, differently so in different social worlds, according to their different cultural schemes of signification. The converse is also true: histories of different social worlds are globally made in and of specific places, for, to a greater or lesser extent, their cultural schemes of signification are reproduced in the global production of different local histories.[2] Today's world is one marked by signs of digital capitalism and global capitalist expansion, and China has been increasingly integrated into the global system of production and consumption. Nevertheless, what remains uncertain or indefinite is our genealogical relationship to this staggering social giant—"a new leviathan."[3] A genealogical relation, as exemplified in the segmentary lineage organization of Southeast China, is both lived and written, for it involves inevitably a hermeneutic production of oneself in relation to one's ancestors and siblings, consanguineous or affinal. A hermeneutic production

1. The term "moment" is used in the Aristotelian sense to indicate the inseparability of a part from its whole, such as in the case of the color from a tree. In other words, what is conveniently called "China" is a color—rather than a branch or a leaf—of the contemporary world. It is an intrinsic part—an organic moment—of the world rather than an element or a separable part of it. See Aristotle (1979, books 25 and 26, 97–98).

2. As an anthropologist might have noticed, these two sentences paraphrase Sahlins's opening words in his *Islands of History* (1985).

3. Hobbes's *Leviathan* ([1651] 1962) is here invoked for the reason that the rise of this social giant seems to pose, once again, the question of knowledge and governance as a generalizable political inquiry into a new type of "commonwealth," global or globalizing. See also Collingwood (1971).

of self-understanding, as we have been reminded by Gadamer and Ricoeur, would constitute a transformative practice of reciprocal conditioning in and through which genealogical knowledge is produced in the production of the subject of such knowledge. That is, the hermeneutic praxis would empirically make the object of knowledge and analytically remake its subject at once.

The past couple of decades have witnessed an explosion in studies of China, although in my opinion such studies have hardly improved our understanding of that social elephant. A chief intellectual error lies in the positivistic-empiricist presupposition adopted by those who would tend to assume that counting or measuring various types of mushrooms alone could lead to a comprehension of their organic nature as an edible plant. They presume that a purely empirical accumulation of positive knowledge about China can lead to a proper comprehension of it. It is therefore no surprise that we are overwhelmed by the explosive accumulation of empirical data, such as in measuring the rapidly growing heights of China's urban space or in calculating the slow declines of its Gini coefficients. We seem to get lost in a jungle of data and facts of our own making. However, such emerging empiricity and positivity, brought about by the global conditioning of "local knowledge," are not yet seriously questioned. These new forms of life and knowledge that are shaping—and being shaped by—the data and facts of contemporary China must be scrutinized. The coming of age in modern development in and of the People's Republic of China has reincarnated a positivistic spirit, for China has provided a new location for the global application of an old set of conceptual schemes. In such an elephantine world of material development, this neo-positivistic spirit—made by, and yet making, global economic transformation—has generated a series of new empiricities that have become the basis for studies of China. On such grounds, as we have recently witnessed, new platforms of public debate have arisen and become institutionalized; new modes of authority and governance have been made or invented; new regions of knowledge and knowledge practice have been created and produced; new disciplines and fields of social sciences have been put into place; new forms of institutions and new modes of institutional practices have come into being and been legitimized. These recent developments still await an anthropological investigation, and such an investigation, going beyond the conventional confines of anthropology (see, e.g., Rabinow 1999, 167–182; cf. Cassirer 1944, 1–20), will make up the central focus of my study.[4]

This project was initially conceived more than a decade ago when the field of anthropology was searching for an intellectual reorientation.[5] The hope of

4. See Ong and Collier (2005) and Rabinow (1996, 2003) for other attempts to lay a new conceptual groundwork for the discipline of anthropology.
5. A series of works could well indicate the path traveled by the anthropologist in the last couple of decades of the twentieth century. See, for example, Boon (1982); Clifford (1986, 1988);

developing "an anthropology of modernity" was one of its goals. This treatise, as a patient reader will see, is a partial response to such a disciplinary reorientation that has sought to step away from older epistemological conventions. However, my ideas have changed over the years, and as a result the conceptual framework of the study has become broader than initially conceived, thus delaying its completion. The original plan was to show how Chinese society became statisticalized in the late twentieth century, and my thinking then followed the line of Ian Hacking's work on statistics and probability theory. His studies of statistical governance and probabilistic logicality as a historically specific mode of social practice, making new forms of authority and surveillance possible in modern societies, continue to be relevant (see, e.g., Hacking 1975, 1990). However, due (and thanks) to the delay in writing it, this book, instead of taking up China as yet another example demonstrating the effectivity of modern technology, focuses on the problematic of life and knowledge in and for the contemporary world by means of an anthropological exemplification of what is called "China." In other words, it is now less about a specific transformation in the world of China and more about the general condition of possibility for "being in the world"—both within and outside the People's Republic. The global world is both larger and smaller than the world of China: larger because the world of China is made within the historical horizons of a modern world; smaller because a particular mode of historical development taking place in the People's Republic has enriched or will enrich the interior space of modernity. This study will try to grasp the significance and signification of China's particular mode of becoming as a symptomatic moment of our being in the world.

The immediate material impact of China is now felt almost everywhere in the world. However, the importance of such an effect, resulting in sentiments that are both old and new, is far from being clearly, or rightly, understood. While the mirage of China is still alluring, we need to comprehend its significance, to see it as a way of understanding our own life and reasoning. This is a key intellectual task of our times.

* * *

Let us recapitulate the argument. This is a study of how China came to put a new dress—seemingly scientific or modern—onto its not-yet-so-new gigantic social body. The empirical object of inquiry is about how the world of China has become statisticalized, that is, how a quantitative mode of self-objectification has come

Fabian (1983); Fardon (1990); Geertz (1988, 2000); Gupta and Ferguson (1997); James, Hockey, and Dawson (1997); Marcus (1998); Marcus and Fischer (1986); Rabinow (1977, 1986); Sangren (1988); Sperber (1985); Stocking (1992). For a synoptic overview of the four main anthropological traditions, that is, British, German, French, and American, see Barth et al. (2005).

into being on the ruins of the Maoist revolution. The ethnographic attempt is to show the emergence of an epistemological fissure that has separated today's China from its Maoist past. In short, it is a conceptual ethnography or, rather, an ethnographic investigation of concepts. It is an anthropological inquiry into two modes of life and knowledge that have made up a "history of the present" for contemporary China.

Three cautionary points should be stated at the outset. First, in terms of its style, this study should be read as an analytical story about the changes that have come to constitute the new face of China. It is a descriptive account of the emergence of an epistemological rift—in both the mentality of governance and the sentimentality of life—that has produced a different outlook for the People's Republic. Since the materials and the object of analysis are concepts or conceptual forces, I have taken "ethnography" to be analytical description in a narrative form. That is, I have presented my argument, albeit highly conceptual, in a storytelling format. The last two chapters, which aim to bring the rift into clear view, could be read as an extended conclusion for the study.

Second, in view of recent social science and anthropological debates, the work intends to address two particular theoretical concerns. In responding to the idea of developing an anthropology of modernity, this study aims to show how "categories" of statistical thinking, by which experiences are (re)appropriated, have arrived in the vast world of China. This is therefore not a study of the country's socio-political or socio-economic development per se; rather, it is an anthropological analysis of the a priori categories of statistical reasoning reborn and relived in the People's Republic. In other words, it is an ethnography of the condition of possibility for a certain kind of experience to become real, that is, to be or to be reckoned as "factual." The second concern is with the problem of "global knowledge" and how the statistical or quantitative objectification of the world came to be crowned as "true" science in another lane of history. The problem of knowledge in the domains of life and governance is central to the intellectual focus of this study. It is the conceptual scheme in change that has made up the analytical core of this project, for globalization, however it may be viewed, should also be understood as a categorical (re)production of certain life forms.

Third, in terms of the choice and employment of materials, I have made use of three kinds of empirical data: ethnography, documents, and interviews. Over the years, in persistently working on the relationship of the empirical to the theoretical, I have realized that there is no one-directional journey of verification of a theoretical point by an unproblematic use of ethnographic "facts," for it is the problematic status of "facts" and "truth" as a historical emergence that I have tried to analyze. In other words, "facts" can become "factual" only under a particular historical condition of emergence. Raw materials are already cooked, in a sense, while "theory," so to speak, is always written.

This book has been composed as a whole, and I hope that it will be read in this way. The prologue begins with an ethnographic account of the emergence of statistical thinking and provides a contextualization of the new face of China, which has become modern in its quantitative mode of self-objectification. Part 1 includes two chapters that show the rise of statistical reasoning, especially in the field of governmental statistics, as described in chapter 1. Chapter 2 deals with the idea of facts and truth, whose importance was revitalized by an official and scholarly appropriation of the statistical datum. Part 2, including another two chapters, reviews the debate on the nature of statistical knowledge. Through a detailed account of changes in the field of economic statistics, which has become a dominant sphere of social knowledge in China today, it shows how an old model of social sciences, that of the Soviet Union, was buried by a new model, the modern or global one. Part 3, including three chapters, begins with an ethnographic sketch of the return of notions such as luck or fate or chance, by which I hope to show that probabilistic theories of large numbers have come to assume a greater function as the logic for social life. As a scientific measurement of marketable reality, the distributive stability of the normal curve, with its x-bar and t-test, could not guarantee who would "get rich first," an official slogan of the 1980s. A statistical theory of random choice thus provided a perfect explanation for China's rapid economic growth as well as its devastating social disparity. Chapters 6 and 7 present the Maoist politics of subjection in contradistinction to the current mode of life and governance, which has become global in its ambition and motivation. My theoretical intent is to capture the epistemological rupture that has separated today's China from its recent past, resulting in a different mentality and outlook for the People's Republic.

Prologue: Making Up Numbers

One late afternoon, on our way to the National Bureau of Statistics, Pannong and I were chatting in a taxi, the least expensive kind, a *xiali*, which cost only one Chinese dollar and twenty cents per kilometer, a favorite choice for most people in the capital of the People's Republic at the threshold of a new century. I was conducting fieldwork for a new project, and Pannong, a businessman based in South China, whom I knew through another connection prior to this trip, was hoping to meet with a friend who worked at the Bureau. After the taxi started moving, the driver asked, "Where the fuck are we going?"

"San Lihe," replied Pannong calmly, showing no surprise or uneasiness at the linguistic habits of the driver, who, as a typical local resident, could elegantly integrate into his manner of speaking a large number of obscene words in such a way that would offend no one but simply enhance the beauty of the dialect of his native town.[1] A faint smirk crept across Pannong's face as he told the driver where the Bureau was located.

"Which fucking part of San Lihe?" the taxi driver asked again with discernible impatience.

"Well, close to the end of it, on the west fucking side." Pannong grinned at me.

"Fine, but where the fuck are you actually going?"

"Do you know the Bureau of Statistics then?" Judging by his tone, I didn't think that Pannong wanted to converse with the taxi driver. However, the driver, friendly and enthusiastic, was talkative.

---

1. For an outsider, this particular linguistic habit might well be considered uncivil, if not barbarian. An interesting commentary on similar scenes in nineteenth-century China can be found in Arthur Smith's infamous study, *Chinese Characteristics* ([1898] 2001, 219–221).

"You mean the fucking place where they make up numbers?" asked the taxi driver. "I know that place for sure, but they don't fucking allow us in. We'll have to stop outside the gate, and you've got to fucking walk a bit."

"Yes, you're right, the place where they *make up* numbers." Pannong laughed at his expression and turned to me. "Did you hear that? The place where Weiping works is called 'the place that makes up numbers'!" Then he said to the driver, "That's fine, but get us as close as possible to the main entrance."

"There are fucking soldiers there, you know, at the gate. I don't know why they have to have soldiers—I mean, security guards. Well, that's what's happening everywhere these days. All the places where rich people live are guarded by the guards. These guys are sometimes worse than the police. Well, that must be the way it is nowadays." The taxi driver would have gone into a longer sociological analysis of the wealthy, but Pannong interrupted him.

"You don't seem to believe these numbers, like the 8 percent goal of national economic growth announced by the government." Pannong was intrigued by the taxi driver's earlier reference to making up numbers.

"Do *you*?" he responded coolly and with emphasis. "Do *you* believe in the official growth figures?"

"Well, to some extent, I must confess that I do."

"Me fucking too. To *some* extent."

"What do you mean by that?"

"I mean, when and who."

"What do you mean by 'when' and 'who'?"

"I mean, *when* I want to believe them, I fucking do, but it all depends on *who* is telling me what to believe."

This exchange gave the driver an opportunity to deliver a speech, which was probably neither entirely invented on the spot nor fully rehearsed. Eloquently addressing an imaginary audience, he began to describe his own life—his personal and familial life—to us in the back seat. In a slightly animated tone, fully confident of his knowledge, he talked about the dilemma of living in the capital and, particularly, his distrust of government statistics.

"You know, you probably don't know anyway. Let me tell you what you should know but don't. You people look like you're from the South. Am I fucking right? I can tell by your manners and the way you dress how much you make. We taxi drivers have good eyes and senses. The fucking salary you make always hangs on your face. A prostitute makes more than a decent man, like my father-in-law. The old man works like a madman but makes almost nothing, you know. You probably don't know anyway. I listened to the news on the radio yesterday. Everyone listens to the radio while driving because there's nothing else to do. Most of them listen to some shitty programs, but I prefer the news. I can't watch television while driving, can I? So I listen to the radio. The news on television is much better, of course, because you can see what is there on the screen. But you have to manage with your radio while you're driving.

"Anyway, where was I? Yes, yesterday's news said that there has been a leap in economic growth, and now our average income is more than thirty thousand a year. Do you think they're telling the truth or making it up? I'm not sure about this. Your people may know better, but I fucking doubt it. Is it something like what happened during the Great Leap Forward of the late 1950s? Everything was made up to fool us. Nobody believes the Great Leap Forward today, but everyone believed it at the time. Don't you see what I mean? I hope we're not doing the same thing. If there is such great development, where's the fucking money? Perhaps in the pockets of all the rich guys. I haven't seen an increase in my earnings for ten years! I work more than ten hours a day but make less than two thousand, and I don't know what the government has been talking about. The news makes no fucking sense to me. The numbers must be made up. Why? Who knows. Perhaps the government fakes just like a woman does sometimes. Don't you think so?"

It is perhaps true that the taxi driver's commentary was triggered more by the social disparity that has accompanied the rapid economic growth in the world of China, a material reality now officiated according to the statistical datum. Had it been a longer journey, we would have been given a thorough sociological analysis of everyday life in the capital. However, we soon arrived at a muscular building, gray and tall—the National Bureau of Statistics or the "place that makes up numbers." We got out of the taxi and went across the street to the entrance. The security guards seemed to be wearing some sort of army uniform, which was probably why they were referred to as soldiers. Pannong asked one of them, who was standing on the left side of the entrance, "Can we get in to see Wang Zhuren, one of your Chiefs in the Bureau?" The guard raised his lower jaw, pointing us to the other side of the entrance, where we saw a reception office in which guests must register the purpose of their visit and identify their host.

"Hello, we have come to see Wang Zhuren," Pannong said to an old man inside the office.

"Which Wang?"

"Wang Weiping, the Director of the Industrial Sampling Survey Office."

The man phoned someone inside the Bureau, probably to check with Chief Wang's office. Idling outside the entrance of the Bureau, I looked around and saw, behind the sleepy leaves of a big tree on the other side of the street, an enormous banner hanging on the wall of another tall building: "Guarantee 7 percent. Aim for 8 percent of GDP Growth." In the media, this was referred to as "hoping for the 8 percent while securing the 7 percent of national economic growth." This was a sentimental official slogan or, better yet, a slogan of official sentiment that, at the turn of a new century for the People's Republic, became a popular sign, an ideological sign that dwelled in a reality of its own making. In the mind of the state, *the statistical measurement of growth* and *the growth of statistical measurement* must mean the same thing. Seeing such a slogan draped on the building, one could not help but reflect that one was standing in the vicinity of the government statistical office, whose chief function, due to its increasing effectivity and efficacy, was to provide reasons and proofs for national economic development. Percentage in this case was less a pure estimation of growth and more a promise for governmental achievements. That is why the term "guarantee" was employed for the slogan: it was a pledge of psychic reassurance for the nation.

Chief Wang finally came out to greet us. "Hello, Pannong, my old friend!" he exclaimed, apologizing to us for the inconvenience. He said, "I did not realize that our security system has been raised to the level of a prison." Although Chief Wang acted as if he were joking, his comment revealed a truth: the security system for his office, which had been fully established in the early 1990s, has been increasingly tightened ever since. As would be made clear, this reflected a change in the Bureau's significance for the official hierarchy as a whole. More and more it has been considered a sacred institution for the production of socio-economic truths. As Chief Wang related later, the value of the National Bureau of Statistics in the governmental hierarchy has increased since the late 1970s. The significance of the Bureau has been increasingly recognized by the state, which sees it as being able to predict economic development.

There are three identifiable layers of officials in the Bureau, and their interactions are essential to its functioning as a whole. The very top layer consists of the directors, a small group of decision makers who work closely with the General Director of the Bureau. Their chief responsibility lies not within but outside the Bureau, that is, they are responsible for communications with the central government. In other words, this group, at the tip of a hierarchical iceberg, is not working on data but is communicating it to the political leaders of the central government. In terms of management of the Bureau, it is they who give orders to the section or division chiefs below them. The second layer of officials consists of division or section chiefs, who are responsible for the everyday administration of the Bureau. According to Chief Wang, those in this layer—to which he belonged—constitute the most important force in the Bureau. Their superiors do not work on the data, and their subordinates do not know where the data should go. The third layer consists of those who actually work on the data. Trained for specific statistical work, they can be easily replaced. Under Chief Wang, who had promoted to Section Chief a decade ago, the main responsibility for a team working on the data of industrial development included collecting data, verifying reports from provinces and cities, and producing tabular matrixes of statistics for various purposes. These office workers have to work on their computers all day long, and they do not have much responsibility outside the reach of their limited task of producing data. They "make up numbers" in the basic categories or the elementary forms, and it is through their hands that the material life of the statistical datum acquires an organic form. It is their labor, which will never bear the imprint of their names, that brings the representation of economic development to life. According to Chief Wang, a most important aspect of the Bureau's daily activities consists of the interactions between the second and third layers of officials. It is at this intersection that the routine business of "making up numbers" takes place.

"Do have some tea," offered Chief Wang when we entered his bright, spacious office. While tasting the tea, Pannong turned around and said to me, "Chief Wang was my college mate, and we used to play Go or Bridge all the time, day and night. The business world grabbed my attention after graduation, and my friend turned himself into an official, as you can see. He has a superb mathematical mind, but in my case, I'm ashamed to say, what I learned in college has totally gone back to my teachers. Nothing is left in my brain—it is entirely empty. Well, I might just add that doing business requires no knowledge but instead a great deal of sense and sensibility of a particular kind. It cannot be taught in the classroom but can be learned only through practice. Business knowledge is *practical* knowledge, and business skills are *practical* skills."

Pannong wished to elaborate on his business experience but was interrupted by a quick knock on the door. It was Chief Huang, Wang's superior and next-door colleague, who had come to inform Wang that there would be a meeting the following morning. Having been briefly introduced, Huang sat down with us and said, "I know that each of you, whether a businessman or a professor, is an expert of some sort. However, we, myself and my colleagues in the Bureau, are also supposed to be experts—a special kind, perhaps, different from other types." We were not allowed a chance to reply, for Chief Huang went on in an exciting and yet unexpected direction.

"What is the difference? Let me tell you—squarely and honestly—the truth: we cannot live our life today without statistics, for we must have accurate and correct figures in order to determine how to develop. This Bureau is not a usual governmental office. It is a special branch of the state, which cannot survive without statistical information. Although we do not make policies ourselves, we make it possible for the central government to make policies. In other words, we serve as the necessary mechanism for decision making by obtaining and accumulating socio-economic data." A man of sharp thought, Huang's manner reflected his confidence and experience. He was an influential chief in the Bureau and a rising star in the perception of colleagues such as Chief Wang. Huang was in his late forties, perhaps one or two years younger than Chief Wang, who was Huang's associate director in the office. Being in charge of the Industrial Sampling Survey Office, capable and confident, Huang spoke in a decisive tone and directed our attention to the problems of the Bureau.

"Yes, you are perfectly right. There are far more people working for the Bureau nowadays than when I came in 1982. It was a small office back then. Its expansion is indeed comparable to the growth of the city itself. The city is different now, and so is the Bureau. But there are many problems in the city as well as in our office. To be frank, I don't think we have done our job as we should have. We are incapable of doing the work assigned because my colleagues don't know what a statistician should be engaged in. This problem has always been with our Bureau, and it has become a most cumbersome obstacle for our performance and progress. Simply put, what we need here are not grand theorists or macroeconomists. We do not need the smartest guys on the earth who consider themselves more original than Marx or Keynes. Instead, what we want and need are people who can work on the numerical details. Do you know what I mean? Chief Wang knows for sure. A large number of my colleagues think of themselves as macroeconomists. They can spend hours talking about their fantastic ideas of development, but they refuse to improve the quality of their tabularized statistical figures. Some of my colleagues might be better politicians than statisticians. The labor of statistical work should be spent on calculation—not on speculation of some theoretical sort."

Becoming a bit agitated in his speech, Chief Huang continued, "What can be done about this? Whenever you talk to your colleagues, they tend to give you a marvelous economic theory about how to change the country, such as the best strategies to reform our financial institutions or the most effective means to curb inflation, etc. Give me a break! My dear colleagues! The truth is that before we make any decisions about what we must do, we need to know the facts in the first place. What is going on will have to be grasped by calculation and computation, that is, by means of statistical tabulation and analysis of data and facts. Our job, as I understand it, is to draw a reality map from the actual statistical analysis and tabulation. In other words, we do not make policies, but we provide the statistical information for doing so. However, my dear colleagues would wish themselves to be in charge of the central government affairs. I must say that in their impractical tiny minds, big ideas have grown that are misplaced and useless to us." Chief Huang stopped for a second to sip some tea.

"Well, I would have thought—which might not be true—that you and Chief Wang would have the opportunity to choose whom you want to work for you," Pannong commented, grasping the chance to get into the conversation.

"Well, yes and no. There is an examination nowadays by which we select those who wish to come to work for us. They are chosen by the Bureau as a whole, and some of them are assigned to our division each year. The way in which new people are selected is not what I'm talking about. The problem is *a habit of thought*, which is my chief concern. No matter who was chosen, almost everyone was trained to think like a politician whose vision would cover the entire world. This is a habit of thought, which is persistent and resilient. We should not have this kind of mind here, and we certainly do not need it. But the Bureau is full of this kind of people—grand and imaginative in scope but lacking attention to accuracy and detail. What can I do? Patience, perhaps. What else? I have kept telling my colleagues what they should do, but they have made no change in their mode of thinking. I am so tired of those who keep talking about national political decisions or macroeconomic policies as if they were in a Politburo meeting with the Premier listening, I mean, across the marble desk."

A noticeable grin crept over his face when Huang mentioned "the marble desk." There seemed to have existed a sort of "private language" between Huang and Wang, for the latter immediately registered the metaphorical mentioning with a corresponding smile. We—Pannong and myself—had not expected such a lecture on the problematic nature of statistical work, especially on the difference between a politician and a statistician, a conceptual division around which Chief Huang had developed a critique of his incapable colleagues. Later on in the course of my field experience, I came to realize that Huang's commentary reflected a governmental anxiety that would express itself in a nationalistic urge for more accurate or efficient statistical knowledge. The need for statistics was a sign of the times as the country crossed the threshold of a new century. Nevertheless, the lived experiences of ethnographic fieldwork, unlike the well-cooked chapters of anthropological writing in manuscript form, consist of a series of contingent revelations, or revealing contingencies, by which a light of life and knowledge brings chaotic experiences into focus. This was indeed such a moment of anthropological revelation and ethnographic contingency.

The reference to the marble desk, as we later learned, involved a joke widely circulated in the Bureau at the time. Let me briefly retell the story. From time to time, those working for the Bureau might be called upon by the higher administration to take up a different job, perhaps more important or prestigious. Young people, or at least some of them, might consider this a good opportunity for moving up in the hierarchy of the official world. A few years ago, a friend of Huang was chosen to be the personal secretary for a top-level official in the central government. This young man, who had graduated from the same college as Chief Huang, had originally been assigned to work for the publishing house of the Bureau, which was considered an insignificant office. Huang's friend was unhappy about being trapped in an office with piles of manuscripts and papers. He wanted to leave, and soon his opportunity arrived. A senior official in the People's Congress—the equivalent of the Congress in the American political system—was looking for a personal secretary, and he was chosen. This young man left the publishing house and moved to work in an office inside the Zhongnanhai, a complex of buildings that serves as the headquarters of the central government. As those who do research on contemporary China are aware, the symbolic value of the Zhongnanhai cannot be exaggerated. The fact that one might bump into the Premier at lunch, as some

believed, would always intrigue every mind at the Bureau. Following his reas-
signment, whenever this young man met with his old friends from the Bureau,
he would casually mention the splendid arrangement of his boss's office. The
marble desk, signifying power and hierarchy, had become a metaphor among
his friends for the difference between their work as statistical laborers and the
work of decision makers at the top level of government.

"You see, the problem is that everyone imagines that he is sitting next to the
Premier, assisting him in making some great political decisions," Chief Huang
continued. "You know, this is 'the marble desk' complex of our Bureau, which
is totally different from what I have experienced in other countries. Whenever and wherever I have visited, statisticians would never consider themselves
as decision makers. Instead, they would always think of themselves as technicians of quantitative knowledge—the carpenters of statistical information
or the gardeners of tabulation and numeration. When I was in America, for
example, where the statistical spirit was most ripe, I saw how they worked for
their governments. They were laborers of tables and figures or slaves of facts
and data. They never intended to think big. Instead, they often looked small in
their ambitions and sounded modest in their projections. This is what I need in
my office: an army of good technicians of statistical knowledge. In comparison
with those advanced countries, I must say, there is a difference in the attitude of
statistical workers: they are detailed, we are grandiose; they are factual, we are
fanciful; they are technical, we are political." Chief Huang stopped for a sip of
tea and then said: "Facts are in the details, let me tell you. Are they not so?"

In this situation, one was reminded of the taxi driver's comment on "making up numbers," which was different only in that Huang's critique was cast
from an official point of view. During the national reorganization of economy
and society as the People's Republic moved into the fast lane of modern development, there came an urgent demand for the acquisition of quantitative and
statistical data. This desire for the rapid institutional expansion of statistical
knowledge was alternately an official and a popular sentiment, which could
be read as follows: facts must be *factual*, which should make them calculable;
and truth must be *truthful*, which should make it quantitative. Putting them
together means that it is in the numerical details that one should be able to find
truthful facticity. And this must or should be the job of the statistician, who
arrived on the ruins of the Maoist revolution like a milkman distributing daily
nutrition to each household in the early morning of another era. In the conventional eyes of political science or sociology, society is usually set apart from
the power of the state, which is often seen as an antagonistic or oppositional
force to civil society. However, considering life and knowledge as epistemology
rather than politics, the sentiment avowed by Huang was not so far apart from
that of the taxi driver, although, of course, the reasons for such a resemblance
were different on each side.

"Statisticians should not—and must not—be politicians," Chief Huang went on. "They should be technicians of knowledge and information. Statisticians should be spending their lives on numerical details. They should be willing to sit in front of their desks working long hours for the perfection of statistical tabulation and computation. This is what we need—or lack, to be more precise, for we do not have this kind of worker in our offices. What we do have are people—perhaps already more than we need—who do not wish to work on the numerical details but constantly fantasize about making changes in our national policies. In this sense alone, I would say, if I dare, that we are behind other advanced countries such as Western Europe or America. We need and will have only one Premier but many technicians of statistical information and knowledge. Otherwise, there will be no way of figuring out what is happening in reality. What is happening can be grasped only by means of statistical work, without which the Premier would not know what is happening to our economy and society."

Among several significant forerunners of our times, Francis Bacon (1561–1626) would have given a favorable response to Huang's passionate reaction. Although not always explicit, Huang's speech did imply that descriptive statistics, an exemplary tool of the inductive method delineated by Bacon, should constitute a new foundation of knowledge in and of the People's Republic. Chief Huang's criticism of his colleagues who behaved like politicians might be compared with Bacon's critique of the old habits of thought, which were not based on empirical facts obtainable by means of induction. Bacon's "idols," deductive in nature, symbolized the conceptual inertia that prevented true science from advancing in the field of empirical knowledge.[2] This was analogous to Huang's opinion that the minds of his colleagues were inhabited by the "idols" of inappropriate political thinking, which prevented statistical work from fulfilling its proper functions. One might also say that this spirit, reincarnated in Huang, was close to the empiricist critique of cognition exemplified in the work of John Locke (1632–1704), who placed sense and sensuality at the center of life and knowledge. The difference is that for Huang experience in its socio-economic sense should be made of nothing but the statistical datum (cf. Locke 1959). There is no doubt that the value of statistical information has increased drastically since economic reforms began in the late 1970s; however,

2. See Burtt (1939, 34–35) for Bacon's definitions of the four classes of idols: the Idols of the Tribe, the Idols of the Cave, the Idols of the Marketplace, and the Idols of the Theatre. For Bacon, the existence of these idols impeded the growth of a true scientific spirit, which must be empirical and inductive. In referencing an old signpost of the modern scientific spirit, I do not mean to argue for a parallel or homology between Bacon's era and the People's Republic today. Instead, I intend to show how an old sentiment can always be remade or felt as new. In other words, the value of antiquity does not lie in its antique value but rather in our antiquarian tastes of the present times. For a philosophical introduction to the socio-historical background of Bacon's thought, see also Russell (1945, 541–545).

in the mind of Huang, the conveyors of statistical information have not yet fully realized the value of their work. What was needed was the inculcation of the empiricist spirit in the statisticians themselves, not simply further expansion of the government's statistical institutions. Various divisions and offices of the Bureau had been put in place, with security guards at every entrance. What was missing, according to Huang, was the right attitude within the building—a place where "idols" of an older kind still occupied a predominant space.

Chief Huang was later called away by a telephone call. While his superior had been engaged in his enthusiastic critique, Chief Wang had hardly uttered a word. Instead of joining his colleague in the conversation, Wang had gone over to his desk by a window on the other side of the office several times to check something on a brand new computer. From where we sat on a comfortable, red leather sofa, we could not see the screen facing the window. "Is it a new computer?" Pannong asked out of boredom.

"Yes, a brand new one," Wang answered. He then proudly continued, "Our team is expanding fast because our job is new and necessary. We do sampling surveys for the manufacturing industrial sector. This is a new division of the Bureau, and it gets all kinds of support from national and international organizations such as the World Bank. They want us to come up with accurate numbers on industrial development. As you might know, we used to follow the Russian model, which was awkward and old-fashioned—suitable only for the old economic system. Under that model, all the information was supposed to be collected directly from each enterprise. It was their duty to report the requested data to us under the socialist planning economy, which is gone now. In this new epoch, governed by 'the invisible hand' of Adam Smith, the sampling survey and census have become the chief means of statistical investigation. This change started with agricultural surveys in the 1980s. In the following decade, our division came to play a more and more important role. We now do sampling surveys across the entire country to collect statistical data from all the manufacturing industries.

"It is natural and appropriate that government statistics should reflect the new market system of production. In a nutshell, the system can be summarized as a change from the 'repose-reportage' model to the 'sentinel-sampling' method of government statistics. As an indication of the growing significance of our division, we no longer have to wait in the office to add up numbers reported by state-owned enterprises. We now collect statistical information by scientific methods, among which the sampling survey plays a key role. The fast expansion of our survey team has been a direct result of China's rapid industrial growth. We do sampling surveys rather than censuses, both of which are the common, governing practices of government statistics for all of the advanced countries. As you might imagine, our team relies far more than any other office in the Bureau on the sophisticated methods of statistical inference, which is, by definition and in nature, different from purely descriptive statistics. Due to the increasing importance of our division and our need for complex statistical tools, we were given funds to replace our computers. This is what I got last month, a Dell."

With a shining forehead, Chief Wang paused for a second and then added, "With this computer, I can play Go with ten guys online simultaneously." Playing Go?[3] Is that what he was doing when his colleague was complaining about the lack of a scientific spirit in the office? "You see, right now I am playing Go with five guys online. I can have this game constantly playing on the computer even when I have guests, and I only need to take a look every few minutes in order to know who made a move and how I should react. My colleague, Chief Huang, is a good man but a workaholic who wants to change the world overnight. I believe, apart from paying attention to details, one also has to be a balanced person in order to be a good statistical officer. The balance between work and play, that is, between bureaucracy and objectivity, is no less important. Otherwise, one will be ruined by absurdities."

No sooner had Wang finished his last word than his telephone rang. "Hello, who is this? Oh, Lao Hu, yes, kind of busy at the moment but it should be fine. Tell me, yes, do tell me what you want to say, yes. Fine, yes, just a couple of friends." While talking on the phone, Chief Wang was also looking at his computer. Having punched a key on the keyboard, he returned to the phone. "This is important, you know. It cannot be this way, I mean—it should not be this way. You know what I mean? This figure is very important, and it will go to the Director's Office, you remember? It may later go to the Premier's office, you know, so we've got to get this right. Of course, you're right, but what I meant to say earlier this morning was that we should not make Little Mu feel bad about this. He is an enthusiastic young man—capable and diligent—and I don't want his pride to get hurt.

"I know that both of you are correct, and nobody is wrong. But we can't have two different growth rates, can we? Nobody is saying that his figure is wrong. I know that he went to the factories many times in order to get a better estimate. Of course, he knows the truth. Do you doubt it? You are far more experienced and should know what I want or mean to say. Growth rates are not only about truth. They are also about face, and we've got to be consistent. He is too young to be able to understand this fully. Please go and talk to him again about this. I also know that you have your reasons, good ones, for why the growth figure should be higher than his estimate. The bottom line is that we cannot take to our Director two different figures for industrial growth. How can that be? If one is correct, then the other must be wrong.

"As a matter of fact, this has nothing to do with truth. It is about consistency and our face. Do you hear me? We will have to start over again until we can

---

3. Go, or *wéiqí*, is a form of chess that is also popular in Japan and South Korea.

find one reportable figure for industrial growth. What is scientific? A fact of science should be one and the same, objectively obtained by each and every one of us. If so, how can we produce two figures for annual growth? As I have made clear, providing two figures to the Director is not a possibility. Little Mu must raise his estimate, which is too low to be reported. On the other side, I think you should try to make your figure slightly lower than you have prepared. We all know that inflations and exaggerations of statistical data have been inherited and carried over from the old days. This is not *our* fault. Yes, exactly, it is what we inherited from previous calculations over the years. They used to add a percentage every year to the existing pie of our economy, making it appear to have grown the way that it should have. But the fact is that development is often uneven, and one should not do simple math, like an algebraic magician, on the head of economic growth. This is what we—I, you, and Little Mu—all know. But what can and should we do about it now? We can do nothing about it—but I mean that we must do something about it. In the long run, such as in a decade or so, I would hope that we could bring these two figures into one by narrowing the gap between them.

"My position is crystal clear. Mu's estimate of growth, the fresh fruit of our own work, may be true, but it is too low to be acceptable. Your estimate, basically based on adding 8.5 percent to the previous year's figure, is probably a bit higher than is needed.[4] In the future, we will hope to use the figure from our own survey work. But at the present moment we should not and cannot make such a sudden change as Little Mu has suggested, because, if we did, everyone would be shocked by our estimate, which is far lower than the national target of economic growth. Listen to me. What I don't want you to do is to hurt Little Mu. He is an excellent young man. Just tell him that we cannot use his estimate without some sort of modification. At the same time, we must praise his enthusiasm and commitment to doing good work. His spirit should be encouraged, but his stubborn and unreflective attitude must be tamed. Last year, if you remember, his friend criticized our estimate as being lower than the true growth, and this year Little Mu is arguing that our estimate is too high. Okay, if it was low last year, we are willing to make it up a bit this year. He is far too young to be able to see the point of maintaining a good balance."

4. Over the phone, Chief Wang did mention adding a percentage to the previous year's growth rates. However, the figure quoted here is not an exact report of what he said, since the conversation could not be recorded, a normal difficulty of fieldwork among officials (cf. X. Liu 2002). With regard to ethnography and writing, my general stance is that the act of writing ethnography is not ethnographic writing. The latter usually involves an academic exercise in which ethnographic experiences are turned into an anthropological text. The former, as I have tried to employ in this study, problematizes the relationship of the textual to the actual and vice versa. In other words, following such a stance, the question of the real will always entail the problem of textualization of the actual experience, which, by definition, is made by "writing" (cf. Sartre 1988).

It was a long telephone conversation, lasting more than half an hour. For the report on quarterly industrial development, an estimate of growth rate was required, and Chief Wang's Office would have to provide it. The problem was that two figures had been worked out by two different means of statistical estimation. One was based on the division's own sampling data, while the other was a modified figure that had been calculated with reference to the accumulative growth rates of the past ten years in the comparative quarterly periods. The former was relying on sampling data estimated by means of statistical inference; the latter was worked out by taking into consideration the accumulative data of the past several years. The result was that the accumulative figure was higher than the sampling figure, and one of young office workers refused to accept any compromise, which was the usual way of "making up numbers." Little Mu insisted on providing both estimates, leaving it up to the General Director to decide which figure should be used for what purpose. This is not to say, as we learned, that the sampling survey estimate would always be lower than the accumulative figure; this would depend on what kind of estimates and which time periods were involved. The point, as we were told, is that whenever there were two disparate estimates, the discrepancy between them would need to be reduced in order to produce a consistent report. The long conversation between Chief Wang and his colleague was about how to create an agreeable, consistent, and acceptable estimation of the actual economic growth.

Overlooking the busy streets full of noisy cars and cumbersome trucks from the window of Wang's office on the seventeenth floor, one could not help but soberly meditate on the significance of these two statistical estimates, each being truthful to its own history of truth. By the turn of a new century, the ideological battle was almost over; however, two modes of life and knowledge, with their dissimilar relations to a historical rupture in time, continued to trouble the collective representations of a scientific consciousness. The socialist planning economy was gone, yet in the technical field of governmental statistics, the inertia of the Maoist past, as a form of life and knowledge, was still alive. The problem that Chief Wang faced is how to transplant one into the other in order to reconcile two modes of life and knowledge into one calendar. The problem, in other words, is not technical but rather epistemological in nature. It is therefore necessary to scrutinize the transplantation, instead of each mode in isolation. Put generally, a central question is, what is the signification of such an infusion of the modern, scientific mode of life and knowledge into the heart of the People's Republic, a societal giant, a new leviathan, breathing an old socialist air but hoping to jump onto a new global platform? Although the People's Republic has climbed aboard the train of modern development, its experience will not be determined by the tracks already traveled by others. Our analysis will focus on China's feeling on the journey, which is nothing but a history of sentimentality—both new and old, both pleasant and painful, both innovative and inertial.

The empirical object of our inquiry is the historical disjuncture that separated the Maoist mode of life and knowledge from that of the present age. The
field of government statistics, reflected in sharp contrast over this disjuncture, provides an excellent entrance into the troubled historical consciousness
of truthfulness and facticity, understood as both ethical and epistemological
problems for "being in the world." The Cold War, the Soviet Union and the
socialist camp in general, the death of Mao and the subsequent reformatory
era, as well as other broader historical shadows, need not be reiterated here.
The cogent story of the National Bureau of Statistics alone supplies a case in
point. Briefly, as an essential aspect of socialist economic planning, the Bureau
used to be under the authority of an overarching institution, the Central Planning Committee, which was supposed to plan out the entire economic development for the whole nation. During the Maoist years, the statistical work of
the state was simply a supplement to the planning work of the Committee.
The economy and its development were in the hands of those working for
the Committee, whereas the government statisticians often felt as if they were
sideliners in the official game of power.

A reversal took place with the arrival of the market economy. Alongside
the decline in function and purpose of the Central Planning Committee, the
National Bureau of Statistics, due to its ability to objectify economic development, came to assume an unprecedented importance in the eyes of the state. In
the process of becoming confident of their place and focus, and no longer feeling
inferior to those in other state economic institutions, official statisticians had
to resolve a technical problem: transforming the Soviet system of government
statistics into a modern and global one. A bridge over the historical disjuncture
was therefore needed, for the calendar of the People's Republic, unlike the Soviet
Union or Eastern Europe, did not restart anew. On the other hand, an epistemological break, no less stunning than the fall of the Berlin Wall, is clearly visible
from a retrospective aspect. It is this "continuous discontinuity"—in and as a
history of sentimentality—that will make up the central focus of this study.

Before leaving Chief Wang's office, having figured out the problem that
would trouble the mind of a conscientious official statistician, Pannon asked,
"Why don't you just report the figure collected by the first-hand sampling surveys, since it is supposed to be scientific and objective?"

"We cannot do that," Wang explained, "because last year's growth rates are
already on record. If we use another figure, however correct or true, we might
end up saying that there is not enough economic growth this year—that it is
lower than the targeted 7–8 percent GDP growth. This would be a political
disaster. Nobody will allow it to happen. Would *you* want to go to the Premier
and say that we made some mistakes earlier and would like to report zero
growth this year because our previous annual reports were exaggerations? This
is an impossible solution. Nor is it true. Obviously, there is growth every year.

Look at all these new buildings from my window! What are they? Growth. If we have discordance in statistical estimations, we will have to make concordance slowly—that is, over a number of years—because we are in transition. One should not try to kill the fish in order to breed the ducks. They have to be in the same pond for a while until we finally work out a solution."

* * *

Let us now draw a few analytical sketches from the above ethnographic experience. The worrying concern about the truthfulness or facticity of government statistics was not a one-sided feeling. It wa s shared by both officials and ordinary people, the governing and the governed, although the reasons that they felt the same were dissimilar. For the latter, as exemplified in the case of the taxi driver, the doubt about official statistics was a refraction of the materiality of social disparity. In other words, this doubt or distrust of government statistics should be seen as a social index for the birth of an enormous gap between the wealthy and the poor, which is growing simultaneously as the country itself grows. Behind it lies the wisdom of common sense: statistics on national growth and the increase in average income tell nothing about the structural problems of distribution or redistribution of wealth. The interest of ordinary people in the truthfulness of official statistics arises from the concerns of social classes and economic interests.

For the official statisticians, now vital to the state, the worrying concern is of a different origin and nature: they are genuinely hoping to develop an effective means for measuring the country's changing materiality while it is being increasingly integrated into the global system of production and consumption. That is to say, their concern is epistemological in the sense that they are trying to objectify the materiality on the ruins of the Maoist revolution. It is therefore no surprise that ideas of science and truth have come to (re)constitute the ground for the official discourse of the present age, for the home of the state, with its expensive furniture and charming gardens, is visible only in the statistical statement of assets and liabilities. As we have seen, within the Bureau there may be contradictory claims as to whether a statistical estimate is accurate or adequate. But these debates are nevertheless about truthfulness and facticity, *not* about "reason and revolution" (see, e.g., Marcuse [1941] 1954). In other words, it was not a new ideology but a new grounding for life and governance that came to be paved and for which the labor of official statisticians was exploited.

"Making up numbers" is not simply about whether a particular figure is accurate or not. It is about whether the surgery, a heart transplantation, would work well or not. It is about whether a new heart of governing and living could function well in the old body of the People's Republic. No one accepts all of the implicit assertions made by government statisticians, yet ordinary people have come to argue more and more in the same way, that is, on the same ground of scientific truthfulness and statistical facticity. Presently, the battlefield of objectivity and truth, which is a different battlefield from the Maoist years, seems to be more and more consolidated. What has united the official view and that of common people is precisely this grounding of new truth claims, upon which different kinds of feet, with or without proper jogging shoes, have left an indistinguishable mess of footsteps. The taxi driver, unfortunately, has no choice but to walk on the path asphalted by the statistical laborers of the state, since, as we were reminded a long time ago (see Marx 1939), "the ideas of the ruling class are the ruling ideas."

Hence, the challenge to official statistics represents a negative response to the positive value of quantitative analysis, which has held up a new plateau of truth claims. The popular consciousness, exemplified in the taxi driver's critique of government statistics, only confirms the mentality of governance during the process of change. This is the heart of the problem: quantification of the social world and statisticalization of everyday experience have given birth to a new life, which would look, in its skeleton or outline, materialistic, narcissistic, and exteriorized if placed in the rearview mirror of the Maoist years. Materialistic it is for sure; it is also narcissistic in the sense that all of the calculations, comparativistic in nature, are driven by the gravitation of the ego, being either a self or a nation. The Maoist years became unbearable under the shining rays of a strong modern light, and the present-day calculations of GDPs or GDPs per capita have come to signify an obsession with self-identification. One cannot rest assured until one has determined a measurable distance, in statistical terms, between oneself and the Other, the modern Other—Western Europe and North America in particular—for "facts will speak for themselves." Narcissistic materialism could not survive without the necessary vitamins of statistical data and analysis that exteriorize life, making it like a thing rather than a living experience, which would otherwise interiorize the habitat of being. One's horizon of seeing and believing—and not simply what is seen or believed—has been re-formed. The elephantine world of the People's Republic has undergone a change in its horizon of vision and involvement. Still on the path of change, it is determined to see as the modern Other sees, not in terms of diverging political or economic interests but in terms of the way in which the condition of the possibility of existence is constituted. Seen from either side of the issue, this is a fusion of particular horizons into the globalizing one. Even if an official might have been wrong in his calculations, his conscience came to be assuaged by faith in scientific objectivity and truth. Indeed, the world of China has been statisticalized, resulting in a radical change in the horizon of being and believing.

In a crucial sense, in today's People's Republic "to know" has come to mean "to calculate." Calculation (of one's salary, for example) would often mean that a person or a group of persons has been designated a position on the newly drawn moral map of economic development. In other words, statistical data have obtained almost an ethical character. In both official discourse and everyday language, this new faith is viewed as progress in science, particularly in the scientific management of society. To document this change of horizon, three analytically distinguishable areas of happenings will be examined, although in these pages they will not be treated in exact succession of one another.

First, alongside the reconstruction of the temple of social sciences, another round of heated debates about culture, history, and development took place in the 1980s. The role of statistics and its applicability to the analysis of social and human affairs came to the forefront of intellectual debates, behind which raged a fierce battle of sentiments—under the flag of scientific objectivity and truth—against the remains of Maoist ideology. Socio-economic statistics as an academic field of training, together with some other social science disciplines, had been labeled a bourgeois pseudo-science and abandoned by the Maoist government. An examination of the return of statistics to the new family shrine of social sciences will be an important step in tracing the history of a national mentality in the process of change, for it was in debates and bitter fights that a new regime of truth was given birth.

The second observation addresses the astonishing speed and scope of institutionalization and bureaucratization of state statistical organizations in the late twentieth century. In a single decade, from 1976 to 1986, the number of formal employees of these organizations increased from 7,000 to 67,360 (*Dangdai Zhongguo de tonji shiye* 1990, 87–111). What is the significance of such an expansion of a particular field of the official labor force? Or, put differently, what are the practical implications of such an expansion for the management of society and the population? This will constitute a crucial aspect of inquiry into the mode of authority and control that reflects, and yet is reflected by, the change of horizon in the mentality of governance.

Third, the systematic collection and use of statistical data have affected not only the ways in which society is conceived but also the ways in which people relate to each other. The arrival of the insurance economy in the world of everyday life, the possibilities of investing in stock markets, the uses of sampling surveys in various sociological fields and government reports—all have combined to produce a different vision for living one's life in the world. Everyday experience itself has been affected by the birth of a "moral mathematics," which, as an old European coin endowed with a new value,[5] has profoundly transformed what people choose to do, who they want to be, and how they conceive of themselves and their neighbors. Apart from the intellectual and governmental reorientation, there is also a popular remaking of everyday experience by a new

---

5. See Hacking (1990, 38–39) for a discussion of the emergence of the idea of "moral science" in post-Enlightenment Europe.

moralizing practice, which derives its energy from the calculation of various statistical means driven by the gravitation of large numbers.

Just as "the predicament of culture" is not only a cultural predicament (see, e.g., Clifford 1988), the riddle of China is not simply a Chinese riddle (cf. Levenson 1968). It is rather the Sphinx of our times—a time of transnational capital and digital capitalism. As an urgent intellectual task, we must take up this riddle as a mirror effect of our own mode of existence in the contemporary world. We must view it as more than a mirage of the condition of possibility of our life today. We must unpack the mystique of a self-remaking by means of the Other in the context of global capitalist penetration. To the mind of modern reason, its appears that a new Philosophy of History, *pace* Hegel (1956), is begging to be written, for the Religion of China, *pace* Weber (1951), looks as if it were enjoying its carnal copulation with the world religion of science and statistical reason. To the eyes of development, it appears that a new testament of an old faith of European origin is being composed on the ruins of the Maoist revolution.

PART I

Moral Mathematics

Chapter One

THE MENTALITY OF GOVERNANCE

Today's "Morning Prayers"

"'Reading the morning paper is a kind of realistic morning prayer.' This remark by Hegel is often cited to illustrate how interests have changed in the modern age: our gaze has turned away from the invisible beyond and toward daily events.... Modern man's sole orison consists in reading the morning paper; for, being a realist, he deems the news to be the first object worthy of his attention at the moment when that attention is sharpest."[1] It seems as though such a realistic attitude, having traveled a long distance from the time of Hegel (1770–1831), has nowadays regained its truest expression in the vast continent of the People's Republic, an enormous social world increasingly permeated by various kinds of contemporary media—particularly television. Yes, it is television—rather than newspapers—that has become the most common means for the modern attitude to express itself. Whether it is the morning or evening news—when one's attention is sharpest—the television will be on, and it is made to supply twenty-four hours of rolling stories and updates about what is happening in the entire world. It is the *news*, rather than the newspapers, that continues in its essential function of securing a realistic attitude toward life, albeit a new form of life, referred to as "petty affluence" (*xiaokang*) by the official church of development.

In the People's Republic today, this attitude, which is believed to be modern and rational, has brought about an excessive focus on the egoistic self, who constantly checks his appearance in the mirror of the modern Other.

---

1. Quoted in Descombes (1993, 3), in which the reference to Hegel's aphorism was made with regard to his German piece, "Aphorismen aus der Jenenser Zeit," no. 31 (Hoffmeister ([1936] 1974, 360).

His life makes sense to himself only through a materialistic comparison with other people, related or not, near or distant. Television, with its vivid colors and animated images, has provided a far better presentation of the world in which our realist can find reliable and yet entertaining reference points. From a sociological point of view, it is an error to assume that the zeal for obtaining a new Panasonic simply expresses a materialistic impulse for consumption. It is also, and perhaps more so, a reflection of the psychic urge for seeing more clearly the world in its pictorial representation—in which one lives a life with and against other such lives. The rapid development of information technology industries and mass media in the People's Republic, encouraged by both official permission and popular support, has been a *collective celebration* of the realistic ideology of "petty affluence." Such an attitude in life, its materiality, as shown on television as well as reported in newspapers, can be grasped only by a measurement of the distance of oneself to the modern Other. And this is the function of news, as a source of existential nutrition, as an assurance of one's knowledge of oneself in the world, as a means of situating one's place through a restless measurement of one's material distance from others in developmental terms. In the realistic mind of "petty affluence," fortunately or not, a metaphysical lane of thought that used to separate realism from materialism and vice versa no longer exists. Thus, for a new generation of the People's Republic, *what is real is material* and *what is material is real*. A new meaning has been added to the old Hegelian observation: digitalized news now represents electronically a truly "real" picture of global materiality.

Once when I was interviewing an official from the Shanghai Bureau of Statistics, he told me about his new habit: as soon as he returned to his house, no matter the time of day or night, he would immediately switch on his television. He explained, with a big smile, "You know why? One has to know the world in order to act in it. This is a plain and immediate reason for watching television, in which you can get access to the real world, its material development in particular. I watch everything, but my favorite programs are news programs. The whole world is now on television, so one can and should know what is happening in every corner of the world. Don't you think so? If nothing is worthwhile watching, I always leave it on the CCTV's news channel, which continuously puts one in touch with the real world and vice versa.[2] A man of knowledge and education cannot afford to be ignorant of what is happening in our society *and* in the world. Television functions as an informational window for us to get access to the real world. Having access to the real world means being aware of new developments around the globe. Thus, we can compare ourselves, our economic development to that of other countries. This is

2. The CCTV (Chinese Central Television), which is owned and regulated by the central government, is the largest and most influential official broadcasting corporation in the People's Republic.

a must for our government and for myself as a government employee." This ethnographic encounter reveals a mind-set in which televised images of other people's lives, particularly those across the Pacific Ocean, have a direct impact on the everyday life of the People's Republic. On television, morning and evening "prayers" are read by beautifully attired anchormen and -women rather than being printed in the newspapers. And it is in one's bedroom, where the Panasonic typically resides, that the world will be baptized into the new faith of "petty affluence."

In turning its attention to the material development of the world, the People's Republic moved away from an older set of ideological concerns. The government's positive embracement of a realistic attitude toward life suggests an implicit denial of the Maoist past, which is seen as historical madness from the viewpoint of "petty affluence." A government statistician, the official in Shanghai whom I interviewed, reminded me of the emblematic slogan, popular in the early 1980s and favored by Deng, the paramount leader after Mao: "Reality Is the Only Measurement of Any Claims for Truth." The farewell to the Maoist past, in its earlier phase, welcomed the homecoming of the pragmatic man. According to the new party doctrine, bearing the signature of Deng, "no matter whether it is a white or a black cat, as long as it catches mice, it is a good cat." The mouse is the reality, a material one, whereas the measurement of such a reality has nothing to do with, for example, the color of a cat. The true judgment of whether a cat is good or not, whether a system of ideas works or not, whether a theory of the world is sound or superfluous, whether one should stick to some moral stance or not—namely, whether a cat is *useful* or not, regardless of its color, its temper, its habit, and our feeling about it—this judgment of its value should and must be practical and utilitarian, that is, it must be based on whether it can catch the mouse or not. It is thus only against the reality of the mouse that a cat can be evaluated or judged. At the beginning of a new century, the official from Shanghai represented the maturity of a materialistic realist, whose principal school instruction had been the pragmatic lesson on how to catch the mouse.

In order to grasp the significance of televised news and Hegel's concept of morning (or evening) "prayers," let us consider the ideology of the Maoist years. During that period, the role and function of the media and news were defined in an entirely different way. The Leninist doctrine, which was adopted by the People's Republic in its adolescence, stated that in order to convey the party's policies to the people, a national newspaper, directly controlled by the government, was necessary for a revolutionary society. By then, already a century after the death of Hegel, the newspaper remained an essential means for national communication. "Lenin, in his earliest major work on organization *What Is to Be Done*, devoted a long section to a discussion of the need for an all-Russian newspaper and states: '*There is no other way of training* strong political organization except through the medium of an all-Russian newspaper" (Schurmann 1966, 63; emphasis in original). Underlying this doctrine was the belief that ideologies or ideological doctrines should not be neutral or objective statements of reality; rather, they should contain a correct and corrective message for the society in order to facilitate change. In other words, reality should not be simply reported on in the news; it should be *made* by the news from the proper source—the party itself.

Franz Schurmann's work, *Ideology and Organization in Communist China* (1966), published during the outbreak of the Cultural Revolution, is an exemplary study of the Maoist understanding of news and media. "All mass media, particularly newspapers, devote a considerable space to the publication of major policy speeches, policy directives, and explanatory articles relating to policy decisions. Dissemination of policy decisions ranges from those which are made at a national level to those made at a local level. As we shall indicate in our chapter on management, all organizations require the setting of policy, that is, the goals of organizational action. Since Communist China is an organizational society *par excellence*, policy statements of all varieties and implications are handed down all the time" (ibid., 63). In this mode of organization, what appeared to be the "news" was in fact policies and directives of the state. A chief function of the news and newspapers was to make reality subordinate to the more important problematic of what it *ought* to be. This is no longer the case: the current conviction is that the news, televised or written, should be a mirror of reality. In a sense, the relationship of *is* to *ought* has been reversed: in today's outlook, *what ought to be* can be knowable only by finding out *what there is* in reality. During the Maoist period, the morning and evening papers ("prayers") were taken as an ideological invocation; in contrast, they are now viewed as a lens through which one might be able to see the world in a better perspective. One used to read newspapers to receive a message from the party, which often involved a personal consecration or sacrifice. It was a "religious" act in the sense that one's reading was a response to the call for a greater good—collective and future-oriented—that was represented by the party as its temporary agent. The morning paper was thus not a prayer *in* the morning; instead, it was a prayer *for* the morning light of seeing and believing. For the party or government, the newspapers functioned as a tool to mobilize the masses; for the masses, on the other hand, they were an essential means of suturing the visible to the invisible, the part to the whole, the personal to the social.

A new day has indeed arrived in the People's Republic. Televised news no longer contains the mysterious messages that used to appear in newsprint; rather, it aims to become purely a photograph of the world in words. Today's realistic reader is more likely to seek out news through digital technology, a medium that is far more sensational and sentimentalized and for which the pictorial presentation is essential. In the fast expansion of the CCTV news programs over the past decade, we have witnessed, among other aspects, a regularization of news reports on economic growth. More and more we have seen official statisticians invited to appear in a beautiful modern studio who speak to the audience about China's economic development. Guest spokespersons, including various kinds of experts, sociologists, and other types of scholars, have frequently been invited by the CCTV to appear on the programs, as have speakers from the National Bureau of Statistics. In addition to publishing statistical monthly or quarterly bulletins, government statisticians, in neat black suits and colorful ties, now appear regularly on national television programs, making statistical analyses or interpreting data to confirm or deny the truth of a matter. The use of statistical data as a form of evidence or a quantitative method for justification has induced a habit of reading that is quite different from the "morning prayer" of the Maoist man. Nothing could make one feel closer to the beating heart of the world than the screen of a Panasonic right in one's bedroom.

Alongside the change in the means of communication, a difference in the use of statistical data and analysis has also arrived. Let us examine the annual government report, a systematic announcement of its achievements, as an exemplification of this difference. By government reports, I mean the official documents first delivered by the Premier and later published by the national media such as the *People's Daily* or the CCTV. The economic life of the People's Republic has gone through a series of drastic changes. Two decades, the 1950s and the 1980s, can be singled out for comparison, as during both of these periods the state was concerned with the regularization and institutionalization of governmental statistics, although the models and inspirations for the concern sharply differed. Starting in the mid-1990s, the second round of official regularization and institutionalization of governmental statistics has more or less completed its mission, by which I mean that an ethical and epistemological equivalence of truth and facts with statistical data and analysis has more or less been established. As a consequence, forecasting or predicting future economic growth has become a new habit of thought for an entire generation that has grown up on the ruins of the Maoist revolution. Retrospectively, in the eyes of today's official statisticians, the Maoist past stands out as an era of madness and barbarism. During the Great Leap Forward (1958–1959) and the Cultural Revolution (1966–1976), statistical analysis, as well as the institutions of governmental statistics, suffered a great deal from its alleged pseudo-science status in the hands of the revolutionary masses led by the Maoist government. In an interview, a professor of economic statistics in Beijing told me, "Can you believe that when I first returned to work in the late 1970s, I found no records at all about our economic performance for the years 1966 to 1968? Because of the Cultural Revolution, no national economic data had been collected. It was really a disaster! Can you believe that nobody collected any data for those years? This should never happen to a country, but it did during the years of the

Maoist revolution! Back then, the first thing we did was to repair the broken chain of economic data. Otherwise, there would be no way of applying regression analysis for future predictions. In a way, we had to make things up. Can you believe it? Crazy! During those damn years, people debated about their loyalty to the country, but the country did not even exist in statistical reports. The material world has to be produced, and such a product can be visible to our eyes only by means of statistical tabulation and classification. Is it not so? Is this not a naked truth?" His remarks are revealing, not simply with regard to the Maoist insanity but also because they reflect a new certainty achieved by means of rationality. It is into such a crevice between the past and the present, between insanity and scientificity, between the primitive and the modern, that a history of sentimentality may be written. The spectacle that would mark this fissure was the official demolishment of the national statistical observatory during the early years of the Cultural Revolution, a truly astonishing phenomenon of the Maoist years. However, it is not true that the Maoist government never made use of statistical data and analysis. The life of numbers as part of a history of sentimentality is far more intricate than it might appear to be today.

The Year 1954: A First Report on Government Work

The 1954 report opened its discourse, representative of the government style of the time in general,[3] by announcing the country's achievements. It said that "We," standing for the nation, the people, the party, and the government, had moved into a new stage of development by overcoming the severe poverty and underdevelopment that had been inherited from the "Old Society."[4] This opening statement carried a celebrative tone, suggesting that, as with political and military victories that had been attained, "We" would achieve a similar victory in economic development. The implicit parallel between yesterday's military successes and tomorrow's economic triumphs was thus drawn. Economic development, the 1954 report stated, should become a primary focus of the government's attention. Interesting to note is that the party, a most crucial political signifier, did not appear in this report. Instead, it employed terms

3. The 1954 report is actually the first report of its kind ever made in the history of the People's Republic—or, perhaps more accurately, the very first report that was systematic and properly entitled to be referred to as a report on government work. See Zhou Enlai's "Government Report," delivered at the first meeting of the First National People's Congress of the People's Republic of China on 23 September 1954.

4. Each reference is made to the year that a government report was issued, not the year of activities or achievements that the report refers to. In this case, the report was delivered in 1954 by Zhou Enlai, then Premier. In it, he discussed the performance of the national economy and the work of the government since 1949.

such as "the central government" or "the state" to convey the sense of a strong, collective "We."[5]

What follows in the report is an explanation of the government's developmental strategy, which emphasized the urgent need for the growth of heavy industries. Other economic sectors, such as agriculture and services, were thought of as secondary and dependent on the development of primary industries such as steel and iron. This developmental strategy, based on a particular reading of Karl Marx and on an understanding of the experience of the Soviet Union, placed its emphasis on the production of "the means of production," seen as the genesis of productive energy for long-term economic prosperity. This developmental strategy was characteristic, in general, of all the socialist planning economies of the times, such as those in Eastern Europe, and its fate as "the economy of shortage" has been well documented (see, e.g., Kornai 1980).[6] In the Chinese case, the need for a great economic triumph at the time was both psychological, speaking to the hurt caused by a series of defeats by the Western powers, starting with the Opium War (1839–1842), and political, responding to the Cold War divide between the socialist and capitalist camps. The report was delivered by then Premier Zhou, who was speaking to the assembly of the People's Congress. For the new government at the time, the question of how to develop involved the question of which sector of the economy should be prioritized. Premier Zhou rhetorically asked: "Which is better? Is it not a good idea for our people to bear some inconvenience and certain temporary difficulties in life at the present moment for the sake of achieving a great, long-lasting prosperity in the future? Or is it a good idea to consume everything we have now, but in the long run suffer from poverty as we have always suffered? We believe that you will agree with what we have decided to do. We must try to establish development that will lead to long-term prosperity."[7] In retrospect, some would argue that this national economic strategy meant sacrificing life and convenience for a focus on the development of heavy industries, for which primary capital accumulation would have to come from agriculture and other likely sectors.

The main part of the report exploded into a powerful recitation of a series of facts and figures, as if Premier Zhou felt the need to demonstrate the details of how such a policy had worked. Through the enumeration and computation of national economic achievements, with facts and numbers cited for verification and proof, the success story of the People's Republic in its cradle years was

5. During the Cultural Revolution, it was the party that signified the nation, whereas the government was often seen as a bureaucratic institution that would have to be revolutionized (see, e.g., H.-Y. Lee 1978).

6. Kornai's work was translated into Chinese in the 1980s; and it made an impact on the mind of Chinese students who were trying to learn lessons from the market model.

7. Translation is mine.

heralded by a symphony of statistics. The tone of the report, utterly confident and optimistic, was reflected in the choice of three kinds of statistical indexes: growth rates, sum totals (of important products for national needs), and various kinds of ratios, such as the proportion or increase of state-owned enterprises in the total industrial growth. Three long paragraphs, full of figures and ratios, showed the purpose of their use. For example, there was a detailed analysis of statistical data on industrial growth, including both annual and accumulative figures. The annual industrial growth rate of 1953 was 33 percent. This was lower than the average growth rate in the previous three years, which came close to 37 percent annually. Of course, one needs to take into account the fact that prior to the establishment of the People's Republic, the civil war and other circumstances had dragged China's economy to an extremely low level. There was also a list of statistical figures of actual outputs for a number of major industrial products, such as coal, electricity, iron, and steel. These sum totals might not appear striking to the eyes of an observer in terms of their quantities, which is understandable given the primitive condition of the country's economy at the time. But in comparison to China's productivity prior to 1949, they do indicate a great achievement. Most importantly, the report included a series of ratios, carefully chosen and computed, such as the one showing a further increase of heavy industrial production in the total economy.

A patient reader of an old governmental report would have to be impressed by such a deft demonstration of statistical data and struck by the notional significance given to the idea of proportion reflected in the active use of various kinds of "ratio" explanations. This was indeed a most important tool of the official thinking at the time. What is proportion? What is ratio? What does it signify? How is it employed in and by official thinking? Plainly, it was an effective instrument for understanding and determining social reality in terms of the Maoist mode of reasoning. Without a market mechanism that allowed economic activities and social services to be adjusted by means of "an invisible hand," the state, with its central planning economy, would have to be in charge of arranging those activities and services for a society whose health was judged by and thought of in terms of its proportional balance. As reflected in the voice of Premier Zhou and recorded in those written pages, the pulse of the government, whose thinking followed the logic of *proportionality*, can almost be felt by an observant reader. Put another way, the state, in its allocation and distribution of economic resources and social capital, labored under a *proportional logic*. This explains why the calculation of ratio was so central to its vision of society and to its future.

To the mind of the state, total economic development should be thought of and discussed in terms of dividing the entire economy into several sectors or segments, such as the industrial sector versus the agricultural, for each of which a deserved share of reinvestment, taken from the national revenue, would be made. The logic of proportionality, as both a *dividing* strategy in terms of investment in each sector and a *uniting* strategy in planning the future growth of the entire economy, was therefore essential for planning economic development. In 1954, the proportion of the heavy industrial sector versus the rest of the economy, in terms of output, was 42.3 percent versus 57.7 percent, which was thought of as healthy for China's development at the time. Reinvesting an adequate proportion in each of those economic sectors, which would maximize total growth, was conceived as an essential task of the government's work. When the question of economic development was posed at the time, it was natural for the official mind to wonder, first, whether the existing proportion of, for example, heavy industry in the total economy was appropriate or not, and, second, how to divide the capital available for investment proportionally into different economic sectors in order to achieve a greater chance for further development.

The idea of ratio or proportion, derived from simple calculations and because of its simplicity, came to constitute a most effective means of conceiving social reality and its movement. This was an essential aspect of Maoist governmental thought, whose logic penetrated the entire social world. To take a political example, seats in most national assemblies, including the People's Congress, even today are proportionally distributed among different social groups. These groups are defined not only by administrative or natural divisions but also by categories such as ethnicity, gender, age, class, official/non-official and military/non-military status, etc. For instance, an officially accepted ethnic group must be given a proportional representation in a major national assembly, regardless of the political function for which such an assembly was originally convened. The underlying thought is that representativeness, understood as an exemplification or extension of the logic of proportionality, in itself serves as a significant political function.

During the Maoist years, the Central Planning Committee, which no longer exists, was responsible for devising economic development plans. It was this committee that used the logic of proportionality extensively for its work. Its favorite notion was that of "balance," by which economic performance would be well-balanced when all of the essential contributing factors were kept in good proportion. Whether the economy was in good shape or not could hence be talked about in terms of whether it was well-balanced. If there were problems, it would be thought that a disproportional imbalance had occurred. It was thus by the "visible hand" of the Central Planning Committee, the right arm of the Maoist state, that the national economy was handled and kept in balance. Disproportional contusions, in whatever forms that appeared or would appear in the economy, were considered an obstacle for growth. As is clearly shown in the 1954 report, the call for more investment in heavy industries was due to the belief that prioritized development of the means of production would create long-term economic prosperity. It was also believed that such long-term prosperity could be achieved only by a proportionally sound reinvestment strategy. The idea of growth, in this governmental report, seemed to subordinate itself to the logic of proportionality. Little attempt was made to foresee or forecast what would happen in the future, while a great deal of attention was paid to verifying and justifying the proportional balance of the existing economy. This logic allowed a double operation of the mind: on the one hand, grasping reality by dividing it into segments or proportions and, on the other hand, conceptualizing society by binding the segments into a totality of which its different parts would be given differential policies or priorities.

Such a form of logic was indispensable even for mass political campaigns. For example, during the Anti-Rightist Campaign of the mid-1950s, the Maoist government declared that around 5 percent of the total population was reluctant to welcome the new socialist society. It was believed that there were definitely more of such "bad elements" in colleges and universities—or even in government offices—than in villages or factories. Everywhere the masses tried to seek out those who belonged to the 5 percent in their neighborhood or village or factory. This Maoist *ratio*—rather than *racial*—politics depended on carving out a proportion of the population for the political mobilization of the masses. Although this was politics rather than economics, the logic of its thought, its rationality, was the same.

The idea of proportion presupposes the calculation of sum totals. It is based on such sum totals, in both the statistical and logical senses, that various proportions can be calculated and therefore made into ratios. In order to calculate a proportional ratio or a pure ratio—that is, one proportion versus another proportion—some corresponding sum totals have to be computed in the first place. However, the relationship of the ratio to the sum total is not reciprocal. That is to say, ratios or proportional ratios may be deceptive if constructed without knowledge of the relevant sum totals. If one were to make a distinction between static and dynamic ratios, one could perhaps conceive of the growth rate as a kind of dynamic ratio, whose proportional difference was calculated according to the increase of the current year's production over the previous year. Unlike the static ratio, the growth rate incorporates into its calculation a temporal movement, registering a *temporal proportional difference* (or increase). It is intriguing to note that in the cradle years of the People's Republic, the government did not pay particular attention to growth rates despite the fact that the entire ideological discourse of the Maoist revolution was built on a socialist vision of a different tomorrow. In other words, time and difference played a decisive part in the formation of the Maoist discourse. A clear reversal has taken place in the People's Republic today. On the one hand, there is a national obsession for calculating growth rates and related statistical indexes, while, on the other hand, the official sentiment, which is not only the sentiment of the officials, has become more and more spatial, that is, geopolitical and global. Apart from dreary slogans, little discursive energy has been devoted to a different conception of time and history. One can easily argue that a comparativistic sentiment, whose eye has always focused on the fashion of the modern Other, is characteristic of the present age in the People's Republic.

This reading of an old governmental document, which is a *reading* of the rationality of the Maoist past, is meant to provide a glimpse through a window at the scenery of difference in the recent history of the People's Republic. Through the window, three aspects must be kept in mind. First, three kinds of statistical figures, interrelated and interdependent, were employed in the making of such governmental reports—themselves documents of the mentality of its governance when the People's Republic was in its infancy. Second, the notion of proportionality was a crucial element of Maoist logic for conceiving social reality and calling for collective action. The calculation of static ratios therefore played a potent role in planning out the new economy and in making sense of societal needs. Third, it was the political usage of descriptive statistics that changed over time, or, more precisely, it was a different conception of the toolbox of statistical representation that made the Maoist logic appear illogical, its rationality irrational, its reason unreasonable. Within a short time span of a couple of decades, the Maoist past would look like a distant foreign country, if seen from the touristic eyes of the present age.

To return to the 1954 report, one finds it divided into two parts, the first concerned with domestic affairs, the second with the role of the People's Republic in the international order. This was the era of the Cold War, and the ideological fight had just begun. The first part was full of statistical figures, covering a wide range of domestic issues and including a lengthy report on the country's economic performance. Well into the second part on foreign relations and international policies, there were very few quantitative illustrations. This part of the report fought an ideological battle in words that could not be supported by descriptive statistics. Nevertheless, in a pensive reading, it did feel as if a mutation or a break in the mode of textual presentation had taken place, as if the textual space of the report had been torn into two halves—one statistical, the other ideological. This change of tone was due to a change in addressees. There were two different addressees presumed by the same report. The first was the citizens of the People's Republic, who were given quantitative reassurances of the success of socialism. In these circumstances, descriptive statistics served the function of providing evidence for great achievements under a new government. Although people knew what was happening in general, in looking around they might have encountered unpleasant experiences in some corners of the new society. They needed therefore to be convinced by facts and figures about domestic successes that were greater in scope and vision than their immediate experiences.

In the second part, the report turned its focus to the world, in which the West was represented as an enemy. Due to the simple fact that there was no common ground between the two worlds of socialism and capitalism, there was little need to employ statistical comparison as a communicational means. The point was not to convince but to denounce the political stance of the Other. One must not forget that 1953 marked the end of the Korean War, in which many American and Chinese lives were lost. The point is that it is the addressees who partially determined the choice of an official representational strategy, as this report has clearly suggested. For an ethnographer of the contemporary world traveling into the Maoist past, this document could serve well as a passport for getting through the checkpoints of a different mentality.

The Year 1957: Changes in Content and Style

Three years later, the governmental report wore a different dress.[8] For example, in terms of its format, it now had a table of contents, which had not appeared in the earlier report. It was an interesting shopping list of the official concerns at the time, which was a crucial moment for the People's Republic as it entered its adolescence. Let us take a brief look at them:

About Socialist Revolution
About Socialist Construction
About Reform in Education
About Advancement toward Science
About People's Livelihood
About Employment
About the Salary System
About the Apprentice System
About People's Cultural Life
About Our Country's Basic [Socio-economic] System
About Domestic and International Alliances

The textual space of this report is marked by the implicating adverb "about," which is *guanyu* in Mandarin. Its meaning is a suggestive one. It is *about* something in the sense that it is not simply what it is; it is what it is *about*, suggesting a problematic or a hierarchy of problems in a given social field. It also means to put a question in the form of a statement: *guanyu* implies a possible answer to a question that is not explicitly articulated. Was there a question or a problem

8. See Zhou Enlai's "Government Report," delivered at the fourth meeting of the First National People's Congress of the People's Republic of China on 26 June 1957.

about the economy and the society? In those frail coming-of-age years, some serious doubts about the way in which the Maoist society was governed were mounting. This implicating adverb, which did not appear in the earlier report, can be seen as an official reaction to the criticisms of its administration. For the first time in the short life of the People's Republic, the Maoist government felt the need to defend itself, which signified a new beginning.

Another significant difference in this report is that Mao was configured as a means of entrance into the text of official discourse, which praised Mao and his guidance as a guarantee that the People's Republic would continue its socialist march forever. From this time onward, Mao came to be conceived as a signifying *author* for all of the official texts and discourses. Put another way, it became impossible to speak publicly without including a Maoist citation, which came to constitute a new Mandarin for the People's Republic. This was the beginning of a new official practice, one of enormous political significance, that characterized Mao as both the founding father *and* the living spirit of the nation. Mao was indeed a charismatic leader in the Weberian sense of the word. However, the ubiquitous citations crediting Mao as the sole author of official discourses were intended to ideologize the social world in a new way, of which an essential characteristic was to speak of *what ought to be* in place of *what was*. That is, denoting reality gave way to connoting what it ought to be. It was an early indication that ideological discourses would be prioritized over or empowered against descriptive statistics, as we have seen in the years of the Cultural Revolution.

The year 1957 was a transitional year. The government had consolidated its control since coming to power in 1949, but the ideological waters that had been previously unruffled seemed to be disturbed by some severe criticism of the Maoist sovereignty. In which direction should the People's Republic continue to travel? And how? The government's promises for a better future were seriously doubted by some people, particularly certain intellectuals who had just gone through the Anti-Rightist Campaign. This was also the time that the countryside was about to be collectivized, which would soon result in the organization of the Chinese peasantry into "people's communes," a historic development of collective production that was unprecedented in such a vast geography (Shue 1980). The 1957 report should therefore be read as a sign of transition. Its chief function, as a highly discursive ideological document, was to call for politico-moral conviction. "Do you not think that the victory of the People's Republic is a victory for the majority of its people and a victory for the future?" This kind of statement, typical of the rhetorical style of the document, was not intended to represent reality, statistically or otherwise. Instead, it hoped to insert into the discourse an ideological conviction.

It is important to note that such a mode of official documentation, which was to become *the documentary officiation* of the Maoist discursive praxis, would dominate the social imagination for the entire epoch of the Cultural Revolution (1966–1976), during which descriptive statistics stood in the shadow of history as nothing more than the remains of bourgeois pseudo-science. In other words, it was a statement that should be taken as the *state-meant*, which *officiated* what was "meant" by the Maoist conviction. Thus, the use of statistical figures was not crucial for this report, and the figures that *were* employed were not used in a straightforward fashion. For example, to counter criticism of the official plan for collectivization, the report tried to show that although the previous year had not been a great one for agriculture, the country's agricultural production had surpassed expectations, due in part to the ongoing collectivization that was being led and encouraged by the government. In order to prove the worth of collectivization, some statistics were shown: the total output of agriculture was 58.13 billion yuan, an increase of 2.74 billion yuan in value over the previous year.[9] It is intriguing to observe that the report did not describe the growth in percentages this time, which would by no means have been significant in statistical terms. The increase was in fact less than 0.5 percent. It is perhaps a bit tarnishing to note that this increase was calculated only in *value*: the report did not announce the output of any actual produce, as it had proudly done in the 1954 governmental report. Even a sympathetic reader of the Maoist years could hardly avoid the impression that the government tried to circumvent the normal use of statistical data and analysis. Instead, a hide-and-seek kind of approach toward statistics seemed to be the government's official response to its critics.

Thus, although the percentage or ratio was still being used, it was being used in an entirely different way. A typical use of proportionalization, which had nothing to do with economic development or industrial production, was to defend official political decisions. For example, the 1957 report related that among those arrested for their "counter-revolutionary" crimes, 16.8 percent were given a death sentence, 42.3 percent were placed in labor camps, 32 percent were put under mass surveillance, and 8.9 percent received no severe punishment. During the early years of the People's Republic, the government had repressed various kinds of "counter-revolutionary" movements. By providing these figures, the state meant to show that such crimes were now being fairly treated and that not every single case resulted in an indiscriminately severe punishment. However, the report avoided providing the actual figure of those punished. Hiding behind a percentage, the total number of people who had been put to death, which could have been very large, was not revealed. In these pages it is not my intention to judge the political decisions of the Maoist government,

---

9. The yuan is the primary unit of Chinese currency. The official exchange rate with the US dollar up to 2007 was about 8 yuan per dollar. From 2007 onward, the Chinese yuan has become stronger against the dollar.

as that would go beyond the scope of the discussion. Nevertheless, it must be pointed out that an official manipulation of statistics seems to have been the case. In short, despite being separated by a gap of only three years, the 1954 and 1957 reports reflect a very different approach toward employing statistical data, with the three types of statistical figures—growth rate, sum total, and ratio—no longer being used more or less systematically and objectively for measuring the productivity of the national economy in the 1957 report.

Denoting is demonstrating or proving; connoting is persuading or convincing. In the three years between reports, the official documentation system appeared to have changed from demonstration to persuasion. It seems as if reality no longer needed to be verified by descriptive, provable statistics; it would have to be changed, by conviction and persuasion, into a perfect ideological state. Statistical descriptions of actual happenings would have to give way to the articulation of a new vision of the world, whose copyright came to be owned by Mao.[10] The official attitude about the usefulness of descriptive statistics for objective measurements of social reality had changed. The following year was buffeted by the storm of the Great Leap Forward (1958–1959), a fanatic mass movement of sacrifice and invocation whose disastrous consequences resulted in a devastating nationwide famine in the early 1960s. A momentary collective intoxication had come into being. The collective phantasm of the Great Leap Forward, seen retrospectively, could be nothing but a societal delusion, mad and unreasonable. However, at the time it did bring a seemingly impossible possibility into life.

One's curiosity should never be satisfied with simplistic explanations. Nevertheless, questions remain: How did such an irrational, almost lunatic uprising come to be seen as a real possibility for historical development? Why were so many people, scientists and intellectuals included, spellbound by such an "unscientific" calling? How could people believe that the agricultural output of a village or a region could increase a thousand times within a year through the sheer passion and force of collective labor? Why did almost everyone think that China would soon take over the lead in worldwide industrial production simply by means of manual labor and sweat under the leadership of Mao? There was a genuine mass participation in the Great Leap Forward, and this "mystic participation" was not just the result of official coercion (cf. Lévy-Bruhl 1975). The 1957 governmental report does not explain entirely the advent of the Great Leap Forward; instead, it is a documentary anticipation of the "mystic participation" of the masses in the following year and during the years of the Cultural Revolution. In other words, the report is a documentary monument in the history of Maoist ideas, when the descriptive or denoting

10. For accounts of Mao's thinking, particularly his vision of human will and history, see Schram (1989) and Wakeman (1973).

function of the governmental report gave way to the prescriptive or connoting function of ideologization and indoctrination. On the official calendar, it
marked the moment for the disappearance of statistical objectification as a
favorable speech genre of the government. It indicated the birth of a different discursive strategy, with which a new mode of citation and recitation—by
which the world would be presented to our eyes—came into existence.

Let us briefly compare the two reports. In the 1954 report, statistical figures
were used in and for themselves, with no further explanation unless of a technical or statistical nature. The statistics stood as evidence to prove what they
represented—that there had been a tremendous increase in industrial production. In contrast, the use of figures in the 1957 report was by no means self-evi-
dent. The numbers had to be explained—contextualized in official terms—as if
they no longer represented reality. Indeed, there had been little actual increase
in production and productivity, insofar as the 1957 report was concerned,
which resulted in the need to defend the official view through contextualized
interpretations of the limited statistical figures employed. Rather than a systematic use of descriptive statistics, there was a careful selection of ratios and
sum totals for particular ideological uses. The awareness of what statistical figures *could* do, and what they *should* do, was clearly evident in the official mind.
In the second half of the 1957 report, few numbers appeared. Its tone reflected
the goal of refuting or confronting anti-government criticisms instead of representing what actually had taken place. And very little was said about foreign
relations. Instead, the report directed its attention to answering criticisms,
complaints, and utterances of disbelief in the new order of things. Several
sections opened with expressions such as "some people said" or "some people
complained" or "some people thought," as if the governed were no longer the
same as the governing in their fundamental identity but had become subjects
running away from the official view of reality who needed to be reined in.

Hitherto, we have had two photographic impressions of the same face, representing two sets of sentiments that originated from one family. Or one could
say that there existed two rationalities wrapped in the envelope of an unruly
history. According to the first expression, descriptive statistics was understood
as a tool for denoting or describing material or economic development, for
which the logic of proportionality was essential to the official planning work.
When the People's Republic was in its childhood, facing economic underdevelopment and political instability, reality, represented by statistical data and
analysis, was indeed recognized in somewhat objective terms. At this point,
the ideological swallowing of reality had not yet eliminated the assisting role
of descriptive statistics, as is made clear in the 1954 governmental report. In
the country's youthful imagination, both sentiments—objectification and ideologization—seemed to have existed together, rather than one being totally
dominated by the other. At the time, prescription still depended on description

and vice versa. With the second impression, albeit of the same face, the two sentiments or the two modes of making sense of reality—denoting and connoting—could not live together in peace. As we have seen, in the 1957 governmental report, a new function was given to descriptive statistics, with numbers now being used mainly for the defense of the country's ideological employer. Being totally subordinated to and sterilized by the power of the Maoist ideology, the statistical datum lost its weight on the steelyard of a different reality. From the mid-1950s onward, "the weight of numbers"[11] became lighter and lighter with regard to any possible objectification of economy and society. Perhaps one could say that in terms of its horizon of apprehension, the People's Republic changed from a double vision to a single vision, from a latitudinarian perspective to a one-dimensional one. The pendulum swing between these two sentiments, almost bipolar, in and of the same social body suggests an inability to manage its temper.

The Obesity of Statistical Yearbooks

The passion and violence of the radical years of the Cultural Revolution put a momentary stop to the routine work of governmental statistics. The National Bureau of Statistics, as it came to be called later, stopped functioning for a couple of years (1966–1968) when its officers joined the mass movement. To the official mind of the People's Republic today, this legacy is a shame, if not a sin. The Cultural Revolution is viewed as a scar of the Maoist past, which in recollection seems like insanity. How could such primitivity and irrationality take place in the modern world? How could a modern state survive more than a few hours without some statistical objectification of its existence and sovereignty? How could the masses participate in such a lunatic, collective delusion? From the official perspective of today, it is indeed impossible to understand this historical absence of rationality. For this absence, which indicated the presence of a different faith in truth and facts, recorded another impetus of power praxis, according to which the empirical validity and evidence of facts had to be validated by the Maoist Red Guards in the first place. It is very hard not to read into the Maoist past a postmodern distrust of the modernistic conception of truth and facticity. This distrust, as an intellectual sentiment, has prevailed in the field of human sciences (see, e.g., Foucault 1997).[12] Awakened from the Maoist nightmare, the People's Republic turned to the modern schemes of things, arguing against the irrationality and primitivity of the past and, in the process, rendering the statistical datum equivalent to facticity and truth. In

11. The term "weight of numbers" is borrowed from Braudel (1981, 31).
12. See Norris (1996) for a critical review of the problem of truth in the postmodern age.

contrast to the intellectual sentiment across the Pacific, the People's Republic has made the official statistician a shaman of objectivity and objectification. In short, on the vast ruins of the Maoist revolution, a new regime of truth has been born: social reality and economic development are now believed to be attainable only by means of statistical data and quantitative facts.

For an illustration of the history of the treatment of facts, I turn to the story of the statistical yearbooks, a special category of publication that has been made available to the general public since the 1980s. During the entire epoch of the Maoist revolution, no such attempt was made for two reasons. First, contrary to the experience of other societies, in which the rise of the modern state with its new mentality of governance saw a tremendous increase in the use of statistical knowledge to manage society (see, e.g., Cole 2000; Desrosières 1998; Hacking 1990; Porter 1986), the Maoist government did not recognize the statistical datum as a scientific means to objectify reality. On the contrary, economic statistics and several other social science disciplines, such as sociology, were looked on as the remains of bourgeois pseudo-science. In epistemological terms, little significance was given to the statistical computation of social reality. Second, under the system of the socialist planning economy, the National Bureau of Statistics acted like a clerk or an assistant to the colossal institution of the Central Planning Committee. Figures and calculations of national production, produce, or productivity were limited to the categories devised by the Committee. Always restricted by coded degrees of circulation, the statistics were almost never distributed outside the relevant government offices.

For the first time, in the year 1982, the National Bureau of Statistics brought out a statistical yearbook of China, which consisted of 337 pages and 337 tables of figures. It was not a small book, but in comparison to today's elephantine publications, the 1982 yearbook would be comparable in size to a small rabbit. More importantly, not only have the length and size of the national statistical yearbooks expanded, but there has also been an explosion of different kinds of such publications. Following the model set up by the National Bureau of Statistics, over the past couple of decades, the National Agriculture Statistical Yearbook, the National Industry Statistical Yearbook, the National Demography Statistical Yearbook, the National Foreign Trade Statistical Yearbook, and many other such publications have been crammed into the libraries. The list of publications has been growing, and every province has also produced its own equivalent series of such volumes. Local governments—that is, cities, districts, or special counties under provincial governance—have also been eager to follow suit. A little math tantalizes the mind: how many statistical figures, wrapped in matrixes and tables, have been produced for the sake of grasping a changing materiality? The expansion and accumulation of statistical information in such a short period of time and in such an explosive quantity, sanctioned by the official will, have been both a result of and a reason for the country's ongoing material transformation, by which facts are made into numbers and numbers are made into facts. Statistics—descriptive statistics in particular—as an effective means of maintaining a certain sense of reality, which is development, has gained an unprecedented power in the world of China today.

Not too long ago, largely due to the lack of systematic socio-economic data, students of China were limited to guesswork in trying to put together the pieces of their sociological puzzle. Proper social sciences, including sociology and political science, as well as economics and demography, suffered from a disciplinary migraine at not being able to obtain trustworthy quantitative data for their object of study. Unable to obtain statistical information about the Maoist society, sociologists spent their time speculating about the average income or the normal size of factory dormitories in urban China, a unique social science problematic for the study of a "mystic" reality.[13] With the memory of the previous difficulties still fresh, the sociological imagination encountered an explosion of statistical data that became available almost all at once. For example, the Center for Chinese Studies Library (CCSL) of the University of California at Berkeley, then under the guidance of Annie Chang,[14] had once hoped to collect, more or less systematically, the statistical yearbooks of China as a library project in the early 1980s. In a span of a decade or so, such a project had become quite an impossible one due to the enormous quantity and growing obesity of the volumes. The CCSL later changed its strategy. Instead of attempting a systematic collection, it hoped to focus on only a few provinces and a few areas of scholarly attention, such as industrial growth. Even if one were to walk into the library today, without any intention to look for these yearbooks, one would not be able to avoid noticing them. Huge in size—usually with hard covers and sometimes decorated with colorful images—they proudly sit on several long rows of bookshelves. The impression of their self-completeness and heaviness, partly due to the crowded space of the library,[15] is immensely striking. In opening a volume, one is intensely impressed by the amount of data contained therein, which would strain the mind of anyone searching for truth and facts.

This kind of systematic collection of statistical information by the state has happened elsewhere, such as in Western societies. However, in those societies the systematization and institutionalization of statistical knowledge have

13. See, for example, Walder (1986) and Whyte and Parish (1984). Both works, as a final testimony to the sociological headache of studying the Maoist society, have included an appendix to explain the source and quality of their data, which were obtained chiefly from interviews in Hong Kong.

14. Annie Chang, a devoted librarian, retired from her position in 2004.

15. Since the time of this writing, the Center for Chinese Studies Library has merged with the East Asian Library to become the new C. V. Starr East Asian Library in a central location of the Berkeley campus.

taken place as a gradual process over a period of a couple of centuries (Hacking 1990)—unlike in the People's Republic, where it came as a sudden rush. What is refreshing, in the historical experience of this social giant, is not its massive construction of a quantitative world of statistical information, nor is it the explicit attempt to objectify social reality in terms of quantitative facts and evidence, which is not a new approach. Instead, what is impressive is its *empathic* shift, in both official and popular imaginations, in embracing the sentimentalized usage of the statistical datum for truth claims. This *empathic transfer*, wrapped up in and yet wrapping up a history of sentimentality, is a new happening on the old track of modern development. Therefore, it is not how the quantitative came to represent the actual or the real that will make up the central problem of our inquiry. In such a case as this, the intellectual task must be a serious questioning into such an *empathic transfer*, which is a global effect of our "being in the world."

The lineage of the yearbook series has now expanded into many sibling branches and extended families that are not only statistical in nature; for example, economic and sociological yearbooks have also appeared in their own series. In fact, the lineage or clan of serial publications reflects a national psychic urge, an unstoppable desire, to summarize, to put everything under a general thematic or annual name, to represent reality in seriality, to mirror the shape of development in its concatenational entirety, however defined. The statistical yearbook has become an exemplary paradigm for an official and yet intellectual fancy for a totalitarian representation of reality in which the manifold world of happenings is squeezed into a serial encyclopedia. In such a synoptic overview of the country's annual progress, the world of the People's Republic is supposed to be thus epitomized by the scientific means of statistical tabulation and summarization, which is, as a new faith, factual and minute, quantitative and objective, scientific in spirit and representational in carnality. Those obese yearbooks of statistical tabulation are not simply data containers, baskets of facts. They are instead models of real development in its representational form, which has become *the form of representation*—quantitative and statistical. Not only the scenery, but also the eye has changed. Just as urban space in contemporary China rises to new heights, the expansion of statistical knowledge, official or scholarly, has made certain conceptual skyscrapers visible and necessary for thinking about life. Like walking in Pudong, a newly developed area of Shanghai, where the crowded high-rise buildings stretch to the ceiling of the sky, one would easily find, in the residential area of a thinking mind in and of the People's Republic, a new neighborhood of statistical tabulation and classification, according to which the world of development is to be shown as hard facts. Both urban development and the growth of statistical knowledge are real, resembling one another in their amazing, empathic steps of reciprocal movement—as if a pain in one would also be felt by the other.

The Law for Statistical Work

Now facing an avalanche of information contained in the officially sanctioned statistical yearbooks, scholars of China began to worry about its validity and truthfulness. Were the socio-economic data of governmental statistics accurate? Was the estimation of the annual growth rates precise? Questions of the sort, both inside and outside the People's Republic, have arisen in recent years, and doubts seem difficult to repress. US economist Thomas G. Rawski (2001) contends that there have been inconsistencies or exaggerations in China's official statistics, especially regarding its GDP growth. This worrying concern also speaks to the miracle—or myth—of China's economic development, of which a key feature is the development of a dubious incongruity between its visibility and reasonability. As a common rule of economic development, Rawski argues, the GDP growth should increase in proportion with a concordant increase in the consumption of energy and resources. However, in the case of China, for example, from 1996 to 2000, its GDP annual growth was 8.3 percent on average, while the corresponding increase in the total energy and resource consumption was only around 2.2 percent. For this to occur, China's productivity must have greatly improved, which means that its unit consumption of energy and resources must have decreased significantly. If this were so, it would explain the growth, which would have been due to a decrease in the unit consumption of energy and resources, thus allowing greater productivity. However, this was not the case, observes Rawski. According to governmental statistics, the unit consumption of energy and resources in these years did not improve very much. Thus, the question arises: what made such a GDP growth possible, if it was due neither to an improvement in productivity nor to an increase in the total consumption of energy and resources? In other words, as Rawski seems to have suggested, is there not some kind of mistake in the official records of China's economic development?

Official responses to such skepticism, popularized in the mass media and verified by my own fieldwork among state statisticians, will often include two main points. One is that, having transformed its industrial infrastructure, China has succeeded in greatly reducing its level of energy and resource consumption. This means that its achievement is *structural* rather than technological. It has saved energy and resources by restructuring its economic infrastructure rather than by improving its industrial productivity. For example, officials argue that a great reduction of waste was achieved by closing down small, inefficient, and redundant rural industries. As a result, it is the *increased scale of production* that has saved on the consumption of energy and resources—and this is not always observable in the statistical recording of the unit consumptions by industries. Thus, China's GDP growth must be seen as an effect of the increased scale of economic production, not solely as an improvement in productivity. The second point is that there has been a growing army of rural laborers contributing to economic growth in a significant way, but the value of their labor had not been entirely taken into account before. Their contribution is now being registered, but obviously this added value did not increase the consumption of energy and resources. The value of rural labor has been an essential factor in China's economic growth, but it was often overlooked. For example, the construction workers who have consumed no industrial energy or natural resources have made a great contribution to China's GDP growth figure, and this labor has been statistically recorded only in recent years.

One might agree with either side in the argument; however, no one could or should refuse to engage with Rawski's economic and statistical logics. Such an exchange demonstrates not only who wins the argument but, more than anything else, *in whose terms and conditions* such a debate is set up as legitimate. The official smile, in winning an argument such as this, seems only to confirm the battleground having been shifted to the Other shore of the Pacific, where Rawski, embodying the spirit of modern economic rationality, resides. The truth is that for such arguments to be possible, governmental statistics must be prepared in the first place, and it is only in the growing volumes of statistical data collected by the state that a different discursive possibility emerges. This emergence has allowed a different mode of argumentation, which has made possible a connecting path traveling from and to the world of the People's Republic: statistical data have built a new bridge between China and the rest of the world. It is hardly useful to spend more time verifying the statistical figures themselves, because the underlying question is not about the truthfulness of those figures; rather, it is about *the truthfulness of truth*, which explains how a new life of data and facts has come into existence. The function of statistical figures, such as growth rates, goes beyond simply denoting reality—it legitimatizes such reality governed by a newly renewed sentimentality of life and knowledge. Having cast off the Maoist logic and reasoning, the People's Republic now embraces modern development by adopting its objectifying language of economics, whose vocabulary is statistical in nature.

That there have been inconsistencies and errors in the governmental statistics of the People's Republic is incontrovertible. Statistical mistakes might have been represented as data and facts in the story of the country's development, and figures may well have been made up. As Mark Twain once said, there are three kinds of liars: liars, damned liars, and statisticians. "Do statistics lie? How many people are really unemployed? What is the real rate of productivity? These measurements, which are reference points in the debate, are *also subject to debate themselves*" (Desrosières 1998, 1; emphasis added). The point is that what is subject to questioning should not simply be the GDP growth rates, as in the above debate, but also *the objectification* of the statistical representation as objective truth and scientific knowledge. Rather than moving within the space of thinking circumscribed by statistical reasoning, we must interrogate this circumscription. By questioning what constitutes the facticity of facts, we may be able to gain a better vision of a *life of truth* that has dressed itself up as the truth of life.

It is unfair to blame the current government of the People's Republic for the fallacies and errors of statistical information on record. This government has in fact tried hard to ensure that the process and results of data collection are scientific and correct. Behind this attempt lies a positivistic spirit, according to which facts have nothing to do with opinions or policies and are entirely *separable* and/or *separated from* their use in policy making. The presumption of a total divorce of data from their production and presentation is an intrinsic principle of the positivist doctrine (see, e.g., Lenzer 1975). Unfortunately or fortunately, this doctrine has come to prevail in the official mind of the People's Republic, despite the fact that Auguste Comte's positive science and Durkheim's rules of sociological method have perhaps never been heard of. Seen from the political horizon of China's recent history, the importance of treating "facts" as *facts* signals, among other things, a desire to advance science or scientific reason against Maoist ideological errors. These errors of ideology and socialism, the Maoist inheritance, are conceived *in total contradistinction* to today's scientific approach, which can be best exemplified in the quantitative and statistical analysis of hard facts. The official language of the People's Republic, its new Mandarin, may not be flawless, but the sentiment thus avowed represents a historical innovation for the world of our time. The positivistic spirit of modern science, which came to be understood as global and rational, has allowed the People's Republic to depart from the Maoist primitivity and irrationality.

For an official statistician, certain moments of the Maoist years would appear incomprehensible or unbelievable. Students and scholars of contemporary China know well that during the Great Leap Forward (1958–1959), there were appalling exaggerations in the statistical records of the country's economic performance. The political environment encouraged people to overstate the output of their produce for the purpose of demonstrating their enthusiasm for and loyalty to the Maoist government. This political passion or collective insanity, which cannot be easily understood from an "objective" viewpoint beyond its historical boundaries, produced both sacrifice and accolades. It can also be argued that the lunatic ambience gave birth to a large pool of opportunistic encomiasts. During those years of zeal and violence, individuals had few alternatives but to follow the political prescriptions of the day. Other possibilities were blocked, and one would have to compete on the new political ground paved by the Maoist ideological state (see, e.g., Burns 1988).

In order to illustrate the atmosphere of the time, let me relate an anecdote told by an interviewee who had found the most explicit version of it in a literary magazine. It was a story about how local cadres urged village leaders in northern Shaanxi to exaggerate their production figures during the Great Leap Forward. This kind of narrative, a popular mode of representing the Maoist past, came to dominate both scholarly and literary imaginations from the 1980s onward. The story concerned a peasant leader and other village heads who were called upon to report to the local cadres about the village's total output of grain production in the autumn of 1958. In the tension of the moment, with the Maoist government proclaiming that China's economic production would catch up with America in fifteen years and Britain in seven to eight years, village heads were under extreme pressure to exaggerate their productivity. After persuasion and coercion, most village leaders agreed to say what the local cadres wished to hear. The exaggerated figures, which were not verified, would bring disastrous consequences later on: the local government would use the reports to demand that more grain be handed over than the villagers had actually produced or possessed. Peasants wanted to produce more for the new society because they believed that they had greatly benefited from it. This enthusiasm was taken up and encouraged by the Maoist state, which responded with its plan for a "great leap forward" in economic production. This was a vicious circle, with the local cadres caught in between the two genuine passions. The marriage of the official dream with the popular fantasy produced the deranged mass movement, in the course of which local officials made up inflated numbers for agricultural productivity and production in order to demonstrate their own loyalty and achievements.

As the story goes, our hero, Lao Ma, entered a room where a group of local officials sat around a large table. Other village heads had been already there, and each of them had reported to the local officials on their village's outputs for the year. Whenever someone said something, truthful or already exaggerated, a coarse, low, and serious voice would ask: "Is that all? Is that all you have produced? Could that be possible? In such a great mass movement of leaping forward, how can your village only double last year's production? Is it true? Or are you cheating? I can tell you that your neighboring village has produced ten times more than it did last year. Just tell me what is happening in your village. Is there someone who tries to delay our socialist progress? Or is someone cheating? Or is there someone who is trying to work against our country?" This kind of logic and reasoning, pronounced in a harsh voice coming from a stern countenance, made people uneasy, and one by one each village head would try to come up with an acceptable figure in order to pass through the meeting. A village head would not be allowed to leave until he produced a number that would satisfy the local officials. This meeting had been going on for a couple of days, and most village leaders had conceded to the pressure to make up numbers.

Lao Ma, the last one remaining in the room, refused to surrender. "That is all that we have produced," he said repeatedly.

"That cannot be all that you have. You must have produced more than that. Have you not seen how much other villages have produced?"

"They are they, we are we. We are not they." Lao Ma was not very good at public speaking.

"How come? Your village is even bigger than theirs. This cannot be true, Lao Ma. You need to think about yourself. You are making a serious mistake." Threatening words indeed. Nobody spoke to him for a while, and then they asked Lao Ma to squat on the brick bed, which, characteristic of northern China, was heated from inside.[16] The local cadres did not question him further but added more fuel to heat the bed, which soon reached almost a burning point. The officials scattered in the room, sitting around the table, smoking heavily and tasting their tea, while waiting for Lao Ma to change his mind. But he never did. He stayed on the bed in his bare feet for more than ten hours without even blinking.

"Lao Ma," an impatient cadre finally said, "it cannot be true that your village has made only a 30 percent increase. Is this because you want to keep some extra grains for yourself or your village? If that is the case, you will be in shitty, shitty big trouble."

"That is all we have grown, believe it or not. I can bring everyone to my house to see whether I have hidden anything. This is the truth." Lao Ma's resistance succeeded in the end, and the local officials gave up their attempts to force him to say what they wanted to hear. In this story, a retelling of a fictional figure as a peasant hero against the Maoist insanity, Lao Ma was treated, in the 1980s, as a local legend for enduring the burning heat. When the national famine arrived in the following years, Lao Ma's village could have survived a little better than other villages, because, by not making a gross exaggeration, his village had managed to keep some extra grain for itself. The year 1958 was a great year for agriculture. It was also a mystic or mythical year for "making up numbers," an unprecedented historical experience.

It is against such a mythical and mystical past that the Law for Statistical Work,[17] a legal declaration of the authority and legitimacy of governmental statistics, came into being in 1983. Implicitly or explicitly, the law spoke a language critical of the Great Leap Forward, or, more generally, the Cultural Revolution, whose spirit ran entirely in the opposite direction. The immediate attention, at an early stage of economic reform, to the problem of governmental statistics—which ought to be, as is now believed, governed by law—is an

16. See X. Liu (2000, 42–47) for a discussion of the heating system of a northern Shaanxi house.

17. A direct translation of the Chinese in this case would be confusing. It would become the Law of Statistics or Statistical Law, which would make little sense to an English reader. This law is intended to officiate the government statistical work and therefore is more appropriately referred to as the Law for Statistical Work.

indication of a shift in the mentality of governance from a prescriptive and connoting mode of official thought to a descriptive and denoting one.[18] The 1983 Law for Statistical Work was revised in 1996, when several amendments were added. This new version, consisting of six chapters and a total of thirty-four articles, was an essential part of the official effort to set up a legal framework for the country.

The first article is an official statement about the need for establishing such a law, and the second article explains the task of government statistical work, which is said to function as a supervising agency for the surveillance of socio-economic development. Following the two preliminary articles, a crucial message arrives in the third article: national institutions, social groups, industrial units, private enterprises, and all other legal subjects or representatives of statistical surveys must act according to this law and other relevant government regulations. These representatives or institutions are requested by the law to provide truthful and honest statistical information. They *must not* make up, hide, refuse to deliver, or delay in submitting statistical data. They *must not* fake or purposely change the statistical information. This is an unmistakable reaction to the man-made errors of the Maoist data collection, which was neither scientific in its procedure nor objective in its production. The National Bureau of Statistics may today still record an incorrect number; however, if so, it is due to chance and probability, for the statistical method will allow random errors to be regulated and calculated. The chief concern of the law is to eradicate intentional errors and misrepresentation of data in the government statistical work.

In other words, the truth or truthfulness of statistical information should be secured by the law (see, e.g., Articles 5, 6, 7, 8 in the first chapter). For example, the law addresses the issue of how to protect statistical workers from illicit instructions or intimidation that may come from their advisers or superiors (Article 8). The law means to protect those working first-hand on the data, to prohibit those in higher offices from influencing the truthful collection of statistical information, and to punish those who dare to manipulate statistical data (Article 27). It is a law that speaks a universal (or global) language to a particular historical experience. There are, of course, other concerns, terms, and technical regulations, but the very spirit of this law, which is *not* the *Spirit of Laws* of Montesquieu, hopes to establish *the authority of facts* against the ideological errors of the Maoist past, in order to achieve an objective, quantitative, and statistical representation of socio-economic reality. Behind such a legal establishment lies the absolute presupposition that, contrary to the Maoist mode of thinking, reality always exists independently from the eyes observing it. That is, facts should not be mixed up with opinions or points of views.

18. There was a similar law in Republican China, established in 1932.

Therefore, obtaining and maintaining a truthful representation of social reality—by means of statistical tabulation and taxonomization—must be the essential hope of the law. The language adopted by the law is global and modern, but its message is instead addressed to the Maoist years, when, as it is believed, a lot of man-made errors were produced. From today's perspective, the problem of the Maoist years was due to both its ideological bias and its lack of an objective measurement of reality in statistical terms, which has now been put into place. According to the official view, there are five main functions of this law. First, there is an instructive function: it discourages one from playing with statistical information, which must be truthfully reported and recorded. Second, there is an evaluating function: it allows one to judge whether the collection and processing of statistical data is adequate or not. Third, there is a regulating function: it guarantees the collection of data by a legal authority and its institutional means. Fourth, there is an educational function: it makes people understand the importance of government statistical work. Fifth, there is a punitive function: it provides a legal framework to punish those who try to alter governmental statistics. This is what the law intends to do and what it has tried to achieve. Reading the law and listening to the official explanation of its functions, it is hard to resist the pull of "truth" and "fact," which have been born once again, in a strenuous struggle for modern development, by an old woman but a new bride—the People's Republic of China.

Chapter Two

THE FACTICITY OF SOCIAL FACTS

A New Life of Facts

A primal shift has taken place in the field of governmental statistics of the People's Republic: statistical information is no longer considered purely an *official* asset, sacred as well as secret, entirely made or prepared for the state's use. Against the long and somewhat rusty Chinese tradition of thought, statistical data have come to be seen as a source of neutral, objective knowledge about the economy and society. This knowledge is now owned, as common property, by both officials and ordinary people. To say the least, this indicates a change in the relationship of the governing to the governed, of the sovereign to its subject, of the state to society. To a large extent, to govern nowadays means to convince the governed that what is being done is for the general good, which can be proved by statistical comparisons of various sorts. Statistical knowledge, with its neutralizing and objectifying power in producing "hard facts," has become a bridge on which officials, scholars, and ordinary people can walk from one side to the other in the hope of making a reasonable and rational argument. This signals a redefinition of the means of legitimization for sovereignty in which the public use of statistics has become a necessary condition for effective governance. The mind of the state, the heart of governance, has come to be dominated by the mode of statistical reason. Its appearance, to the eyes of a naive observer, might seem to be nothing more than a modern "long march" toward an objective, rational, and scientific destination.

However, beneath the surface lies a *history of sentimentality*, which signifies a change in the mentality of governance. The rise of statistical reasoning, in both the official and popular imaginations, denotes a critical reaction to the Maoist past and a coming of age in modern development.

Let us look at the scholarly attitude as an exemplification of this change. A couple of years ago, a leading sociologist from China was invited to speak at the University of California at Berkeley on social stratification in the People's Republic today. He was confident and eloquent, and his speech was well-received. After his talk, an audience member asked about what was off-limits to researchers in today's China, the sort of question that could be expected from people who had not been to China in recent years. The question carried, intentionally or not, an ideological tail that meant to suggest the limits of sociological objectivity within the political confines of a dogmatic state. The sociologist took the exchange into a slightly different direction and responded proudly: "My research, both its procedures and results, are superior—far superior—to many of my colleagues. And I have never been scolded by the government. Why? Let me tell you the reason. The truth is that government officials always want to know what I have discovered in my studies. They want to know my opinions about what is happening. They trust my judgment and findings because I let the numbers speak for themselves. I use quantitative methods for my studies, which are fact-based rather than judgment- or opinion-based. I will never act like some of my colleagues do. They are basically expressing their own opinions or stating their personal judgments, which are always arbitrary and false. Instead, what I have done over the past two decades is to provide the government with quantitative analyses, to give the officials or my superiors data and facts, which will never lie. Let them examine what I have found out about our society. Any judgment should be theirs, not mine. My job as a sociologist is to collect data and facts and then submit them to a scientific analysis. My principle is *data, only data, nothing but the data*. My findings are nothing but truth because they are always made of hard facts."

Data, only data, nothing but the data. This is indeed a new expression on the not-so-youthful face of the People's Republic, made visible by a famous sociologist whose confidence in statistical data and quantitative analysis was shown by his eloquence. His intention was clear. First, he meant to say that the researcher in sociology or other social science disciplines has a responsibility to work on the real happenings while putting aside his or her personal opinions. Selection or abstraction in the representation of real happenings, in quantitative forms, is not, according to this view, subjective or judgmental. In other words, statistical or quantitative analysis, such as random sampling, will provide an objective method for understanding society. Second, the sociologist also suggested that there are perhaps some areas of social or official concerns that are not yet entirely open to academic research. However, nobody,

including the officials themselves, should or would deny the need for collecting truthful data about what is happening. In the end, judgments and policy
decisions should be made by the government, but in order to facilitate such
decisions or judgments, one must collect hard facts in the first place. The sociologist or the social scientist in general has become the medium for making
and maintaining truth about the world by producing first-hand quantitative
observations. This outspoken confidence in the quantitative method reflects
both the official and the popular perspective of the real as a statisticalizable
world of hard facts.

Now that socio-economic development has grasped the government's
attention, sociological research has become an official method for observing
material changes in society. Casting a governmental vision, Li and Mo's *A
History of China's Statistics* (1993) has provided an intriguing sketch of official
concerns about the collection of socio-economic data over a *longue durée* history of more than 3,000 years. The book is no doubt a useful account, especially
with regard to tax and population figures, which were vital to the success of
any ancient dynasty. However, one should not expect, despite the book's title,
to encounter those such as Laplace or Galton (see, e.g., Hacking 1975), who
paved the modern path for probabilistic and statistical thought. Instead, Li
and Mo's work, lighting up another historical lane of thought, should be read
as a guidebook into the mind of the People's Republic today. They argue that
statistics, by which they mean economic or governmental statistics, should
belong to the field of general economics. In doing so, they maintain that governmental statistics is something more than simply a collection of data. This is
their reason for placing the origin of statistical work or governmental statistics
in the general domain of economics, rather than tracing its foundations to the
gamblers' games that had troubled a number of great mathematical minds.

Going through Li and Mo's text attentively, the reader would be tempted to
attribute the advancement of statistical thinking to emperors who realized the
importance of statistical knowledge for effective governance. With no need to
inquire into "the politics of large numbers" (Desrosières 1998) or "the power of
large numbers" (Cole 2000) or any other similar histories of statistical thought,
Li and Mo (1993) established the view that connected the modes of control to
the modes of knowledge. Central to their vision, which was semi-official, was
the value of governmental statistics for economic development. According to
their logic, economic development is dependent on a correct evaluation of its
healthfulness, which in turn relies on the truthful diagnosis of its bodily conditions. These conditions are observable only by means of statistical figures and
numbers. Therefore, political leaders must make use of governmental statistics,
rightly and wisely, for their decisions on socio-economic development. Those
who fail to do so will fail the national economy. In their view, the Maoist economic failure was first of all a failure in government statistical work. The true

value of (descriptive) statistics, according to the authors, is its official and economic value, because it is necessary for decision making. It is interesting to note that, being critical of the Maoist years, they re-evaluated the Republican period (roughly 1920–1940) with regard to its improvement in governmental statistics, about which they made three observations. First, scholarly research regarding the development of statistical methods was developed during this era, and a large number of books were translated or written on the subject of statistics. Second, the Republican government institutionalized official systematic statistical work. In comparison to earlier institutions, such as those in the Late Qing Dynasty, the newly established institutions were superior in organization. Third, the Republican government also tried to provide a legal framework for statistical work, which anticipated the later attempts by the People's Republic.

Li and Mo were not alone. It was a commonly held view that the Maoist years had failed to create a modern system of governance because the official statistical work was either neglected or, worse, molested by those in political power. Overlooking the historical gully, X.-B. Liu (1997), a recalcitrant freelance writer known for his sharp and entertaining essays, goes further in arguing that the lack of a scientific, statistical (digital?) administrative system in China must be the reason for its failures in modern socio-economic development. It is *the lack of means*—that is, of the means of statistical measurement and surveillance—in the history of a *longue durée* that effectively explains its weakness and underdevelopment. This diagnosis, shared by a large pool of other scholars, would direct one's attention to the differences between the scientific, objective, quantitative mode of modern governance and the lack of it in the People's Republic. Orientalizing or not, in crossing the threshold of a new century, the People's Republic took up an old comparativistic scheme of the nineteenth-century evolutionist model, which assumes the existence of a great chain of modern becoming, a hierarchy of a developmental order of being. It is according to such a great chain of being and becoming that the meaning of self can be defined in relation to the Other, the more advanced modern industrial world.

Liu's essay, in fact, was a response to the point made by an economic historian of China, R.-Y. Huang. Trained in America, Huang specialized in the history of the Ming Dynasty (1368–1644), although his fame largely came from popularizing history for the Chinese audience in the 1990s. Straddling the old conceptual divide between the West and China, Huang (1997) argued that Chinese rulers never properly developed a system of quantitative or statistical administration. For example, the Chinese system of taxation and tax collection, both past and present, is far less developed than the complicated system of the Internal Revenue in the United States. According to Huang, the error of history in the case of China is its lack of a sophisticated administrative system, one that is statistical or quantitative (i.e., objective and scientific) in character, and minute and accurate in practice. The mentality of governance also differs from one to the other: that of the West is quantitative, specialized, technical, and hence attentive to every single detail, whereas that of China is qualitative in style, poetic or humane in spirit, grand in manner, and ideological in its practice (cf. Weber 1951). Not an entirely new thesis, this argument retained its force in the 1990s to an impressive degree. Huang suggested that *the Confucian order of things* was built on the *order of Confucian things*, which was concerned with value, ethics, and the morality of family and society. Such an approach did not lead to a modern system of computing and accounting. The West, according to this view, stood in the opposite: the spirit of science in administration must be its quantitative character, which China lacked. The problem for the Ming emperor, as for other Chinese rulers, is that he did not know what was happening outside his palace because he *could not* know—for he lacked the necessary means of knowing it. It was impossible for him to get access to reality without an established system of effective statistical or quantitative administration.

Huang's point was well-taken, although Liu slightly disagreed. He suggested that the quantitative, statistical model of administration would not work without the *right* adoption of such a system, which depended on the gradual cultivation of a scientific spirit for the whole nation. However, common to both authors was a sense of the People's Republic at the time, which came to view the history of China in terms of its place in the world's development. Statisticians may lie, but as a means of historical comparison, the quantitative versus the qualitative came to bear the weight of a most important conceptual distinction. In such a scheme of conceptualization, which is dichotomous in character, history is no longer, as shown in Huang's work, simply a backward-looking operation; it is also a forward-looking one, taking the modern Other as one's potential future. Thus, notional areas concerning science, modernity, quantitative administration, and rational government have become central concerns for a new mode of thinking, which, comparativistic in essence, will produce a series of dichotomies, such as science versus ideology, quantitative versus qualitative, etc. In this way, the modern Other, its positive image, has become an indispensable and immediate reference in intellectual discussions and everyday conversations.

Of course, this modern Other is not just anyone—not Portugal, for instance, and hardly Spain—but rather those capitalist countries, such as the United States and Germany and Japan, that are the most advanced. For example, in daily conversation in the 1990s, when someone from America inquired of a friend in Beijing about his life and work, or his health, a most likely answer would be, "Well, not too bad, which of course cannot be compared with what you have in America. I am doing quite all right." One was also likely to find out later that this man had just bought another suburban apartment and drove a brand-new BMW. This is not what he meant; he did not mean *to compare.* But this way of making sense of life has become habitual, fostering an inertness of which he was perhaps not fully aware. According to a local newspaper report, a few years ago, when then President Jiang visited Daliang, a beautiful seaside city in North China, he praised the elegant redecoration of the city's urban architecture as follows: "Oh, it is lovely, a truly pretty scene. Everything looks so handsome, it can almost be compared to San Francisco." President Jiang certainly intended to pay a compliment to the mayor; however, it is also true that such a compliment could be but a comparative flirt with the modern Other. Across the Pacific Ocean there has been erected a standard of development against which one can measure reality for oneself.

Facts will become "factual" when and only when an empirical-quantitative ground for conceptualization has been constructed. This comparativistic vision of the world is dependent on the vast accumulation of statistical knowledge. To the official mind of the People's Republic, for example, in order for the country to develop fully and properly, the national accounting system should make possible statistical comparisons between China and the rest of the world on all social and economic matters. This comparativist impulse or complex, which makes facts "factual," took a new lesson from history after the People's Republic awoke from its Maoist nightmare. In a panorama, several interconnected or overlapping undertakings got underway. Firstly, there was a systematization of government statistical work and a systematic expansion of institutions and organizations at a pace that was unprecedented in the history of the People's Republic. Secondly, laws and other official regulations were passed to regulate or try to regulate such work, which was to be conducted in scientific ways. Thirdly, and perhaps most importantly, an epistemological and ethical ground was opened up for producing equivalences of facts with quantitative data and for making statistical analysis the guiding light of social sciences. For the younger generation of students in social sciences, to know has almost become to calculate. That is, the statistical datum has been taken as the most real reality of socio-economic development.

Socialism and Statistics

To argue against the country's increasing economic disparity, one could still return to the Maoist model, but it will hardly be possible to defend the primitivity and irrationality of its mode of authority. A fragment of debris from the old mansion might be picked up and used in the construction of a new one, but the new building itself is designed by totally different structural principles. One could continue to employ the Maoist vocabulary to talk about life in today's China, but one would not hope that such a dialogue would retain the same objectivity, for a new sense of self and reality has licensed the "objective representation of reality," its epistemological legal right, to statistical quantification and comparative analysis. In other words, truth and validity—what is factual and what is not—will today depend on the use or abuse of the statistical datum, the legitimate status of which the Maoist discourse utterly denied.

An example will be explanatory. A residual attempt to evaluate the Maoist achievement positively, *Zhongguo shehui zhuyi yu tongji shuzi* (Chinese Socialism and Statistical Data) (1991), an anthology by fifteen authors, tells an interesting story about the impossibility of retaining the Maoist vision of the world. Up until the mid-1990s, a persistent question for the People's Republic was the question of whether or not to change its direction of historical travel, for example, whether or not to develop a market economy and whether or not to continue some sort of socialist practice. The question of "whether or not" is not a practical or technical inquiry but a political and epistemological one, which, however, lost its force later on. Especially after moving into a new century, the relevant question for the People's Republic is no longer "whether or not"; it has become "how"—how to progress, how to learn about modern development from successful models. In a way, this means that questions about history and social existence have given way to questions about economy and material development. Even today, despite the changes that have taken place, one can still find the remains of socialism in some back alleys of life in the People's Republic. However, the key thing is that the dominant ideology has changed. Socialism is no longer a living force; it has become a dying device struggling to retain its last breath on the ruins of the Maoist edifice. *Chinese Socialism and Statistical Data* intended to make a final defense of the old sentiment, socialist or Maoist, which was fading away. As its preface says, "Against the wrong view that capitalism is better than socialism, believed by some people, we have combined theoretical arguments with statistical data, and compiled this scholarly study as a practical and educational social science reference book and as a political propaganda text."[1] One should not forget the date of its publication—two years after the crackdown on the student anti-government movement in Tiananmen Square.

The "whether or not" question is characteristic of *Chinese Socialism and Statistical Data*. What is intriguing, however, is not its ideological claim that socialism is good for China, but rather its way of proving it. The title of the book consists of two phrases, "Chinese Socialism" and "Statistical Data," connected by an "and." Neither "Chinese Socialism" nor "Statistical Data" is an unusual signifier; however, placing the two together is a rare occurrence. What is the function of the "and" in between? Is it not an attempt to build a bridge across the two realities that are already separated from each other? The phrase "Chinese

1. See *Zhongguo shehui zhuyi yu tongji shuzi* (1991, i). The translation is mine.

Socialism," if used before the time of this publication, would have required no verification or proof. Everyone would have known what it meant: the development of a new China led by Mao. It was a positive signifier, a politically correct expression of what China was. However, its signification became unclear with the passage of time, and its positive connotation could not be assumed among a new generation. With socialism no longer a firmly accepted reality, the sacred socialist doctrines were no longer divine; instead, they had become the subject of comparative sociology or historical economics. Unfortunately or fortunately, in the early 1990s, the value of socialism needed to be proved rather than simply accepted, as the book would have to admit. Then came the scientific need for an objective re-evaluation of history, which would be based on statistical comparison. In reading this work, it seems comparable to asking a Catholic priest to prove the existence of God by measuring the height of his church. This is indeed the irony of the book, for it tries to show how an apple is different from an orange in their respective weights. The fact that the Maoist order of things did not allow a place for the "bourgeois pseudo-science" of statistical comparison is overlooked. Now the bourgeois pseudo-science has returned, with full energy and objectivity, to weigh the weight of socialism on the scales of a capitalist conception of development. The title of the book, with its problematic placement of an "and" between the two rival epistemologies, betrays its argument. It hoped to show that even according to the developmental measurement of statistical data, socialism in China was still a success. Yet it is clear that socialism cannot be defended by such a quantification; ideologies cannot be ideologies if they have to be proved in quantitative terms. This is an intriguing and yet inherent paradox of this book, a last attempt to defend an impossibility.

The first chapter of *Chinese Socialism and Statistical Data*, "The Practical Meaning of Combining Chinese Socialism and Statistical Data," is a good place to trace the logic of a falling spirit. What is meant by the phrase "practical meaning"? It seems to suggest that the success of socialism is provable by statistical data. It is "practical" in the sense that this has to be done empirically, in order to show what is right for the People's Republic of China. This chapter begins with an old story about how a socialist victory took place in China. As usual, there is a discussion of some basic categories of Marx, pertaining to a particular reading of Chinese history, and some statistical numbers are used to show this victory. The next section, titled "Statistical Data and Their Function," offers a concise discussion of the purpose of statistical data and analysis, expressing a view on the nature of statistical analysis: "Statistics collects, displays, describes, and analyzes data. It is a form of art that makes inferences from a set of samples." A form of art? According to this view, the term "statistics" may refer to three things: statistical work, statistical data, and statistical science. *Statistical work*, as it is explained, should include all statistical practices, official and non-official. *Statistical data* are the quantitative information accumulated in and by statistical work. *Statistical science* is the theory that will provide guidance for statistical analysis. This typical view of the triple function of statistics, developed in the 1980s, became a common lesson for students of social sciences.

How does such a view reconcile statistics with "a form of art"? A slip of the collective tongue? Curiously, there is also a reference to Marx, Lenin, and Mao, claiming that they all emphasized the importance of statistical information as a necessary tool for comprehending social reality. It ought to be noted that the three-fold definition of statistics is to be taken as a whole, inseparable and mutually dependent: data make up the material of analysis; science is its method; statistical work is its praxis. That is, statistics must be thought of as a ternary entity consisting of truth, method, and practice. Having stated that statistics means three different but related aspects, the book goes on to explain the importance of collecting data for the government, which must develop proper statistical institutions. The function of the government statistical work, they insist, is to collect data systematically; to collect data systematically will in turn be dependent on setting up official statistical organizations. Of course, data have to be collected in the first place in order to be analyzed; it is also true that data thus collected should be as accurate as possible. Is this not precisely what the government has been trying to do? What does this redundant tautology mean to say?

The last section of this chapter, which serves as an introduction to the entire book, is titled "The Practical Meaning of Statistical Data for China's Social Development." A reader will immediately notice that "social development" has replaced "socialist development" as a crucial signifier for the authors' discourse. The discussion now seems to be less about socialism and more about development. This section argues that since the birth of the People's Republic, China's socio-economic development has been superior to that of India. In making this inept analogy, the rationale seems to be that, comparing development among developing countries, China should prove to be a socialist success story. But it has excluded any mention of superior developments, such as post-war Japan or Taiwan, which are considered exceptional cases due to their access to the world market and American assistance. The comparison of China to India seems to defy itself in that it does not draw a conclusion from the facts. Although the importance of statistical data is acknowledged, it has performed little role in the actual analysis. In fact, there is no need for the argument to be supported by any statistical data. Reading this book, one feels compelled by a bipolar movement, running from socialist doctrines that are heralded on one side, back to claims for the objectivity and neutrality of statistical analysis on the other, without being able to stand firmly on any ground. The book has not made a good case. One would then have to ask, why did the authors write such a work, given their failure to prove what they believe? As a prudent reader would soon realize, in their struggle against the spirit of the age, the authors have taken up the wrong weapon.

Throughout this text, there is an unmistakable attempt to bridge the growing gap between the falling (and failing) socialist ideology and the rising conception of socio-economic development and the market economy. The book
implicitly admits that data are not simply facts—that they have become the
new tool for grasping reality. By the time that it was published, the National
Bureau of Statistics was in the process of expanding its institutions in order to
meet the standards of the World Bank and other global organizational requirements. There was no way to stop the movement toward a universal, scientific,
modern system of governmental statistics, which would work through "the
average" or "x-bar" to reach the heart of each economy—regional, national,
and global. This book was a stand against the winds of change, a final effort
in a losing battle that symbolized a schizophrenic moment in the life of the
People's Republic. Socialism had not yet entirely disappeared in practice; nevertheless, "the pleasures of the Maoist past" had become a representational
pain. The authors' labors were in vain: the book is rather a proof that an epoch
has indeed "gone with the wind." Mao and his images could still be used for
particular purposes, for example, to point out social injustice; however, the
foundation of socialism had collapsed, its epistemology being reformed, or
rather deformed, by the new conception of materiality. The farther one reads
into the book, the less one feels convinced by it, for the Maoist ideologies cannot be defended by statistical analysis. In the face of a new regime of truth,
the ideological power of socialism, both as discursive and material practice,
has lost its legitimacy and allurement. Despite the authors' attempt, statistical
objectivity cannot prove that China has done better or equally as well as India.
Instead, it will only show—according to the system of global production and
consumption, the basis of any econometric comparison today—that China is
behind Japan, Western Europe, and the United States.

Chinese Socialism and Statistical Data may be read as a momentary reaction to the historical transition from an ideological questioning about social
existence to an empirical inquiry about life and economic development. In the
new century, there has been little concern with the question "whether or not."
What occupies one's mind in today's China is how to run fast and faster in the
race for wealth on the global market. To know came to mean to calculate; to
calculate should mean to sell well. Contrary to the intention of its authors, this
book demonstrates the phenomenal triumph of statistical reason, considered
objective and scientific, which has come to function as an ideological platform
of socio-economic reality. The case for socialism as an alternative possibility of
being and becoming seems to be closed. It is difficult to prove its merits in the
language of statistical science. One cannot demonstrate the worth of the Maoist years by an empirically justifiable historical mathematics, just as one cannot
demonstrate faith by counting heads at the door of a Protestant church. It is
undeniable that a different moral mathematics, developmental and global, has

arrived in the vast world of the People's Republic, and that this new regime of data and facts, with its new logic of truth and its new law of facticity, will never embrace the Maoist ideas.

"Let Facts Speak for Themselves"

The times have changed, and a different mode of discourse and awareness has arrived on the scene—one that seems to be, in its immediate appearance at least, possessed by a reincarnation of positivistic spirit. This change of scenery reflects first of all a change in the infrastructure of attentions and concerns, which is now composed of global and developmental categories. A rapid process of statisticalization played the midwife's role in the parturition of a new moral mathematics that has constantly spoken about the need to separate facts from opinions and arguments. It is now believed that facts are facts, out there, waiting to be collected, as someone goes to a forest to gather strawberries or mushrooms. They are not, and should not be, opinions, which are subjective judgments that should be made only after the facts have been gathered. Mushrooms or strawberries have to be collected in order to be cooked or consumed; such a vision of the world has privileged the raw over the cooked. This privilege has prioritized government statistical work in the reorganization of the official hierarchy, for statistical knowledge came to be conceived as the knowledge of *first truth* in providing facts about the economy and society. A result is that the National Bureau of Statistics has gained an unprecedented recognition in the People's Republic: the logic of statistical analysis has prevailed; the supposed laws of the economy have empowered themselves as regulating rules of history and society; a new moral mathematics has become the necessary algebra of everyday life. What has happened is an *epistemological rupture*: the facticity of a fact is claimed everywhere; to prove is to calculate; to speak means to introduce or invoke statistical reasoning. The life of data now provides assurance and certainty for living in a world of socio-economic phantasmagoria. The fact and the judgment must be differentiated, for they are distinct from each other. Stand firm and walk a bit, however tentatively, and then talk about the grounds of reality. This is the present sentiment, which has favored the raw, the fact, the data, the first order of truth, which must be statistical.

Behind this faith in truth and facts lies the second proposition of the positivistic doctrine: there exist general laws of economy and society. Hardly anyone in today's China would doubt that there is a universal law of development, or that the modernist and materialist path should be the only route to follow, or that the vast province of the People's Republic has for the first time embarked on the right train of modernity. While it is acknowledged that there may be incorrect conceptions about these laws of economy and society, the laws themselves are

deemed valid. However, let one not be confused by the double layers of the doctrine: data and facts constitute the necessary tools for the discovery of the laws,
but the tools are not the discoveries. The first order of truth is obtained by the
collection and organization of raw data, while the second order of truth must
be uncovered by studies of the raw materials in hand. Without the first order
of truth—the raw data—one could never arrive at the truth of society and history. However, the first order of truth does not automatically lead to theoretical
discovery. Let me quote from Auguste Comte (1798–1857), the father of philosophical positivism, to illustrate how old such a new social philosophy may be
(quoted in Lenzer 1975, 332; emphasis in original):

> On reviewing this brief sketch of the intellectual character of positivism, it will be
> seen that all its essential attributes are summed up in the word "positive," which
> I apply to the new philosophy at its outset. All the languages of Western Europe
> agree in understanding by this word and its derivatives to the qualities of *reality*
> and *usefulness.* Combining these, we get at once an adequate definition of the true
> philosophic spirit, which, after all, is nothing but good sense generalized and put
> into a systematic form. The term also implies, in all European languages, *certainty*
> and *precision*, qualities by which the intellect of modern nations is markedly distin-
> guished from that of antiquity. Again, the ordinary acceptation of the term implies
> a direct *organic* tendency. Now the metaphysical spirit is incapable of organizing; it
> can only criticize. This distinguishes it from the positive spirit, although for a time
> the two had a common sphere of action. By speaking of positivism as organic, we
> imply that it has a social purpose, that purpose being to supersede theology in the
> spiritual direction of the human race.

If Comte were alive today, he would probably add "and Mandarin Chinese"
to the phrase "all the languages of Western Europe." It is Mandarin Chinese
that is imbued with the spirit of positive philosophy in this global age; it is the
global age that has allowed Mandarin Chinese to add itself to those languages
that initiated the advent of materialistic science; it is this materialistic science
that has brought Mandarin Chinese to the clan of Western Europe. This is
indeed a global tour of a local circus.

In the evolution of the official and popular discourse of development, it
is evident that *reality* and *usefulness* are precisely the ideas that the People's
Republic has embraced. This pairing of notions has been made use of today
in the world of China exactly as it was used by Comte in promoting the new
philosophical spirit of positivism in the nineteenth century. The new spirit
of positive philosophy, which reoriented itself toward reality and usefulness,
was, as Comte argued, indeed different from the metaphysical critique of reality in antiquity. If one were to replace the term "antiquity" with "the Maoist
revolution," one would have little difficulty in publishing Comte's writing as an
official statement of the People's Republic today. History often repeats itself as

a parody, and the argument against "the Maoist antiquity" does resemble the tone of Comte's discourse. It says that reality is not composed of metaphysical or ideological speculations. Reality is *real*, out there, and made up of hard facts. The metaphysics of antiquity and the Maoist ideologies failed to recognize such a simple truth. As Comte witnessed in his own time, metaphysics had lost its power to grasp reality, becoming merely an airy breath of critique that no longer shared the same sphere of action with his new philosophy.

Exactly the same can be said about the People's Republic today, for socialism has become purely a rhetorical device, removed from material reality and constituting an ineffective gesture. Use or usefulness as a notional basis has been essential to the formation of the new reality. It is the usefulness of things that people must struggle to attain. Furthermore, reality must be grasped with certainty, and usefulness with precision, just as Comte proclaimed for "all the languages of Western Europe," which struggled to achieve *certainty of reality and precision of usefulness*. Are these terms not familiar to scholars working on contemporary China? Are these terms not what have been treasured as scientific progress by a societal elephant? Are these terms not exactly what are hoped for by the government of the People's Republic today? The historical circumstances are different, but the mentality of argumentation does sound similar. Certainty and precision cannot be generated unless quantitative analysis and statistical data are made central to the measurement of reality. This seems to be the exact reason why the People's Republic has turned to quantitative science—in order to measure social reality with certainty and precision. This is, as Comte would have said, not for the benefit of one group or nation but for all of them. Society cannot have order and progress unless we place the metaphysical (i.e., ideological) debates behind us. In a sense, the real burial of Mao was taken care of by a new figure, an important statesman—the official statistician—who put the final nail in the coffin. As Comte argued: "Till a certain number of general ideas can be acknowledged as a rallying point of social doctrine, the nations will remain in a revolutionary state, whatever palliatives may be devised; and their institutions can be only provisional. But whenever the necessary agreement on first principles can be obtained, appropriate institutions will issue from them, without stock or resistance; for the causes of disorder will have been arrested by the mere fact of the agreement. It is in this direction that those must look who desire a natural and regular, a normal, state of society" (quoted in Lenzer 1975, 83). A "natural and regular, a normal, state of society" is the outcome of possessing a positive philosophy, which should provide exactly what it has promised. This is not only what the People's Republic demands today; it is also what all societies will most likely turn to after turmoil and revolution. Without such a doctrine, a society will persist in a revolutionary state, by which Comte meant that the social order will remain unstable and impractical, with no hope of attaining certainty and precision.

The message from this page of history is that the organic relationship between the spirit of a new philosophy and the making of a modern society should be evaluated in terms of practicality and usefulness. This is what the Maoist society lacked. The Maoist years were passionate and violent, but they were not useful in any practical sense. Comte put the argument in the following way: "As the chief characteristic of positive philosophy is the preponderance of the social point of view through the whole range of speculation, its efficiency for the purposes of practical life is involved in the very spirit of the system. When this spirit is rightly understood, we find that it leads at once to an object far higher than that of satisfying our scientific curiosity—the object, namely, of organizing human life" (quoted in Lenzer 1975, 334). Clearly, Comte hoped for an organization or reorganization of human life in practical and scientific terms, and this is precisely what is desired today by the People's Republic, a new leviathan, crawling out from a turbulent past after having suffered a great deal from its descent into passion and violence.

In such a changing context of history, with the turn away from the Maoist past and toward a quantifiable future, came the cry: "Let facts speak for themselves!" Sadly enough, one may have to argue that the positivistic spirit has been reincarnated in the material development in and of China, which is globalized and yet globalizing. There is nothing spectacularly innovative about its ideology of development. What is instead refreshing is how an old man came to be baptized in a new belief system. This is not to say that today's indoctrination of an aged ideology may not *appear* new to the people involved. It is simply that such an ideology itself is not an invention but rather a transplantation. What is new is not the content of this spirit; it is its *form*, its historical *becoming*, both in and as a vital manifestation of yet another self-remaking. The bitter memories of the Maoist years have given rise to a shifting sentiment in favor of the factual and the statistical. Global pressure alone has not made China what it is today; an interior refurbishment has also allowed the People's Republic to walk on the global pavement. Its developmental ideology is not original in terms of its conceptual schemes and logical operations, but it feels new and refreshing to the People's Republic, still struggling to sever its ties to its own disturbing past. In order to be able to sweep the Maoist remains into "the dustbin of history," that is, to refocus its attention on its present socio-economic development, which has produced egocentric and materialistic individuals, the People's Republic has turned to the philosophy of truth and facts, for which the quantitative method and statistical knowledge are indispensable. The slogan "let facts speak for themselves" serves a double function: it is an ideological declaration of a materialistic conception of the world and a psychoanalytic proclamation of an individualistic doctrine of believing as seeing. It is an official call to abandon the Maoist past and also a popular appeal to a comparative scheme for understanding the global order of things. Let us take an example. The book *China in*

Numbers was published in 2002 by the Institute of Beijing International Urban Development, and its subtitle reads *A Notebook for Reading China's Statistical Figures.*[2] The juxtaposition of the two words "reading" and "statistical" contains a key message: society is now supposed to be comprehended by reading its statistical figures, which would imply a different kind of hermeneutic practice. Reading is to *read* statistical figures and numbers, which would appeal to a person who believes only in hard facts. For such a reader of society as this, the world of reality exists only in statistical yearbooks.

It is probably premature to argue that the People's Republic has been statisticalized to the extent of institutional and official satisfaction. From the official or scholarly point of view, the case might be quite the opposite. Some scholars and officials contend that there still exists an enormous gap between China and the rest of the world in terms of the scientific management of society, and that China is still behind its modern Other in the organization of its government statistical work. However, this belief only confirms my argument that in the People's Republic today, the epistemological fight—a clash of two antagonistic historical sentiments—has been fought on the battleground of the factual and the statistical. Those in the field of statistics or economics in particular may feel that the power of facts has not yet fully worked its way into the heart of the official world. During my fieldwork in 2004 among professors and students in Beijing, I interviewed scholars and graduate students in relevant fields about their thoughts on the function of official statistical institutions. When asked about her opinion on the application of statistical information to government decision making, Professor Li, an assistant professor of economic statistics from Renmin University, replied:

> Despite what other people believe or intend to argue, our society is not yet *statisticalized* at all. Statistical figures and hard facts continue to be ignored by most government officials, whose decisions about things such as building a road in the city are totally dependent on arbitrary and subjective considerations. They have not yet realized the value of *real objective* statistical thinking. What statistics does, as we teach our students, is to help us reach an objective understanding of reality by means of data and facts, the comprehension of which are crucial for government decision making. Statistics is a powerful weapon for working on reality.... I will never forget this, although I heard it a while ago when I was in graduate school. I do not agree with the view that nowadays our leaders, especially at the provincial or local level, possess a statistical vision of society. They tend to make arbitrary decisions without knowing the facts. We must teach them a lesson about the truth of statistical knowledge, without which decision making is blind and capricious. This is why we have had so many mistakes in our development, which are due, at least partly, to the failure to use statistical knowledge in decision making. Those officials

2. See *Shuzi Zhongguo: Zhongguo fei baomi xing shuzi duben* (2002).

make up their minds by bumping their heads into their doors! They never consult us for help. Let me tell you the truth: most officials still do not understand the value of statistical knowledge. They should and need to learn more. They must consult with us. They will do much better if they read our analyses before making any decisions. This is what I think of our society: our officials are incapable of employing the weapon of statistics to handle the country's development. This must be the reason that we are behind the advanced industrial countries.

According to this view—a popular professorial view, a view from the profession of statistical analysis, or a statistical view of society—"development" has become a machine to be worked on by the tools of statistical data and analysis. A weapon is a tool, albeit a particular kind of tool, without which one would be defeated or perhaps even eliminated from history. Still lagging behind the new mentality, government officials do not appreciate the value of statistical knowledge, which could help them achieve the goals they set for themselves. This is the regret of a young professor, a dedicated and promising scholar of the field who has a desire to see society managed scientifically and statistically. What continues to go wrong in development, according to her, is due to official ignorance and negligence of statistical data and facts. From another side of the same coin, the scholar has urged the government to respect the value of facts.

PART II

STATISTICS, METAPHYSICS, AND ETHICS

Chapter Three

DISCIPLINE AND PUNISH

Professor Dai and His Statistical Revolution

"The law of tragedy requires a death before a hero can come onstage." With this amusing observation, François Dosse (1997, 3) opens his account of the history of structuralism in post-war France. The hero of his story was Claude Lévi-Strauss, an anthropologist, while the tragic figure, who experienced a moment of intellectual death, was Jean-Paul Sartre, an existential Marxist during the early 1960s. Intellectual battles, past and present, here and there, are also fought on political grounds. This means, as suggested by Dosse's apt account, that political struggles, both within and outside the academic world, often underlie emotive intellectual debates. The effort to rebuild the temple of social sciences in the 1980s in China confirms such a view. Political sentiments were drawn into an academic battle and played a potent role in the debates on the nature of statistical science and the status of governmental statistics. Our own hero in this story, Professor Dai, a self-made champion of science and a gallant defender of truth, led a statistical revolution that, on the immediate ruins of the Maoist past, destroyed the Soviet system of statistical knowledge. The tragedy of death, in this case, involved the demise of a profession.

Professor Dai, who left a definite mark on Chinese intellectual history, was an economic statistician who taught at Renmin University.[1] His idea for a statistical revolution, not unlike the Maoist revolution in the sense of its

---

1. The ethnographic description in this chapter is based on interviews and conversations with Chinese scholars that took place over the course of more than a decade. I want to express my gratitude particularly to the following scholars and friends: Dai Shiguang, Yuan Wei, Ren Ruoen, Ma Baogui, Zheng Yao, and Wang Wenying.

formation, was conceived one afternoon in the autumn of 1978, just after the Gang of Four—the name given to Madam Mao and her comrades as political devils—were brought to trial by the new government of reform. Society was beginning to change, yet at the time it was still encumbered by a historical inertia, burdensome and almost rusty. Excitement was stirring within, while the surface of society was still painted with old colors. The atmosphere of social life was far from what it would become in a decade, although, as people recalled, there was a sense that a new wind would soon blow away the old odor. Buoyed by the breath of fresh air, Dai went to see his old friend, Professor Chen, in another department, to talk about how to revolutionize the field. This conversation took place in an old red building that had been built in the early 1950s to accommodate Russian colleagues and experts. When the People's Republic, after its birth, developed a close tie to the Big Brother of the socialist camp, Renmin University played an important role in hosting experts and academics from the Soviet Union. The early 1950s, in hindsight, was a happy hour in what became a long, troubling relationship of distrust between China and Russia. It was not until 1989, when General Secretary Mikhail Gorbachev visited Beijing, at the moment of a massive student demonstration, that the two social giants would resume normal conversation. The old buildings in Renmin University, albeit renovated, have remained a witness to this relationship. Professor Chen, who lived in one of those elegant and sturdy buildings, had been trained in the United States in the 1940s, as had Professor Dai. Their similar backgrounds fostered an unusual friendship through the hard years of the Cultural Revolution, which promoted an anti-intellectual sentiment (see Yuan, Ren, and Gao 2000, 232).

When Chen was still taking his afternoon nap, as most professors did, Dai paid him an unexpected visit. Dai eagerly walked straight to Chen's study room, pulled over a chair, and began to talk about his idea of making a statistical revolution. According to Dai, the current statistical model, which was borrowed from the Soviet Union and taught in college, was unscientific and should be abolished. As mentioned previously, prior to the 1980s, government statistical institutions and work had been organized according to the model designed for economic planning learned from the Soviet Union. It consisted of two essential features. First, by taking statistics as a branch of economic knowledge, government statistical work had been considered a kind of theoretical work, as a particular branch of economic theory. Differing from the academic tradition of Western countries, the model created a necessary and substantial connection to the government statistical institutions by training students in universities for possible official employment. In other words, more generally, there was a historical association between government offices and academic departments in the construction of such an organization of knowledge. This is different from the treatment of statistics as a quantitative method in the applied domain of mathematical knowledge. Second, due to the nature of the planning economy, the purpose of government statistical work was chiefly to collect data from officially organized units of material production, such as state-owned factories or collectively owned communes. Since production, as well as consumption, was planned out by the government, its statistical work, operating entirely within the official domain, needed only to collect reports of production from the productive units of the state. In terms of method, therefore, statistics was not considered to be linked to probabilistic theories; it was made part of an official theory of political economy. This model no longer exists, but it had constituted the dominant system of economy and society during the Maoist years. Its disappearance was due in part to Dai's statistical revolution, which aimed at demolishing the Soviet model and replacing it with the universal model of statistical science that Professor Dai had learned in his youth at American universities. Seen by today's standards, this achievement does not appear to be spectacular. But at the time it was foolhardy to make such a move, which could be seen as an intellectual assault on the socialist ide-ologies of the nation. For these reasons, Dai wanted to consult with his friend first before launching an attack. Perhaps he also sensed a quickened pulse in society and felt that the time was right for change. Dai excitedly emptied his basket of ideas, impatiently waiting for his friend's response and approval.

Perhaps only half awake, Professor Chen, after careful thought, replied in a low voice: "Well, you know, you must know where my feet are. They are on your side. I do believe that you are right. Statistics is nothing but a scientific method for quantitative analysis, which can be used for government work or any other work. There is no need to say, therefore, that it is an essential part of the official political economics. It is a *method* for quantitative analysis, and this is the common view of all the advanced modern societies. The Russian view is problematic, for statistics has nothing to do with socialism or its economics. Yes, economics will employ statistical analysis, but the latter is not the former. Because of our training back in America, we already knew this. Statistics is a tool for economic analysis, but it is itself not a constituent part of it. This is exactly what went wrong with the Russian model. I agree with you. But, since you asked, I will say that there is some danger involved here. Even if the Rus-sian model is wrong, it has led to a profession that has supported people's lives. If you say that what your colleagues teach is not knowledge but official defini-tions of the world, I am pretty sure that they will get hurt and take it personally. I am a bit worried about the consequence of your ideas, to be frank."

"For the sake of truth," uttered Dai, clenching his teeth.

"Well, I see what you are trying to do. You want to hit two birds with one stone. By saying that there is only one statistical science, which is a branch of mathematical and probabilistic knowledge, you are aiming to demystify our governmental statistics and to strip it of its ideological illusions. You are also saying that what we teach here, to fulfill the need of training governmental officials, is not scientific work—and that this must be changed. What we do, in your department in particular, is basically an extension of government work, around which universities must accommodate their programs. Over the years, many of our colleagues have worked on government doctrines and ideologies, not on quantitative method or statistical science. They are officials and political economists but not statisticians in the scientific sense of the term. I agree with you, but it will be hard for your colleagues to accept the truth. You will definitely hurt a lot of people who were trained by the Russian experts, for they believe that what they do is scientific work. We have been told all along that statistics is a special branch of economics, that it is socialist social science. You yourself have said this in classes, too. Now you want to tell everyone that there is no such thing as socialist economics, no such thing as socialist social science. To be honest, I think you might get yourself into trouble. For almost thirty years now, both government officials and our colleagues have made a life out of what you want to destroy. As I see it, by creating a statistical revolution, you will make many enemies among your colleagues."

"A scientist must confront the truth, shouldn't he?" Dai jumped in rhetorically. This is, of course, not a new attitude for a truth maker, at least since the Renaissance. However, such a sentiment, resembling that of Copernicus or Galileo but in an entirely different socio-historic location, was truthful to the thought of a professor of economic statistics who wanted to redraw a conceptual division according to the modern tradition of Western science. The categories employed were not new; what *was* new was the concept's historical application, its social transplantation, its cultural translation. Science as a notion is different from its technical applications in practice. The notional power of science lies in its regulating ability to designate and (re)locate different departments of knowledge in a general or generalizable mode of truth claims. By hoping to relocate economic statistics away from the way it was being taught in colleges to the notional area of "government work," Professor Dai was trying to re-establish the scientific nature of statistics as a branch of mathematical and probabilistic knowledge. European in origin, this conceptual division of labor—statistics as a quantitative method and governmental statistics as official work—is practiced almost everywhere today. But at the time, facing an enormous socialist inertia, Dai's move was considered and talked about as a "revolution" in both theory and practice.

A revolution may start from a personal, rebellious reaction, and Professor Dai's motivation was definitely associated with the particular history of his university. Renmin University was closed down during the Cultural Revolution (1966–1976) and reopened in the late 1970s when the economic reform was launched. In a sense, it was a state school where government officials were trained. Different from other universities or colleges, Renmin

University, that is, People's University, was established by the state when the People's Republic was born. Due to its statistics program, it was considered a main training school for employees of the National Bureau of Statistics. In the early 1950s, Renmin University received much attention when it hosted Russian specialists of social and economic sciences. Its graduates, whose teachers had been trained by the Russian scholars, were destined for official or academic posts in other places. As we know, the planning economy of the People's Republic was modeled on that of the Soviet Union, according to which economic activities, either productive or consumptive, were supposed to be planned out by the government. The Central Planning Committee, which possessed great power in investment and distribution of capital and other economic resources, was the direct, superior institution to the National Bureau of Statistics. According to such an official division of labor, up to the late 1970s, there was no independent department of statistics at Renmin University. Instead, there was the Department of Planning and Statistics. The "and" inserted in between the two kinds of knowledge, one ahead of another, or one superior to another, indicated the subordinated status of statistics to planning. This is no longer the case today.

At the time, statistics was taught in college not as a quantitative method but as a way to learn how to perform specific statistical work for government offices. Professor Dai accused the teaching method as being little more than helping students understand the classificatory schemes and indexes of official economics, which had been chiefly worked out by the Central Planning Committee. Very few statistical methods or probabilistic theories were taught; instead, students were required to take old-fashioned political economic theories, whose aim was to prove that planning economies were superior in design to market ones. Professor Dai's revolutionary goals were to reorganize the field of knowledge according to the modern model and to teach statistics as a mathematical method. In trying to get rid of the Russian tradition, Dai did not deny that students should learn how government statistical work was organized, but he refused to accept that such work—which every government, socialist or capitalist, would have to do—should be classified as science. He insisted that science should be knowledge outside the government office and that statistics should be taken as a quantitative method built on probabilistic theories.

Following the conversation with his friend Chen, Professor Dai published two essays that revolutionized the field. The first one is titled "Actively Engaging in Developing the Scientific Discipline of Statistics: In Order to Realize Four Modernizations Sooner." At the time, to "realize four modernizations" was an official slogan, referring to agriculture, industry, defense, and technology. In the essay's opening paragraph, Professor Dai quoted President Hua to characterize himself as an advocate for socio-economic reform in general.

This was part of Dai's strategy. The government was pushing for reform, and so was he, as he suggested with this official posture at the beginning of his essay. However, his essay had nothing to do with modernization. It simply took advantage of the government's agenda in order to be seen as politically correct. At several decisive junctures of the essay, Dai made references to the idea of modernization in order to justify his argument that there should be only one statistical science, that is, mathematical statistics. According to Dai, two sciences of statistics had been developed in China, one of which was supposed to belong to the field of social science. How did this come about? Dai asked. The reason was that in 1954 the Soviet Union defined statistics as an independent social science, which should be studying the quantitative aspects of social phenomena. This definition, in Dai's view, marked the beginning of the Russian tradition, which was called, with some degree of contempt, the "Soviet Union Theory." A key question was whether there should be one or two statistical sciences. Dai's response was that there should be only one statistical science. The Soviet Union Theory was wrong because it mistook the routine work of governmental statistics as a science. It was an intellectual mistake, a deadly epistemological error, a metaphysical misrecognition. Dai's criticism, it seemed, targeted not only the Soviet Union Theory but also his colleagues who believed and practiced it. During the 1980s, a somewhat positive image of the Soviet Union was being replaced by the rising sign of the modern Other, typically symbolized by the advanced Western countries. Dai's revolutionary attempt was both a result of and a reason for this change.

Indeed, Dai's stance was a terrible offense to his colleagues, who had been students of the Soviet Union Theory and now taught this theory to their own students. His denouncement, in a sense, denied them as social science guardians, rejected their life's work as having contributed to the birth of the People's Republic, and liquidated the value of their knowledge. Hence, Dai's attack was fatal. In a couple of paragraphs later in the essay, Dai developed, in the narrow space of this short article, no more than a few pages long, a devastating critique of what he perceived to be the falsehood of the Soviet Union Theory. He claimed that it was not a theory at all, that it was simply pseudo-science. It did not have a scientific object and did not possess a scientific method. It existed only as office work to be taught in college. The only circumstantial evidence Dai provided, by which he made these strong and emotional claims, was his reading of a translated Russian text on the nature of statistics as a branch of socialist social science.

Trained in the United States and Great Britain, Professor Dai's main focus was on demographic statistics. When the Soviet Union Theory was embraced, from the early 1950s onward, his knowledge was trivialized and marginalized by the new ideological force. During the Maoist years, there had been no possibility for his idea of statistics to emerge onto the main stage of academic learning. Sensing that the time might be right, and drawing on a spirit that had been submerged but not extinguished, Dai, now almost seventy, was ready for action. He wrote another essay, "The Only Criterion in Testing [the Nature of] Statistical Science Is Its [Actual] Practice," a sequel to the first, in his continuing battle for truth.[2] This essay was more elaborate and made a theoretical distinction between statistical method and statistical data. Dai argued that government statistical work was concerned chiefly with collecting data; it was the job of universities to study and develop statistical methods. This distinction, albeit simple as it looks, is of vital importance, for it allowed Dai to argue that collecting data is but routine office work that has nothing to do with academic discipline and science. Any society or government, in order to assess how it governs, must collect statistical information about its economy and population. But Dai felt that it was erroneous to refer to such routine governmental work as science or theory, a position that incurred the bitter reaction of his colleagues. For an entire generation of professors, especially those at Renmin University, the prefix "Soviet" had functioned exactly as that of "science" or "scientific." To eliminate it meant more than losing their professions; it meant that the value of their life's work was being brought into question. Professor Dai, perhaps not unlike other revolutionaries, showed no mercy and pressed on with his mission. Dai was not a mathematician. Perhaps slightly more familiar with descriptive statistics than most of his colleagues at the time, he was in fact an expert on governmental statistics, such as comparative analyses of national incomes and demographic changes. Nevertheless, Dai's sentiments were clear: ideology is not science, the Soviet Union Theory must go, truth has to be made true. A "happy consciousness" of modern development would then soon come onstage in the vast continent of the People's Republic.

In 1979, when professional organizations were being restructured as a result of the new ideology for reform and development, Professor Dai was elected the Vice President of the Chinese Association of Statistics (CAS). In 1983, the CAS

2. For a good summary of Dai's two essays, see Yuan, Ren, and Gao (2000, 6–28). There is a definite difficulty in translating the Chinese word "practice" into English. The English connotation, insofar as it is used in scholarly works, such as Bourdieu's use of the word, carries an implicit contradistinction to the idea of theory. And such a conceptual application, which stemmed from a long tradition of intellectual conversation running, say, from Aristotle to Marx, does not necessarily presuppose that theory is always derived from practice (see, e.g., Lobkowicz 1967). However, the Chinese connotation, in the early years of Deng's reformatory era, came to mean that any idea or thought must be able to be proved useful or right by its application in an actual situation. This implies not only that theory should come from practice but also that it must conform to a changing reality. It is clear that the Chinese word "practice" then conveyed a strong sense of reality, which was taken up by the post-Mao government to correct the Maoist fallacy of trying to put an ideological straitjacket on social reality.

held a meeting in Kunming, a city in Southwest China, to re-elect its leaders and to discuss future programs. This meeting, known as "the Kunming conference," was important for setting up agendas that would re-establish economic statistics as a field of knowledge, a crucial aspect of the effort to normalize both governmental work and educational programs. However, the conference was held at a time of political unrest. With the opening of Chinese society to the world, there also arrived a set of "Western" values, such as individualism and democracy, which had been considered bad or evil according to the old official doctrines. In order to assert control, the government launched, in the early 1980s, a political counterattack on what was called "bourgeois spiritual pollution." Still suffering from the Maoist nightmares, most professors did not wish to run against the political tide, which had proved to be perilous. Intellectuals were cautious at the time, to say the least. This was the political environment at the time of the Kunming conference, which would become an unfortunate setting for a political fight among academics. Put simply, Professor Dai was attacked by his colleagues—proponents of the Soviet Union Theory, whom he had attacked in the first place—for "spiritually polluting" the field of statistics by surrendering to capitalist pseudo-science. In the eyes of his colleagues, Dai was nothing but a traitor, because he had taught the same Soviet Union Theory for many years. Psychologically speaking, the possibility for revenge could be realized in the heightened political atmosphere of the early 1980s. While the Kunming conference was in process, during its general discussion for developing "statistical science and theory," someone hit Professor Dai on his head—metaphorically.

It was a beautiful afternoon, with a ray of lazy sunshine creeping into the conference hall where all the important figures of the association were gathered. Suddenly, a relatively young but stern man stood up and interrupted the meeting by putting an unexpected question to the attendees. His question was whether the total denial of the social-socialist nature of statistics was meant to be an assault on the political system of the People's Republic, and whether it should be considered "bourgeois spiritual pollution" in the field of economic statistics. The young man said this with all seriousness, as if he had just dropped a bomb into the heads and hearts of the audience, who were predominantly senior members of the association. Such a question would no longer be relevant today, but in the political situation at the time, this was a lethal question. Professor Dai was in total shock, astonished and shaken. He knew that he was the target of this attack in the middle of a peaceful conversation among the members of the association, of which he was the Vice President. After a trying moment in which he collected himself, he responded to the political charge and became a bit angry. He explained that he did not intend to lead an assault on the doctrine of socialism. Instead, he wanted to advance statistical science in order to help the country along its path to modernization. While Professor Dai was sophisticated as a scholar, he was perhaps a bit naive with regard to human nature. In any case, he always saw himself in retrospect as a person truly dedicated to advancing the scientific spirit in the field of economic statistics.

At the time of the Kunming conference, Dai felt that he was being criticized unfairly. It may be true that he did not mean to attack the principles of the country, but he did attack those who believed that they promoted those principles. As if there had been some sort of prearrangement, the meeting went in an unscheduled direction, turning into a political discussion of the possible danger of "spiritual pollution" in the field of statistics. A large number of the attendees agreed that Dai's new theories did in fact represent an evil wind of "spiritual pollution." This seemed to be the tone of the majority at the Kunming conference. More unbearable than the collective criticism was a hit from the back. Professor Dai suffered the most humiliating moment of his professional life when a colleague of his own department from Renmin University stood up and said, "Yes, if I must say something, I would have to say that I am on the side of the majority, whose understanding of the nature of statistics is correct. Statistics is not simply a method but a weapon, as Lenin once said, a weapon for correctly comprehending social reality. Reality and the weapon of its comprehension are developed together. It is not simply a method." This was also a senior member of the department, an influential figure in the field who was among the very first to be trained by the Russian experts in the 1950s. A generation younger than Dai, he used to refer to him as his own teacher. This colleague continued: "If I must say something, I would have to say this. I love my teacher, as every student does, most affectionately. However, more than the affection I feel for my teacher, I love, and believe in, truth. Comrade Dai is wrong. Statistics is a special social science, closely tied to class struggles. Our teacher has brought 'bourgeois spiritual pollution' to our field."

Nothing further needed to be said after this adamant denial of one's teacher for the love of truth. However, one should note that it was on this same ground of truth claims that Professor Dai had originally laid his charge against the Soviet Union Theory. It appeared that this attack was an academic maneuver for the politics of truth (cf. Berreman 1981). The agenda of the Kunming conference was rescheduled in order to produce more sessions and panels for criticizing "spiritual pollution." Stripped of his official role by the association, Professor Dai did not know what to say. Sitting there hopelessly, trying to concentrate on what was going on but often failing to hear anything, Dai felt exhausted and could not bear it any more. He left Kunming early. One of his students went with him to the airport, and, while waiting for their turn to check in, said to him: "Professor Dai, please do not be disturbed by such behavior, which is nothing but an old habit. Scholarly debates were made into political arguments. Please forget them. The hope should lie in the future, and a new generation of students will be able to understand what you have said." Indeed, it is students rather than colleagues who will carry on one's thinking.[3] After returning from Kunming, Dai devoted his time and energy to training students for a new mode of knowledge.

In China, the authority to allow universities to have doctoral programs in certain fields belongs to the Ministry of Education, which evaluates the quality of each university and its programs in order to decide which should be allowed to offer master's and doctoral degrees. The assessment depends in particular on an ad hoc evaluation of the qualifications of the professors involved. Thus, not every university could have a doctoral program—for example, in the field of economic statistics—even if it wished to. In the universities where there is a doctoral program in such a field, again, not every professor has the right to supervise those students. The qualifications for supervising doctoral students must be proved by the Ministry of Education. This is why, on the name cards of those who were given such a privilege by the Ministry, there would usually be a line underneath the professorial title reading: "Supervisor of PhD students." Thus, one may become a full professor but still not be able to supervise doctoral students. In 1981, Professor Dai was one of the very first who earned the title; however, he initially refused to take any doctoral students. At the time when he was granted the right to supervise doctoral students, he was the only one qualified to do so in the whole department of his university. The department urged him to take on a couple of doctoral students, because doing so would benefit the department as well as the university by increasing its prestige and promise. At the time, there were only two or three other schools across the country that were allowed to train graduate students to be teachers for other universities and colleges. It was an immense privilege, but Professor Dai chose to forgo it. His reluctance was not entirely due to his modesty. A chief reason, as he said, was that his department at Renmin University was not yet ready for it. He probably believed that the department was still predominated by the Soviet Union Theory, and nobody else, except himself, could help train doctoral students if they had been taken in. Training, according to his view, should be a collective endeavor, but, looking around, he found few among his colleagues qualified for such teamwork. However, the Kunming conference, which forced him to step down from the Vice Presidency, changed his mind. The first group of his doctoral students was admitted in 1985.

After a long career of over half a century, Professor Dai passed away in 1999, with peace and tranquility, a year after his ninetieth birthday party, which had been organized by his students and the department at Renmin University. The birthday party for Dai was a true joy, because his students and students

---

3. In an entirely different context and for a different reason, my colleague Paul Rabinow (2003, 87) at Berkeley seems to have shared the same feeling: "Somewhat unexpectedly, it strikes me that essential aspects of the genesis of my work in writing and thinking are eminently imaginable (to me) without direct contact with colleagues."

of his students firmly believed in what he wanted them to believe. Within two decades, the field had been totally transformed. There is no longer any doubt about viewing statistics as a quantitative method that is different from government statistical work. In an interview with an economic statistician, who was Dai's first doctoral student and then Vice President of the CAS, Professor Yuan said in 2000 that what his master, the late Professor Dai, was hoping and fighting for has become a truth of his day. Statistics, with regard to both its academic teaching and governmental work, has followed Dai's envisioning, that is, it has been remade according to the modern model, the global one. No one questions the nature of statistical knowledge as a quantitative method any more; instead, scholars have increasingly employed statistical analysis for verifying the claims of other kinds of knowledge—social and economic, political and historical. This is a radical change in the recent history of the People's Republic. The epistemological status of statistics as a quantitative science, neutral and objective in itself, has been fully established. From the interview with Professor Yuan, it seems evident that nothing remains vague or unclear: there is no longer any myth about governmental statistics; probabilistic theory and statistical science have finally prevailed across the country; students of statistics have moved on to travel the road of science and truth. While the Soviet Union Theory may have deserved its demise, what has been lost in the confidence of a new generation seems to be an awareness of the historical nature of knowledge, quantitative or otherwise. In today's China, statistical analysis has become in many ways a naked-truth-making machine, available for both government and scholars.

This is a *history of conjuncture* (see Braudel 1980), that is, a *conjuncture of historical forces*, in which the notions of science and truth played an important role. Although the language was not new, the *addressees* of this critique, *internal and historic*, generated new impulses for a different audience. The modern scheme, with its variations and change, provided a discursive storage from which an old weapon was borrowed for winning a new battle. There was nothing better than the language of truth and science for disengaging from the Maoist antiquity, although to a postmodern ear, Professor Dai's vocabulary might sound more tedious than that of his opponents. This is perhaps an apt lesson for a student of modern development: in a short span of time, the Soviet Union Theory and modern statistics switched status as a pseudo-science, with almost the same amount of handwringing and tears.

The Colonization of Social Sciences

It is one's students, rather than one's colleagues, who will march on toward a new world of ideas. This revelation came to Professor Dai only in his later years. He realized that it is the next generation rather than the current one, with which one is struggling, that will carry forth a teacher's posterity of thought. Do not waste much time in trying to change the minds and hearts of one's colleagues; instead, put energy into teaching young people, who represent the future. Professor Dai succeeded in this plan, but his success was partly due to the wider changes in society. Within a decade or so, governmental statistics came to be seen as official work and was no longer taken as a theory of economics. Supported by the rise of a market economy, academic departments for statistical education were reorganized so that students would be trained as statisticians rather than government officials. Statistics came to be considered a quantitative method, not a special branch of social science. With all the changes and happenings taking place in society, quantitative data and the statistical method have attained a sanctified status due to their scientific and objective character. Behind the empirical expansion of statistical knowledge lies an epistemological equivalence: facts are naked and truth resides in numbers. Other social science disciplines, such as sociology, came to view statistics as an essential means of analysis, a method for extracting truth from the reality of social change. In a sense, the spirit of statistical quantification came to colonize the minds of social sciences, which, having buried the Soviet Union Theory, hoped to be adopted into the family of the New Continent, with Professor Dai as their Columbus.

With the changes taking place in the 1980s, a few of Professor Dai's colleagues began to introduce the idea of statistics from a different intellectual trajectory. As some recalled, there was a class taught by Professor Gao on the history of statistics, which meant to show the rise of statistical thought in Europe from the sixteenth century onward. Russia seemed not to be part of Europe in this treatment, and the Soviet Union Theory was implicitly criticized. Not many students were fortunate enough to take the class because Gao soon retired in the late 1980s. According to the recollection of several students, who became scholars themselves, Professor Gao was a brilliant storyteller. He always began his lecture by telling an entertaining story, and one was particularly remembered.

Gao said that when he was in college, a long time ago, a room was shared by four students, his classmates, who were infamous for their smelly feet. They played all day long and never took the trouble of washing their socks, and therefore their room became known for its notoriously bad odor. Each of them had several pairs of socks, but no one ever saw them washing the dirty ones. Every morning they would simply pick out the least dirty socks to wear, and at the end of the day they would put them back into the same basket. Their everyday rationale consisted in trying to pick out the cleanest or most tolerable pair of socks from a pool of dirty possibilities. Although they changed what they wore everyday, the odor they carried into the classroom seemed to remain a constant. The smelly feet story was not intended simply to induce hearty laughter from drowsy students. Instead, it was told as a prologue to set up an important idea in the history of European statistical science and to introduce the powerful figure of Adolphe Quetelet (1796–1874), a Belgian astronomer who was arguably one of the most influential people in the nineteenth century with regard to statistics. As Professor Gao would say, the smelly feet represented a fact of truth that varied from day to day in experience but, taken as a whole and treated in statistical terms, could constitute "an average" of a given set of social facts. Put another way, in terms of who was the worst of the group for a particular morning, there might have been variations both from person to person and from day to day, and this variation was *random*. However, taking the variations as a whole and considering the average quality of each in the whole, the odor of their feet could be rendered as a *constant* in statistical terms. The smelly feet story, albeit hilarious, was meant to introduce a serious concept: *the average, the mean, the x-bar*, a basic but essential concept for modern statistics. When students laughed at the story, which might have reminded them of their own habits, their heads and hearts began to accept the idea of "average" as an essential quality of the basket, thus opening a magic path to a new conception of humankind and society.[4]

Gao's intention was to praise the conceptual discovery of "the average man" as a great development in the history of ideas, and it was Quetelet who opened up this new theoretical possibility for understanding the relationship of the individual to society, as well as the qualitative to the quantitative. It was through his concept that an epistemological equivalence was established between the quantitative average and the common value in society. Put in the old European language prior to the nineteenth century, Quetelet gave birth to an epistemological equivalence between the objective and the subjective mean. The objective mean and the subjective mean come from two different sources. For example, a person trying to measure the distance from the earth to the moon will need to take several such measurements and obtain the estimated distance by calculating the average, which will be the mean of several measurements. The average in such a case as this should be and is an estimate, due to the random variation in each measurement of the real, objective distance of the earth to the moon. This is the objective mean. On the other hand, there is no such objectivity in trying to determine the degree of tolerance or intolerance for smelly socks, and therefore the judgment is subjective in its measurements. In other words, the measurement of this social fact is subjective. What one can derive or calculate, in cases such as this, has no objective value in itself; it is instead a common value dependent on subjective evaluations of the odor. This is the subjective mean (see Desrosières 1998, 73–86; see also Hacking 1990).

---

4. Renmin University retained a unique place in the hierarchy of higher education in the 1980s. It was an important school for training officials and college teachers in the fields of economic statistics and social sciences in general. With the further development and marketization of education, Renmin University today no longer enjoys the prestige and power that it used to have.

These two numerical and calculable series are different in nature, and it was Quetelet who made them into a conceptual equivalence through his invention of "the average man" as a *man of the average* standing for the whole population. With this notion, he gave the statistical quantification of subjective values an objective outlook. It was this objective outlook, this possibility of quantifying the qualitative, in making an individuation of the whole as its true representation, that made a difference for China in the early 1980s. The role of statistical objectivity and its power of representing social reality began to be understood, via a tale of smelly feet, by a new generation of students whose minds were fascinated by the name of Quetelet and his notion of the average man.

With the resurrection of Quetelet from his European graveyard, the Soviet Union Theory could not survive in the existing family of ideas, for its fundamental presumption was to deny the possibility of rendering indiscriminately the qualitative into the quantitative. According to such a theory, which shared its premises with the Maoist ideological assumptions, an analysis of class relations in any given society must precede the statistical calculation of the average man. Perhaps a bit old-fashioned in its assumptions, it retained the primal separation of the objective from the subjective, conceived as a gap that was almost impossible to be bridged. In such a theoretical vision of the world, the objective mean is to be derived from the qualities of the physical world, whereas, the subjective mean, a tendency induced entirely from the calculations of moral facts, as in opinion polls, will come from society. The essence of the matter, regarding such an old debate, was concerned with the question of cause. What makes things appear to be what they really are? Is there an underlying reason why they appear as they do? Is the final cause a constant basis for how things are perceived? These were underlying questions for the debates on probability and statistics in eighteenth-century and nineteenth-century Europe (see, e.g., Hacking 1990, esp. chaps. 19–21). Quetelet's decisive stroke, in the invention of the average man, allowed a statistical transgression of the boundary between the physical and the moral world. Establishing an epistemological equivalence between the two worlds was a momentous step in producing a modern outlook by means of statistical objectification. Quetelet was almost a dead man in the European family of ideas when he was called upon by the People's Republic to speak against the Maoist subjective politics, allegedly ideological and arbitrary. It was therefore not the truth of the modern doctrine but the moment of a historical need that re-established the fame of a dead man, an authority on objectivity and statistical science. It was in the interest of attaining a scientific understanding of social reality, rather than the quality of his banal thesis, that Quetelet, among several other figures, was brought back to life. By unearthing the graveyard of European traditions, via Quetelet, Professor Dai's children, the students of a new statistical science, hoped to establish two propositions. First, human or subjective qualities should be quantifiable in order to reach an objective understanding of them. Second, moral facts, despite their difference from physical facts, should also be studied scientifically. The propositions were not new in themselves, but they were refreshing to an entire generation that had grown up on the ruins of the Maoist revolution. This resulted in a renovated belief that society must not be run by arbitrary ideologies and must be understood by statistical science and objective analysis.

Thus, the "smelly feet" stepped onto a different path in a peculiar intellectual history. The status of Quetelet as a positive sign of scientific development was remade in the People's Republic of the 1980s, whereas in his hometown, "the notoriety Quetelet enjoyed in the nineteenth century contrasts with his relative oblivion during the twentieth century" (Desrosières 1998, 80).[5] The European history of science is only part of the story, for the People's Republic in a later hour saw a dead man walking again. The residency of the average man, an abstract figure of concrete reality, an imaginary man of real life, was reissued by both the intellectual and the official authority in China. The notion was essential to the development of a conception according to which the calculation of the average man across the world would make up a moral map of development. The core of such a notion, put in a slightly different way, was defined by the sociological master, Durkheim. Working on his idea of "mechanic solidarity" in his *The Division of Labor in Society*, originally published in 1893, Durkheim (1984, 264–265) developed the notion of "average type," which bore a close relationship to the average man of Quetelet:

> The average type *of a natural group* is that which corresponds to the conditions of average life, and consequently to the most ordinary conditions. It expresses the way in which individuals have adapted to what we may term the average environment, both physical and social, that is, the environment in which the largest number live. These average conditions were more frequent in the past, for the same reason that makes them the most general conditions in the present day. They are therefore the conditions in which most of our ancestors were placed. It is true that over time they may have changed, but generally they are modified only slowly. The average type thus remains appreciably the same for a long time. It is consequently this type that is most frequently and most uniformly replicated in the series of past generations, at least in those generations that are recent enough to bring their influence effectively to bear. It is because of this consistency that the average type becomes fixed, making it the gravitational center for hereditary influence. The characteristics that go to make it up

5. On Quetelet, Desrosières (1998, 80) continues: "This, too, is partly explained by the fact that, from the standpoint of the history of the mathematical techniques of statistics, his contribution seems far weaker than those made by Gauss and Laplace before him, or by Pearson and Fisher after him. But the celebrity he enjoyed in his own time came from the fact that he had managed to create a vast international sociopolitical network, by connecting in a new way worlds that were previously quite separate."

are those that are most resistant, and that tend to be transmitted most powerfully and precisely. On the other hand, those that deviate from this gravitational center survive only in an indeterminate state, all the more indeterminate the more considerable their degree of deviation. This is why the deviations that occur are never other than temporary and never succeed in lasting for any time, save in very imperfect fashion.

In such a mode of explanation, as happened in the People's Republic, the whole, such as society or the economy, is no longer seen as a complexity of totalization of which its evolving parts, its organic layers, are made of irreducible qualitative differences that will change over time. Instead, a social world would be thought of as a whole in the *statistical* sense—a quantitative whole, a statistically verifiable whole, or a whole in the possible quantitative estimates of its type or of its average quality. The average man is supposed to be conceived of as living evidence of the quantitative quality of the whole, or should *represent* the qualitative quantity of a population. To take a further step in one's epistemological assumption, one would arrive at where Quetelet was in the People's Republic: the concept of the average man is not simply a symbolization of the whole; it is its essential representation. In a sense, according to such an epistemological stance, statistical analysis is not simply a means of understanding; it has become *the understanding* itself—for the whole can live nowhere except in the house of the average man. The distance between understanding and representation of facts seems to have been reduced by statistical quantification to the same thing. This series of conceptual transformations was brought to the People's Republic by Quetelet and others, who provided a powerful weapon in the fight against the Maoist remains.

Nothing will be better to show the face of the average man than the statistical index of GDP per capita, an important figure that represents the entirety of a national or regional economy in a quantitative epitome. This epitomic representation of the whole as the average man, by way of computing the statistical mean of national income per capita, has become a most effective way of seeing and living with the world. No longer simply an economic conceptual operation, it has become the developmental lens for the eyes of the state. In generating a comparative connectibility to other such national economies in the world and, at the same time, internally, it allows oneself to evaluate one's own socio-economic status in a particular social world. Outward-looking, this index will allow global comparability, supposedly objective and scientific; inward-looking, it will create a possibility for oneself to be reflected in the mirror of the average man, which is the x-bar of the *normal* condition of a given economy.

We shall call "normal" these social conditions that are the most generally distributed, and the others "morbid" or "pathological." If we designate as "average type" that hypothetical being that is constructed by assembling in the same individual, the most frequent forms, one may say that the normal type merges with the average type, and that every deviation from this standard of health is a morbid phenomenon. It is true that the average type cannot be determined with the same distinctness as an individual type, since its constituent attributes are not absolutely fixed but are likely to vary. But the possibility of its constitution is beyond doubt, since, blending as it does with the generic type, it is the immediate subject matter of science. It is the functions of the average organism that the physiologist studies; and the sociologist does the same. Once we know how to distinguish the various social species one from the other ... it is always possible to find the most general form of phenomenon in a given species. (Durkheim 1938, 55–56)

The idea of normalcy from "the rules of sociological method" brought a conceptual intersection where students of statistical science and those of sociology could perhaps meet. They indeed smiled at each other when they met in the 1980s in China, possessing almost the same confidence in statistical methods. For the sociological mind of the People's Republic, it was the statistical mean, the x-bar, that would allow quantitative classifications of "morbid" or "pathological" individuals to be scientifically made. During the last couple of decades of the twentieth century, there were many stories, in newspapers and on television, indicating that the quantitative requirements of weight or height had become a main concern in areas such as employment or school entrance. Many job advertisements came with a height specification, even for common office positions. According to a newspaper report, two teenage girls were rejected by a nursing school because they were a bit heavier than normal. Many others could not get in because they were one centimeter short of the required 1.65 meters in height. In addition to normalcy, standardization of features also became a matter of concern, among other fascinating aspects of sociological change. Age, weight, height, the shape of one's nose, one's eyelids, and every other aspect of one's physical attributes were often measured according to a certain standard of the "normal" or a "normalizing" requirement by the employer. Of course, this may not be due to the teaching of Professor Dai and his colleagues, but the statistician's doctrine of objectifying the social world in quantitative terms, in this way creating arbitrary standards of a most vicious sort, did function as an initiation ritual for the training of the sociologist, a good representative of the general figure of the social sciences.

Durkheim later modified his position on the question of normalcy. His view of Quetelet and his notion of the average man changed in the work *Suicide*, originally published in 1897, in which Durkheim (1966) no longer equated the average type to the collective type, by which he meant to introduce a certain notion of society. He took a turn at criticizing Quetelet for mistaking the average type as the only type that did not deviate from itself. In particular, Durkheim argued that what had occurred with reference to the stability of the frequency of death rates across a number of European countries was a stable deviation. In other words, variations, considered by a statistical science of a new kind, such as that of Bernoulli and Pearson, cannot be deduced from the calculations of individual qualities. The idea of variation pointed to the structural relations of a given set of quantitative data and began to form a new basis for statistical thinking. This was shown in Durkheim's reaction (ibid.: 300–303) to Quetelet's notion of the average man:

> According to him, there is a definite type in each society more or less exactly reproduced by the majority, from which only the minority tends to deviate under the influence of disturbing causes.... Quetelet gave the name *average type* to this general type, because it is obtained almost exactly by taking the arithmetic means of the individual types.... The theory seems very simple. But first, it can only be considered as an explanation if it shows how the average type is realized in the great majority of individuals. For the average type to remain constantly equal to itself while they change, it must be to some extent independent of them; and yet it must also have some way of insinuating itself into them.... But the social environment is fundamentally one of common ideas, beliefs, customs and tendencies. For them to impart themselves thus to individuals, they must somehow exist independently of individuals; and this approaches the solution we suggested. For thus is implicitly acknowledged the existence of a collective inclination to suicide from which individual inclinations are derived, and our whole problem is to know of what it consists and how it acts.... In short, Quetelet's theory rests on an inaccurate observation. He thought it certain that stability occurs only in the most general manifestations of human activity; but it is equally found in the sporadic manifestations which occur only at rare and isolated points of the social field. He thought he had met all the requirements by showing how, as a last resort, one could explain the invariability of what is not exceptional; but the exception itself has its own invariability, inferior to none.[6]

What an excellent departure from the average man as essentially individualistic in his statistical objectification! According to such a view, we should depart from the arithmetic mean of individual qualities in order to arrive at frequency and stability of distributional statistics. Distribution and frequency, as structural qualities of the quantitative whole, be it society or the economy, should be taken as a collectivity in and of itself. This was an important message of *Suicide*,

---

6. Desrosières (1998, 98) comments: "In *Suicide*, in contrast, the statistical average is repatriated into the world of methodological individualism, and the 'collective type' is no longer compared to the 'average type.' In this case, Quetelet's rhetoric produces nothing more than a holistic trumpery: the average statistical man is often a rather sorry figure, who doesn't want to pay his taxes or fight in a war. He is not a good citizen. This was perhaps the first time that a clear separation appeared between two heterogeneous discourses in regard to the support that statistics could provide the social sciences. For one such discourse, they provided incontrovertible proof. For the other, they missed the essential. The paradox here is that *Suicide*—a work generally considered to have founded quantitative sociology (mainly on account of the massive use of statistics concerning causes of death)—*also* introduced a radical condemnation of the holistic interpretation of Quetelet's average type, and thus of these same statistics."

which had not been on the reading list of Professor Dai's students, whose minds were crossed firmly with the x-bar for anything and everything quantifiable. In the 1980s of the People's Republic, Durkheim's later claim would not have been heard, for it sounded a bit too similar to the Maoist ideologies: society is entirely different from individuals in its origin and function; it is transindividualistic by definition; it cannot be reduced to the sum total of individual qualities, etc. The hope of a new generation that was trying to depart from the Maoist holistic vision of society was to look for a bridge that would connect the earth of individual life to the holy totality of society. For Professor Dai and his students, such a bridge maker was Quetelet and his notion of the average man.

Of course, this is not to say that students did not later obtain more complicated tools of statistical analysis. On the contrary, assisted by various kinds of specialized computer programs, statistical methods have come to make up a diverse field of knowledge these days, to be taught at different levels for different social science disciplines. However, as a notion or a notional gravitation of sociological knowledge, nothing was more powerful than the idea of the average man for interring the Maoist conception of society. In the decade of the 1980s in particular, the average man enjoyed, and yet was taken care of by, an intense interest in the statistical technique of survey sampling, a proven science of data collection. The rising interest in the method of survey sampling, an elementary mode of statistical thinking, was due to the emergence of a different official need for information and governance, which came with the arrival of a market economy. The average man of various kinds, rather than Maoist proportional politics, came to the attention of the state, for which a regular but *partial*, albeit supposedly scientific, estimation of the whole—the economy and society in perpetual movement—made up a new nervous system of the government. From the other side of the same current, it was the scholars, such as Professor Dai and his students, who performed a ritual of justification for the official change of mind. From the late 1970s onward, there came into existence a new monarchy of truth claims, which derived their objective proofs from data collected in various kinds of survey sampling— both officially sanctioned and scholarly produced—on the average man. In this case, random sampling, an old tool of statistical method, was adopted as a new mode of seeing and believing.

In such a moment of rebellion against the arbitrary Maoist ideologies, the objectivity of survey sampling, a mathematical treatment of the parts to the whole in random choices of sampling units, played an essential role in making the subject a quantity of the average man, for whom only the table of random digits would mean a fair law of government. It was believed that no lie could be told by way of survey sampling. In the initial moment of reform, facts were not supposed to be judged but only surveyed or collected by means of random sampling. The only risk in this method was that of running into a random error, which should not be viewed as an error but as a necessary sacrifice for believing in the statistical laws of truthfulness. It was in the hands of Professor Dai and his earnest students that such problems of random errors would be worked on and solved. Recall the ideology of the reformatory era: "Let us find truth by way of facts." At the time, this meant that one should stop quarreling over human values and subjective opinions in order to get to the social facts, naked and quantitative, that were necessary for comprehending reality. To understand was to know what had happened in the first place. This came to be represented by a scientific conviction: the random choice of sampling units would secure neutrality and objectivity in observing social reality. Only in this way could one avoid, it was believed, the systematic errors of human fallacies, such as those that occurred during the Great Leap Forward. In the sociological scholarship, where mathematical training was weak, the method of survey sampling came to be viewed almost as a scientific myth—as if by employing it, one would be guaranteed to reach truthful reality. The guardians of random errors in the "objective science" of statistical analysis would screen out any human faults or subjective slips, such as those produced by the Cultural Revolution. This was a key message from and for the average man, whose sense of reality was not only constructed but statisticalized (cf. Berger and Luckmann 1967). The world of the average man was formulated not just by language and culture but by the systematization of various quantitative qualifications built upon the statistical data of survey sampling.

Somewhat later on, in the wider field of social sciences, economics in particular, the average man came to possess a zealous interest in regression analysis, a particular statistical method. There was a deliberate but unconscious twist in embracing such a method: it was employed chiefly for forecasting future economic performances of various kinds. The scholarly and official obsession with regression analysis indicated a growing urge to measure China's distance from the rest of the world in developmental terms. By means of a scientific approach, both the scholar and the official sought to know the future in terms of material growth in quantitative measurements—for example, to determine when and whether China would become developed in terms of its GDP or GDP per capita. While this was not an entirely new concern for the People's Republic, the use of statistical analysis made it for the first time a "scientific" or "objective" object of official thought. In a sense, regression analysis became part of the scholar-official lexicon, producing conditions of possibilities for speaking and conversing. Regression analysis, in its initial configuration as a statistical method, was meant to show the tendency of "regress"—returning to the mean of a deviating tendency in situations such as biological or agricultural experiments. The meaning of the method—in the hands of Professor Dai and his students, for instance—had nothing to do with "regression"; instead, it was made to mean almost "progression"—or perhaps one could call it "progression analysis." For it was the progressive development of China in relation to the world that came to occupy the scholarly and official attention.

Perhaps there is a legitimation crisis for the current government of the People's Republic, for it has to employ growth rates to prove the rates of growth, for which regression analysis has become its perfect machinery. The growth rates will index governmental performance, but, more importantly, they have become a self-vindication of *government* in its developmental and moral discourse. Clearly, this sense of development, a future orientation, so to speak, which is numerical and material, produced by regression analysis and grounded in statistical terms, is different from the sense of tomorrow during the Maoist years. At that time, the future was enveloped in a metanarrative of historical necessity that was *internal* to those who were ideally both its *authors* and *subjects*. The socialist futurity was *internally* temporal in the sense that the past, present, and future were conceived as an organic chain of dialectical movements enriching human life. Its mechanism was, to borrow a term from Hegel, "the negation of negation." The scientific mind of the present age, with its incestuous affair with regression analysis, seems to have run in an opposite direction: it demands to understand everything in external terms, statistical in essence, which would falsify any ideological mystification of human existence. Ironically, for example, the growth rates were measurements or representations of reality, external to the real movement of life, but this externality, produced by regression analysis in particular and the statistical method in general, came to be taken as the reality of life itself. Professor Dai and his enthusiastic students played the role of midwife in bringing this approach to life for the People's Republic.

No matter what kind of measurement one employs, and regardless of the situation in which a measurement is applied, the general principle of statistical reasoning is that a person has value only in being *someone*—an entrepreneur, a docile female, a millionaire, a European man or a blonde, a government official, a Cantonese businessman, a party member, a mistress, a professor, a homeless beggar, a Muslim Chinese, a university student, a Wenzhou migrant, etc. This "someone" can be defined only by the categories that have already gone into the statistical yearbooks. That is, people have to fall into certain categories in order to be counted, and these categories, either official or sociological, are not an a posteriori derivation from the facts but an a priori condition for recording. Under a new banner of scientific administration, value has come to be calculated from a social science objective point of view. Value is no longer *internal* to man himself; instead, it has become *external* to him. It is his possessions, measurable and calculable, that will stand for him as his true value and self, constituting an exteriorization by means of statistical objectification of worth according to the current market price. The rise of statistical thinking, insofar as the People's Republic is concerned, signifies both an acceptance of a particular conception of life and a historically specific mode of reasoning. In the life-world of everyday life and in the discursive formation of a new official mind we have witnessed the advancement of a global sentimentality of being, which is, in the case of the People's Republic, in the form of a "becoming." The arrival of a taxonomic and/or classificatory scheme driving and yet driven by governmental statistics, scientific and objective in its ambition, is nowhere more evident than on the altar of the rebuilt temple of social sciences, in which sociology was identified as a cross cousin of the state.

Professor Dai can rest assured in his grave, for his dream of a statistical revolution has been realized today. By this, one should imagine not a completion of the process of statisticalization but a more or less complete destruction, by statistical objectification, of the Maoist understanding of the world. Both within and outside the People's Republic, the voice of social sciences could be heard, often in classrooms and conferences, celebrating the coming of age of "objective science." As one would hear, repeatedly and vehemently, facts are facts, which will fool no one, not even the government. Finding out the truth about reality came to be viewed as the job of sociology; this is what social science, we are told, should and must engage with. Many scholars may not have obtained a high command of statistical knowledge, having worked in other fields, historical or literary, but they show a sense of awe and reverence for those who do. The honorable gentlemen hoping to live in a good corner of the temple of social sciences, almost a decade after Professor Dai's funeral, could no longer think of a truth claim without the support of statistical facts. For facts will not lie. There is supposed to be no ambiguity, no partiality, no bias, no preconception in the strict quantitative reduction of social reality. This is indeed a new faith for those struggling on the ruins of the Maoist revolution.

Sociology or social science in general has become a handmaiden of the state that has given birth to such sociological knowledge. Perhaps not everyone has been allowed into the temple yet, but it is almost certain, especially for students of social sciences, that the worship of quantitative facts will mean almost the same as getting access to knowledge. For it is the official knowledge, in its very form, that has defined the truth of social science or sociology in particular. The People's Republic has become a safe haven for sociological research—quite contrary to the opinionated view of its political restriction on academic freedom—insofar as the research is conducted in the scientific mode of statistical analysis. If one should step into the muddy field of potential political troubles, it is usually the case that one's research is deemed not scientific enough, that is, not factual or quantitative enough, to be published or publicized. The state has nowadays made sociology or social science in general its concubine (*ernai* in Mandarin) because they share the same epistemological stance as that kind of a couple does, and it enjoys more than anything else the quantification of reality as an official pleasure of sociological engagement or entertainment. The process of statisticalization is therefore, as I shall argue, both an official and a scholarly reorientation that has made the life-world a different one.

Even if one wished to, one would not be able to avoid hearing the frequent utterance of "number" (*shuzi* in Mandarin) at various kinds of sociological workshops in and on contemporary China. It refers to the statistical number, that is, either numbers in a large quantity being reduced to a few tables or matrixes, or the result of survey sampling aimed at estimations of certain qualities of a statistical population. The difference, a crucial one, between a regular number and a statistical one is that the latter can be tested according to the laws of probability and mathematically proved (cf. Corbett 2000). A regular number, however calculated, can be employed in descriptive statistics as a way of representing a certain fact. However, if one wishes to use inferential statistical tools for analysis, one must be aware of the fact that all inferential statistical figures are *estimates* according to certain probabilistic laws—and one should not forget the difference. In the attempt to quantify the social world, the scholar-official of the People's Republic would often forget the probabilistic theory of estimation; instead, he or she tended to treat all statistical figures, descriptive or inferential, as simply a factual representation of reality. Statistical analysis, including its functions of inference and forecasting, is in the strict sense of the term guesswork, which, albeit scientific, requires sound judgments for its evaluation. In the sociological mind of the People's Republic, two premature equations were often made: first, an equation of the quantitative with the factual, and, second, an equation of description with inference or prediction. Similar processes of statisticalization of the social world may have happened in other places, past and present (see, e.g., Porter 1986). However, the fusion of these two basic models of statistical thinking seems to be especially characteristic of the People's Republic, which has sought to reorient the basis of its existence on an epistemological ambiguity between representation and prognostication. Representation has become, in a sense, prognostication, which in turn will demand further representation. A vicious circle seems to have resulted from the conceptual fusion of these two basic modes of statistical knowledge.

According to the sociological mind of the People's Republic today, there may be multiple ways of representing social reality, depending on differing subjective points of views or perspectives, but there should be only one statistically verifiable, truthful reality, which an objective social science should be able to reveal.[7] There is no difference, in such a vision of the world, between the sociological

---

7. For a discussion of the spirit of sociological research, see, for example, Lu (1989, esp. 1–25). This should not suggest that the sociological field, in terms of its varying questions and problems, has been plowed by only one technique. However, the point is that its very spirit, which strives to be scientific and objective, has been predominantly nurtured by the coming of age in statistical thinking.

and the governmental view. Contrary to the anti-intellectual sentiment of the Maoist years, the scholar and the state—that is, sociological knowledge and official authority—are again united by the science of quantitative or statistical analysis. In a union of knowledge and authority that is an interesting addition to the history of modern science, the sociologist now stands on the Maoist ruins, proclaiming the scientific mandate of the state. In the last decade of the twentieth century, there was a widely circulated story that was almost too popular to be entirely credible. Then Premier Zhu Rongji, known as the economic tsar of China, would suddenly single out a provincial governor at a high-level national meeting and ask him to recite a specific economic figure for a particular industrial sector of his province. Not every governor could remember every single figure even for his own province, and the unfortunate official would be subjected to shameful derision by the premier in front of many colleagues. Premier Zhu had a very good memory, especially when it came to national or provincial statistical figures. Perhaps there was an element of performance in his attempts to embarrass the governors, who began to avoid sitting in the front rows at such meetings. However, the truth is that such a story as this, demonstrating a new confidence of governing, reveals the desire for the official to become a scholar as well. The glittering face of the scholar, when telling this story, reflects pride in his possession of knowledge that is now granted by the state. This story, from either side of the telling, came to be taken as an example of scientific knowledge penetrating the sphere of governmental administration, or as a signpost for a transition taking place in the vast continent of the People's Republic: governing has moved from the "management of people" to the "administration of things."

Facing the new faith in statistical science, the Maoist years stood in a shadowy background as a fading refraction. In sharp contrast, those years were characterized by an extreme awareness of self-positioning in society, such as in terms of class or class struggles, which denied the objective validity of "pure" quantitative analysis. It is against the "arbitrary ideology" of the Maoist revolution that a positive sociology or social science, with its ambition for scientific advancement, was born. Curiously still, one might ridicule Auguste Comte for his conceptual naivety; however, a true postmodern pain would be to see the floating signifier returning to a fixed position. Having placed the Maoist spirit in "the dustbin of history," it seems even harder to "rescue history from the nation," to borrow a term from historian Prasenjit Duara (1997). When the temple of social sciences was rebuilt in the 1980s, a peculiar combination of conceptual schemes, a number of which were European in origin, arose in the People's Republic. In the manner of a *combinatory* practice of historical forms, a rejuvenating spirit has been brought back into the "history of the present," which is nothing but a history of sentimentality. What is surprising about this outcome in particular is the willingness of sociology to enter into a union with the official powers under the name of objectivity. It does not seem to matter much whether one calls it postmodern or "neo-traditional" (cf. Walder 1986). The key thing is to notice that on the docile body of sociological knowledge, traces of official saliva have been left all over the place.

A number of sociologists or other social scientists such as economists have tried to prove the need for the People's Republic to have a middle-class stratum, characterizing it as an important factor in maintaining long-term stability for economic development. Needless to say, this has been a central concern for the government: put simply, in order to develop, there must be stability; in order to have stability, there should be a responsible middle class whose interests will then coincide with the interests of the state in the process of material development. Holding hands with the official powers, sociologists and economists have tried hard to prove the existence or the arrival of a middle class on the ruins of the Maoist revolution. This attempt has produced a vast proliferation of calculations, such as GDP per capita, Engel's coefficients, and other statistical indexes.[8] The "poverty of theory," in such a case as this, is not its lack of statistical sophistication; what is missing seems to be a critical impulse (cf. Thompson 1995). The "sociological imagination" has become a dull imitation of the old conceptual schemes without any critical reflection (cf. Mills 1959). That is, sociology in and of the People's Republic has become, in a word, the emperor's new clothes. Perhaps one should say that the reconstruction of the temple of social sciences, of which sociology has been its exemplary pillar, has come to nothing but a *simulacrum* of ideas and arguments, in which nothing original can be detected (see Baudrillard 1983). In a hodgepodge style, everything edible, both raw and cooked, has been thrown into the same boiling pot (cf. Lévi-Strauss 1969).

There seems to have been a happy marriage of the social sciences to the state via the introduction of statistical science. In epistemological terms, this affinity is nothing but a *contiguity* of social thought that has brought the scholar and the official into the same family of rationality and objectivity. Their intercourse, in the hopes of further material development, is dependent on the statistical edification of the family. In all this, one should understand that the mentality of governance is the governing mentality, a suffusing force that diffuses across boundaries among different spheres of social establishments while making or producing science and knowledge. Sociology or social science in general, in its epistemological character and function, has had no real effect on reality. It has become its parody.

8. From this critique of sociological thinking, one should not infer a disciplinary bias or prejudice (my own field of anthropology would have received an even more radical critique). Instead, this is a call for a critical reflection in epistemological terms. Criticism in and of China—which has been ample and often political in its intent—even if it is well targeted and delivered, will still not solve the epistemological problem that we are facing. What is happening is not simply a case of political and economic devastation. It is also a situation in which the political subject cannot think of itself in any other terms than those of statistical reasoning. Anthropological studies must be, as they should be, an epistemological awakening of the drowsy subject from his or her present-day slumbers.

Chapter Four

THE SPECTER OF MARX

A Marxist-Leninist Statistical Science?

Professor Dai was a believer in science, not particularly in statistical science but in the *notion* of science understood as the iron laws of materiality and development. However, it would appear that he had not always believed in such laws, because in his early works, those written during the Maoist years, he tried to make the Hegelian/Marxist dialectic a theoretical foundation for statistical knowledge. A couple of decades back in time, Dai had hoped to demonstrate the dialectical nature of statistical knowledge. Like his colleagues at the time, he tried to show that the Marxist theory of historical and dialectical materialism should be taken as the theoretical foundation for all scientific thought, including statistical science and probabilistic theory. In his works written in the 1950s, Dai did not take up Hegel or Hegelian philosophy directly but engaged with Hegel's dialectical method by way of Marx. For example, Dai made use of the notions of "contingency" and "necessity" in order to show that the probabilistic laws of large numbers must be understood as a *statistical* manifestation of *dialectical* thought, which was considered the essence of Marx's teachings. For Hegel, contingency and necessity would constitute a dialectical pair of notions. The dialectical play of this notional pair was what Dai had tried to bring into the conversation about statistical analysis and probabilistic theory. Once upon a time, seemingly so remote in history, when everyone was learning from the Russian experts, Dai followed the ideological suit and did not appear to be different from his colleagues. It may still be arguable that the nature of probabilistic theory is dialectical, whether Hegelian or Marxist; however, in the new, imaginary virgin land of the People's Republic, traveling on the global path, it is altogether impossible to sustain such an argument.

The movement from the Maoist years to the present age could be seen as an abrupt alteration in two contradistinctive modes of truth claims. It is as if an epistemological chasm had emerged, in the relatively short history of a long historical duration, separating two possibilities of life and knowledge. The difference and opposition between these two moments, rather than the moments themselves, will explain each as a moment making up the relational whole of opposition and difference. In other words, it is neither the Maoist years nor the present age alone that will be sufficient for understanding; the meaning of each lies in the middle, in the sudden emergence of a chasm that has separated the old sentiments from the new. It is in the fissure of an epistemological difference that we will be able to find the assigned character for ourselves on the global stage.

The tides of society changed, and a couple of decades later, Professor Dai became an earnest advocate for a new statistical science. However, not everyone, including several of his colleagues, was ready to give up the dialectics of Marx. In the 1990s, perhaps the last attempt ever made in the history of the People's Republic tried to provide a solid foundation for a Marxist-Leninist theory of statistics, which meant to restore the basic theoretical possibilities of dialectical/historical materialism in the field of statistical analysis. This was done by Professor Ma, a colleague of Dai. Ma, a lenient man with a stern mind, spent all his life working on the Marxist-Leninist theory of statistics. He was not swayed by the new tides; as some would say, he continued to walk on the pavement when everyone else had taken the bus. In the 1990s, a different taste for science and truth had emerged, leaving little room for the development of such a project, which was considered obsolete and obstructive. Against the tides of the new sciences, which were indeed old in the European context, Ma (1994) went on to publish his work, *Makesi Zhuyi Jing Dian Zuojia Tongji Sixiang Yanjiu* (A Study of Statistical Thought of the Marxist Classic Scholars). Since the world of scholarly publication follows the same logic revealed by Roland Barthes' semiological study, *The Fashion System* (1983), it is very hard to publish anything that is no longer considered trendy for the field. To publish a text on Marxism in the 1990s would mean to swim against the ideological current. No publisher showed any interest in such a manuscript, and Ma, out of desperation, had to seek help from his students who had moved into the official realm. Below is the story told by one of Ma's students, now an official for the National Bureau of Statistics, who helped to get his teacher's book published.

It was hard, you know, very hard, I mean, to publish a book like this in 1994! Who wants to read this sort of thing these days? But, you know, Professor Ma unexpectedly came to my office one day. It seemed that he had something to tell me but could not figure out how he wanted to say it. I prepared a cup of tea for him. He sat down, nervously, sitting on the edge of my sofa, a brand new sofa. He was drinking my tea, very good tea, one cup after another, and was smoking my cigarettes, one after another as well. Professor Ma said nothing at first except to ask what I had been doing after graduation. He was my adviser when I was in graduate school back in the 1980s, but I hardly studied with him. We'd had almost no contact after my graduation. And here he was in my office. Although he had been my adviser, he taught me very little, I must say. Some time passed, and it was about time for lunch. Professor Ma stood up and said that he should not take up anymore of my time. He had been there for an hour without saying much, and then, at last, when we were walking to the door, he asked whether I could help him publish his manuscript.

I knew, and everyone else knew, that he had been working on the Marxist thought on statistics. He had spent all his life on these materials, but, sadly, they are no longer relevant or useful today. Nobody would publish his book, and that was why he came to see me. He had been laboring on it for twenty years since he went back to Renmin University to teach in the late 1970s. He was not prolific and was about to retire at the time when he came to see me, but he was still unable to get his major study published. This was his lifelong work, which he had conceived in the early 1950s as a graduate student. When he was murmuring to me about the possibility of publishing his manuscript, he did not look up at me. He looked downwards, as if he were checking the hygienic condition of my office. He was embarrassed, I knew, to have to seek help from a former student. What could I do? I could not refuse, and so I said yes to him.

I regretted it a bit later on. I do have friends and connections, and this would help me get the book published. But who was going to read it? If nobody wanted to read it, it would become a matter of how to finance this publication. Anyway, I went to talk with a friend who had been my roommate in graduate school and who now worked in the publishing house of our Bureau. He told me that if I wanted to do this, it would be fine with him, but I had to come up with the money to cover the publication costs. He was certain, as an experienced editor, that this kind of work would never sell. Essentially, we—or I—would have to buy up all of the copies in order for it to be published. How much would it cost? I asked. He said that he could manage it with two thousand yuan, which is about three hundred dollars and was about two months' salary for a professor at the time. I did not have the money, but I could and would find it. Of course, not just from my own pocket. I contacted another student of Professor Ma, and he said that it was fine for him to pay half the amount. He was in charge of a small office in a southern province, and he could get the money from his office account. I collected all these contributions and went back to the publisher, and he agreed to publish the book, which came out in six months.

In general, the publication of academic works had become more difficult due to the market pressure for commercialization that had begun in the 1980s, despite the fact that most publishing houses at the time were still "owned" by the state. Ma's book in particular would appeal to no one—neither the public nor the state. But thanks to Professor Ma's students, the book was published and can thus provide us with a textual trace of a repressed sentiment. The opening pages read like a government report: the book begins with a statement of what Marxism means to us today, followed by praise of the rightfulness of the official doctrines. "Let us try hard in order to produce a socio-economic statistical theory with Chinese characteristics," Ma urged (1994, 1). For scholars working on contemporary China, this wording should sound familiar. The phrase "with Chinese characteristics" reflected an official stance that persisted up to the early 1990s, although it is no longer relevant in the new century. Ma's text, despite its obsoleteness, did not mean to contradict the official ideology of the time. This opening gesture contains within itself a contradiction, and this contradiction is a double contradiction. On the one hand, Ma attempted to stand in line with the state, but the state had moved away from its own line. By the time that Ma's book was published, the ideological notion of Chinese (or socialist) characteristics had begun to lose its signification. The book was a work *of* time, which came out too late to be *in* time. On the other hand, if Ma's work were to be seen as a critique of the ideological state apparatus, it would mean a self-defeat, for its basis was that of the older official vision of the world. Contributing neither to statistics nor to Marxism, Ma's book was a souvenir of history within which a historical contradiction of modern development has been encapsulated.

Ma asked rhetorically at the beginning of his book whether it was necessary to undertake such a study. According to what was happening at the time, this study was *of course* necessary, in his view. What Marx, Lenin, and others said about statistics should constitute *necessary knowledge* for us today, as he saw it. The second question concerned the urgency of such a study. Implicitly rather than explicitly, Ma was calling for a theoretical reconsideration of the Soviet Union Theory. If it was wrong, one must be able to determine which part of it had gone wrong, for Marxism and Leninism, from which the Soviet Union Theory derived its theoretical liturgy and energy, could not be wrong. This was Ma's starting argument. Although his work resembled an official document in form, if one were patient enough to go into the depth of its textual space, one might uncover a repressed struggle trying to provide an alternative understanding for the nature of statistical science. Clearly, as Ma intended to argue, statistics as a field of knowledge should not be viewed in terms of a simplistic development of scientific method. Instead, as he insisted, it involved a socio-economic history of real struggles that constituted the essential background for the development of statistics and probability theory as a science. Such a point is banal to the post-structuralist and deconstructionist mind; however, in the social sciences of the People's Republic, it came to be seen as a superstitious residue from the graveyard of Maoist ideologies. What was missed by the sharp eyes of a new generation was precisely the historical nature of "global knowledge." Just as that madness has a history in Europe (Foucault 1965), statistical science tells a good story about the People's Republic.

However, with Professor Dai's statistical revolution in place, no student paid attention to Ma's work. As a matter of fact, Ma was often humiliated by his students in class. Back in the 1980s, a student, after having attended Ma's lectures, which became the basis of his book, said to his teacher: "Professor Ma, you are right in saying that these are great revolutionary thinkers. Marx, Lenin, and others are revolutionary in thinking about revolutions, but they are *not* statisticians. Their knowledge of statistics is minimal, superficial, and shallow. Being a revolutionary leader does not guarantee one's place in statistical science. In terms of statistical knowledge, you and I are far superior to Marx, I believe." By that time, the defeat of the Soviet Union Theory had become irreversible. The rebellious student, who later trained at the Harvard Business School and became a businessman, acted as a symbol of the time, whose message was that scientific knowledge is practical knowledge owned by experts in specific fields. Historical or dialectical materialism might be a good theory for revolutionary thinking, but it has nothing to do with the specific knowledge of statistics. With this change in attitude, students came to consider statistical analysis as a quantitative method rather than a social theory. The notion of *method*, by its implication and inclination in the modern sense, meant objectivity and abstraction, which are *not* historical or cultural qualities.

Professor Ma was late in history, and his message could not be heard by a new generation of students, who were busy preparing for their graduate school examinations and English literacy tests in order to go abroad. There was little point in arguing whether Marx had made a contribution to science, for there was no *practical* or *official* need to do so. Scientific and statistical thinking had come to signify the *non-ideological*. During this period of economic change, a utilitarian ambition arose among university students, who hoped that getting a degree in North America or Western Europe would be a way of securing their position in society. The initial global impact on academia in the People's Republic meant no more than the desire to go abroad. This is to say that reactions to the dueling scientific claims were not pure and simple; Professor Dai might not have won the battle so quickly and completely if the power of economic allurement had not been on his side. Ma not only failed to win the argument, but, more importantly, he failed to meet the a priori conditionality for arguing. Nevertheless, I am certain that if an Ian Hacking or a Thomas Kuhn were to compare Dai's work to Ma's, he would find more sustenance in the latter rather than in the former, for there is nothing in Dai's work that has gone beyond Quetelet or Saint-Simon.

Professor Ma maintained that Marx transformed the nature of statistical analysis, with particular reference to William Petty's idea of political arithmetic. He argued that Marx followed William Petty (1623–1687) rather than

Adam Smith or others in assigning economics or political economics the status of a sub-field of mathematical knowledge. One should remember that when Ma was writing his first few paragraphs, the official ideology had begun to take a pragmatist turn away from the credo of the revolutionary period. Ma seemed to have wished to include this official stance, brought about by the new government, into his reading of Marx. The important point, Ma emphasized, is that Petty, who was wholeheartedly praised by Marx, explicitly stated that data should or must be the language of reality. The achievement of Petty, according to such a reading, was his attention to the quantitative aspects of the social world. As we know, it was Marx himself who said that the degree of the successful application of mathematics should be seen as a measurement of scientific development in different fields of knowledge. Petty should therefore be considered the father of (socio-economic) statistics, Ma argued.

The general point of Ma's argument—the conceptual link between William Petty and Marxism—is based on two particular propositions. First, by stressing the importance of numbers and statistics in outlining "the political anatomy of Ireland," Petty provided a *materialistic* approach to statistical knowledge. Thus, Marx's discovery of historical materialism, especially its scientific spirit, seems to have had its roots in William Petty. This is what Ma hoped to establish. Second, in reading Petty, Marx realized that quantitative or statistical representations of reality are objective in the sense that his historical materialism cannot do without them. One should note that Petty's thought, presented in this way, presents nothing new. In fact, it came very close to what Dai wished to make everyone believe, although his approach was entirely different. Ma perhaps did not misread Marx, but he *overstated* Marx's thought on Petty in order to accommodate the official discourse of his day. He hoped to argue that statistics is a means rather than an end in itself for theoretical arguments or policy making. This is, once again, interesting. Regarding the *methodological* value of statistical analysis, although his gesture was different, Ma's essential position was not far from Dai's. The only difference, in his tiresome treatment of William Petty, is that Ma hoped to deny the independence of statistics as a science. As he argued, since it is a *method*, a form, a tool, statistics cannot be detached from its theoretical content. In other words, statistics has to be part of the socio-economic knowledge, which would constitute its theoretical content (see Ma 1994, 16).

Ma's reading of Marx's analysis of the working-class condition in nineteenth-century England was intended to emphasize the importance of the *qualitative* meaning of quantitative analysis. Statistical analysis can be useful only when a *correct* theoretical understanding of social reality is in place. One cannot, or should not, calculate without knowing what is to be calculated. This emphasis on the qualitative value of quantitative analysis, which would not be refuted by statisticians, is discussed via the Hegelian-Marxist language of dialectics. The example that Ma took up is a classic one: adequate classifications should precede the calculation of group means. The average is or should always be the average of a class—understood in the double sense of both a classified sub-group and an actual social group of economic differentiation—which has to be defined and analyzed in the first place by qualitative analysis. Few would refute this argument explicitly; however, Ma seemed to assign little value to the development of statistical tools. To say that calculation depends on a correct understanding of certain class categorizations, such as what Marx did to Europe, does not mean that such an analysis must always be statistical, as a student of Professor Dai would have argued. However, considering the timing of its publication, Ma's book could have been read as a critical warning. But it did not get read at all. At the time, students were being introduced to computers, and all things social and economic were being analyzed by means of statistical software packages. Using computer software programs such as SPSS (originally, Statistical Package for the Social Sciences), students of statistics were drawn into a different—almost heavenly—universe of calculation and computation.

An economist, who had graduated from and now taught at a major university in Beijing, recalled his experience of working together with several students of statistics, who had just discovered how to do multi-linear regression analysis on the computer. "At the time," he related, "everything was crude. Whenever I came up with some ideas, I would rush to share them with my friends in the statistics department, where new methods were being developed. They were truly the superstars of economics, I mean, in the graduate school of the 1980s. Econometrics came to mean everything sacred in our analysis. Their methods appeared new, and few could understand them completely. Their professors did not even know how to operate the computers. It was this small group of students who spoke, first and for all, the language of econometric analysis and whom we were all madly hoping to learn from. Most of the time, it worked well, but not all the time. Of course, these statistical tools are nothing now, and everyone knows a bit about them today. All of my young colleagues know how to run a regression analysis. Statistical knowledge has become a routine part of economic teaching, at least in major universities. But in those days, back in the 1980s, it was different. The economists had to consult with students of statistics and ask for their help in running those damn statistical programs. Once I went over with my plan for studying economic growth and its associated environmental problems, and I ran into this stupid little guy who was one of the best graduate students in the statistics department of our university. I tried to get him onto our team, but he looked at me, with his eyes almost closed, and said plainly: 'Yes, I would be happy to join you, but I do not care about your problems, which are not mine. In fact, I do not care at all. How you will use your data is your problem, not mine. My job, if you want me to join your team, is to run the statistical machine for you. I will help you run the quantitative analysis. As for the result, its meaning and significance, you will have to figure that out your-selves.' Having said this, he went back to reading a book on cluster analysis. A little bastard of statistics! I was shocked by his attitude at the time. If he wished to be part of the team, he had to know what kind of problem we were hoping to deal with. But he showed no interest in whatever we were trying to do. In his view, the data could be run through his computer programs regardless of what they stood for. However, this was a time of radical change: computers and statistics were looked on as magician's tools rather than a scientific method. We have hardly come out from under its spell even today."

From the time that Professor Ma had begun to work on his book up until it was finally published, a decade of rapid socio-economic change had transpired. His work would probably have been taken more seriously if it had come out a decade earlier, for time had come to run according to a different clock in the 1990s. It seems that Ma reacted to a historical sentiment that was no longer alive. For example, in Ma's work, there is an interesting discussion about how Marx commented on Quetelet, especially on his notion of the average man. Marx once remarked on Quetelet's estimation of the crime rates in France in 1830, which, as shown by Ma, was a case in which Quetelet employed historical data and calculated the possible means of crime rates as estimates for a pre-diction for future years. Using the existing data, Quetelet was able to forecast the types of crimes "with amazing accuracy," as Marx said (see Ma 1994, 32).[1] However, the problem of Quetelet, according to Marx, was that he could not perceive the true sociological reason for the crimes, despite his accurate quan-titative predictions, because he did not recognize the exploitative nature of his own society. The quantitative description of crime rates was at best an initial stage of observation, but the point was *how* to explain it. Crime in such societ-ies was a reflection of unequal socio-economic relations, according to Marx. In his treatment of Quetelet, as Ma argued, Marx showed a dialectical relation of quantity to quality and vice versa. Quantity, as a phenomenal expression, must be understood as an expression of an essential qualitative phenomenon. The quality or the essence of social relations must be the end of our analysis, accord-ing to Ma's interpretation. Quantity can make sense only if we know what it stands for. It is the qualitative nature of things that determines their quantitative appearances (ibid., 32–35). Let us note here that this treatment of quality versus quantity resembles the Maoist teaching, which made class struggles its foremost ideological concern. Ma's book could be read as a reification of an old spirit in a new context, in which the qualitative—the organic and the holistic, namely, the question of class and class backgrounds—was prioritized.

Ma went on to proclaim that it was Lenin who completed the Marxist the-ory of statistical science. Lenin had once said that statistics was a crucial means

1. Ma's reference was made to the official translation of Marx's entire work in Chinese.

for comprehending society, and this became a popular quotation for scholars during the Maoist years. Ma went further by claiming that Lenin revolutionized statistical analysis, because, as Ma asserted, Lenin believed in facts upon which social analysis must be dependent. Ma's argument seemed to be straining in this part of the text: due to the revolutionary needs of Russia, Lenin paid close attention to the importance of collecting accurate data for social or socialist analysis. The Russian Communist Party's victory was dependent upon an adequate understanding of the social, political, and economic conditions of Russia. In Ma's view, it was precisely this sharp awareness of the revolutionary need, coupled with Lenin's acute attention to quantitative facts, that marked a new theory of statistics. It was in the historical organicity of making facts *socialist* that Lenin discovered a new social science. Organic historicity marked the nature of this new science, and this was how one should understand what Lenin said about statistics as a weapon for comprehending society. The second revolutionary contribution made by Lenin was, according to Ma, that Lenin developed the "Marxist dialectical reason" into a concrete analysis of quality versus quantity. Without the Marxist dialectical method, statistics was no more than simply a mechanical means of purely quantitative description, as Quetelet and all other bourgeois statisticians had envisioned it. In such a treatment as this, as well as in Professor Dai's early work, the theoretical foundation of statistics should not be probabilistic theory but rather Hegelian/Marxist philosophy.

Even a Marxist scholar—a truthful one—would find it difficult to accept Ma's contention that Lenin had discovered a new theory of statistics (cf. Althusser 1971). Lenin might have commented on the calculation of statistical means or on the method of statistical classifications, but was he the father of statistical science? Derided by his students whenever he made such allusions, Professor Ma could not properly defend his own position. Unfortunately, he could not have said that the truth of knowledge would require the conditioning of knowledge-truth in a certain "order of things" (see Foucault 1970). In the new temple of social sciences, Ma, whose time had passed, found no place for himself to sit, for, as Bacon once said, "time is the author of authors." In an insignificant part of his book, at the very end of a chapter, Ma (1994, 73–74) wrote:

> It should also be pointed out that, today, some scholars denied statistics as a branch of social science knowledge and argued for it to be a sub-field of mathematical knowledge. They have their reasons. These reasons include that they could not find a coherent theoretical treatment in our textbooks. In our textbooks, they found only specific methods in calculating statistical figures and organizational principles of government statistical work. They therefore doubt that statistics should be considered as a social science. On the other hand, they have seen a wide application of mathematical statistics in many fields, in addition to the fact that we misunderstood the nature of mathematical statistics during the Maoist years; therefore, they came to argue for statistics to be a mathematical science. This is understandable. However,

one must know that the application of mathematical statistics to the studies of social phenomena is different from whether there is an objective need for developing socio-economic statistics as a branch of social science knowledge. Mathematics can be used for studying many things, natural or social, but they cannot replace those fields of knowledge, either of natural sciences or of social sciences. Hence, the total denial of the existence of the Marxist-Leninist socio-economic statistics, which is built on a concrete history of social practice,[2] is not acceptable. This is a historical fact. To apply mathematical knowledge to studying social phenomena is one thing; to provide a true foundation for such knowledge is another.

In referring to "some scholars," Ma was certainly alluding to Dai, for whom statistics stood as a purely quantitative method. In hindsight, this debate, exemplified by Dai versus Ma in the field of economic statistics, should be seen as an index for the historical difference in a battle for life and knowledge, one that indicated the inevitable decline of the socialist imaginary on the global stage. Professor Ma, standing on the threshold of a new epoch, had to admit that there were serious problems in the way in which socio-economic statistics had been taught in the universities, where Professor Dai began to gain his predominant influence. A hero—who was Dai in the eyes of a new generation of students—was born, while Ma experienced the sad end of a tragic figure. Ma tried to rescue Marx and Lenin from oblivion by rereading their works afresh, but he did not succeed in this attempt. He was not aware that, while struggling, some of his counterparts in Europe employed a similar strategy in revisiting an older discursive foundation for intellectual innovations. Insofar as the Marxist tradition is concerned, Louis Althusser's *Reading Capital*, from the vantage point of structuralism, is a good case in point (see Althusser and Balibar 1970). Or perhaps Ernesto Laclau and Chantal Mouffe's (1985) rereading of Gramsci's notion of hegemony could also serve as an illustration. Ma's reading, however, is not comparable to any of these *returns*: Marx and Lenin in his reading are neither systematic nor coherent. The only resemblance is his intellectual gesture to return to the classic scholars in the Marxist tradition.

There is, in fact, little innovation in Ma's reading of those thinkers. That is, no new or additional elements were added to what was common knowledge to the scholars of the People's Republic at the time. This does not mean that Marx or Lenin could not have been *reread* for theoretical renovations. However, Professor Ma did not aim to *reread* Marx and Lenin into a new science; he was simply trying to keep them alive in a changing ideological environment in which they began to be thought of as no more than pure ideologues. For a new generation of students, Ma was viewed not as an evil man but rather as a hopeless figure, a madman, a clown, somewhat like Cervantes' Don Quixote,

2. This clause is not comprehensible in Chinese if one reads word by word, although its meaning is not mistakable. Translation is mine.

fighting against an illusionary enemy that was in fact the sheep of reality. The only difference, with regard to students of a new generation, was that there was no longer—and perhaps never would be again—a Sancho who would be willing to follow the knight whose true love was the love of truth.

"Dialectical materialism and statistics are both theories of epistemology,"[3] claimed Yue Wei, a scholar-official who worked for the National Bureau of Statistics for many years. With a different motive and yet a shared experience, he wrote a small book, *Tongji renshilun* (Statistical Epistemology), which, like Ma's, was published in the year 1994. In it, Yue (1994, 1) states that he has endeavored to use "the Marxist epistemology to study the process, method, and rule of statistical epistemology." Yue's general theoretical or philosophical position was that statistical understanding is part of the *whole* of human understanding. The unique characteristic of statistical epistemology is that it aims at an understanding by means of quantitative analysis; "however, its epistemological action follows the general laws of human epistemological activities" (ibid.). It is only when such general laws are properly understood that government statistical work can be better carried out. Yue's hope, slightly different in its orientation, was to try to discover the general laws of epistemology in order to guide the empirical work of statistical analysis. An official himself, Yue was not only witnessing the wholesale transformation within the Bureau; he was also part of the transformation, in the sense that he was in charge of reforming the institutional functions in his division. The Bureau was going through a series of changes in order to adapt itself to a new system of statistical work that would accord with the United Nations' categories and would be suitable for the market economy. The legitimating word, from the 1980s onward, was "commensurability." Everything had to be made *commensurable* and *comparable* according to the "global" standards. Within a decade or so, the model of government statistical work had altered. It was not simply a change in normal institutional terms; it was a change in the conception of the institution itself, a radical remodeling of institutional principles according to the example set by the advanced industrial countries. Yue was a man who lived two lives. He witnessed both the downfall of the older model built on the Soviet Union Theory and the rise of the new one, globalized and yet globalizing. His book can be seen as an attempt to stitch together his own life, which had been divided by these two moments in history.

---

3. The word "epistemology" in Mandarin is *renshilun*, which bears a slightly different connotation from its English counterpart. To be sure, there are differing philosophical traditions behind the evolution of these terms in their own contexts. The notion of epistemology was not indigenous to the Chinese tradition, which did not build its system of conceptualization on the epistemological distinction between subject and object. For a treatment of the Chinese tradition, see Fung (1948).

In a somber and yet expectant tone, Yue (1994, 1–2) wrote:

> Our great economist, who is also a great statistician, Sun Yefang, once said that if one wishes to understand economics and statistics, one should learn a bit of philosophy, especially dialectical and historical materialism: in order to build a right worldview, that is, epistemology, as well as methodology; in order to know the general rules and tendencies of things that constantly change in the world; in order to be able to understand the essence of everything through its phenomenal appearance; in order to improve one's capability of understanding, analysis, and adaptation. Someone such as a statistician who understands philosophy will be able to free himself from the limited constraints of professional requirements, rising up high, seeing farther than others, possessing a broader understanding, capable of accepting new things and ideas, being able to have a different point of view, developing new hopes and providing new suggestions. This capability is, of course, extremely important to the development of our modern statistics with Chinese characteristics.

Here, as with Ma, there is a Hegelian element in Yue's statement: philosophy as epistemological knowledge should govern specific fields of knowledge such as statistical analysis. Sun Yefang had been an economist in the old times and knew a bit of Hegel by way of Marx. For many scholar-officials of Sun's generation, who helped establish the socialist planning economy during the Maoist early years, Marx was their Hegel. However, in his tribute paid to Sun, Yue's sentiment, representative of an older mode of knowledge and governance, would have to give way to a new model that no longer views philosophy as providing necessary guidance for empirical sciences.

A professor of economics in Peking University, in an interview in 2001, said that when he was in graduate school back in the early 1980s, he attended a talk by a famous professor of economics from Princeton University, Professor Zou. Zou's specialty was in the area of macroeconomics, particularly econometrics. At the time, lectures by world-known economists were considered a valuable opportunity for learning, and scholarly exchanges between China and the rest of the world had only just begun to take place. Zou delivered his lecture with confidence and eloquence and, from time to time, illustrated his points by writing down a few mathematical formulas on the blackboard. Students were especially impressed by this, because few at the time could understand the delicate meaning of a likelihood function employed in econometric analysis. But this master, once the President of the American Association of Econometrics, could easily draw out and write down from memory all the mathematical equations needed for his talk, as well as their macroeconomic implications. Facing this group of ignorant graduate students, whose eyes, and perhaps also mouths, were now wide open, Zou felt that he had indeed done something for their education, which would give new hope to the People's Republic. When he was through, perhaps believing that he had effected a mental revolution, he sat down at a large table, waiting for questions.

A momentary silence occurred because this was indeed new knowledge for those whose training was primarily in political economics. Then a student stood up from the audience and asked: "Dear Professor Zou, what do you think about Marx's labor theory and its applicability for econometric analysis?" The professor's eyes opened wide in surprise, reflecting his distaste and displeasure, and he responded loudly and emphatically: "*Economics is not philosophy!*" Having said this, he looked up at the ceiling, making it clear that he refused to respond to such questions. The embarrassed student, whose training was in the field of Marxist economic theory, had not meant to offend the world-known scholar. As I was told, he genuinely wanted to know whether it was possible to quantify Marx's labor theory. This narrative made a deep impression on me. In fact, reading Yue's book constantly brought this interview back to my mind as I struggled for a proper understanding of such a telling story in and as history. Is it not a good statement for where we are today? "Economics is *not* philosophy." This is a clear-cut statement about what economics *must not* be. It is more than a statement; it has become a crucial part of social reality for the People's Republic. With today's eyes, one can see better the total domination of an economic metaphysic that has thrown Marxism and like philosophies into "the dustbin of history." Marxism is still present, but it is, adopting a phrase from Joseph R. Levenson (1968), "merely *historically* significant." No longer a living force of ideology, it is but a relic inherited from the Maoist past. By stating that economics is *not* philosophy, which was intended to get rid of Marxist philosophy as metaphysics, the People's Republic began to embrace the age of an *economistic metaphysic*, which seems to consign every possible mode of human thought and activity to the steelyard of market calculation based on consumer rationality and cost-profit analysis. In other words, economics, as taught at Cambridge or Stanford or Chicago or Princeton, came to obtain a metaphysical value; it was received and functioned as a metaphysic in justifying social reality.

At the time of Professor Zou's visit to Beijing, this kind of statement still needed to be made, because the People's Republic had only recently begun to change lanes on the economics highway. Students still needed to be taught and reminded that economics is empirical rather than contemplative, that it is observational rather than philosophical, that it is positive rather than speculative—in short, that it is scientific rather than ideological. Zou did not feel the need to explain further what he had said, for he knew that his very presence proved the essential logic of his statement: the sentiment of the People's Republic was on the path of radical change. And he was right. When we compare the confidence in Zou's statement about economics with Yue's reference to the Marxist tradition in the opening of his book, we see a clear difference: the latter was struggling to defend his position because he was looking backward, trying to figure out a way of justifying his early life, which had been spent working on the Soviet Union Theory. The forward-looking professor from Princeton had all the confidence in his pocket and could wait for the testament of tomorrow to prove the correctness of his assertions, whereas the backward-looking scholar-official struggled strenuously throughout the entire text in order to make his point—a point that had value only for the past. This is because there was a new world arising from the historical horizon of the People's Republic, and Zou's statement represented the spirit of this new world, which is now and today. Yue had the harder task, for he was trying to prove the value of the past, which is seen today in the People's Republic only in negative terms.

This is why it is interesting to read Yue's book, which was published in an environment that was no longer of its flavor or favor in an attempt to retain a sense of coherence in life. As Yue argued, dialectical materialism is a universal epistemology that articulates the general laws of human understanding, whereas statistical analysis is an epistemological act that represents a partial, specific branch of knowledge dealing with quantitative aspects of the phenomenal world. In the relationship of dialectical materialism to statistics, it is said that the former governs the latter, although the latter has developed its own particular rules and methods. It is the relationship of the universal to the particular, of a Hegelian kind, that helped Yue say what he wanted to convey. To be accurate, Hegel was never mentioned in Yue's text, and the idea of the dialectic, in Yue's trembling hand, seemed to function as a magic tool of theory that could fix any field of specific knowledge. For example, the basic statistical notions of "sample" versus "population" were discussed in terms of a dialectical relationship of the part to the whole. Yue perhaps did not realize that the relationship of the part to the whole, in view of a long European tradition of metaphysical thinking, was *not confined to* the dialectical reformulation by Hegel. In any case, the relevance of Hegelian philosophy was clear, although not explicitly referred to. If one were to translate into English Yue's writing on topics such as correlation and its statistical meaning, one might produce an effect similar to that of an English student attempting to understand the Hegelian language. Yue's work, in fact, demonstrates that dialectics had been essential to the official mind, characteristic of the Maoist years, in dividing up fields of knowledge and in uniting them into a predominant vision. This treatise presents an excellent example of a different outlook on the world—in the domains of both life and governance—in which the relationship of general knowledge to a specific field of knowledge is considered to be a *dialectical* relation. It is against such a mode of dialectical thinking that Zou's statement came to enlighten us. In saying that economics is *not* philosophy, he meant that economics is analytical and mathematical rather than dialectical or metaphysical. Zou would perhaps say, if pressed, that economics or econometrics or statistical analysis as empirical sciences required *no* epistemological or metaphysical foundation.

By training, Yue was an economic statistician from an earlier time and thus could not have produced a good discussion with a philosophical bent. However, what he sensed, whether through his reading of Marx or by intuition, was right: something greater than data and formulas, whether it is called epistemology or not, should be the foundation for the specific fields of particular knowledge. What he did not realize was that the epistemology itself is *historical* in nature (see Foucault 1970). His struggle to convey his thoughts marked a moment of transition in which the Hegelian/Marxist dialectics gave way to a particular historical invention of scientific metaphysics. Marx and Marxism, which constituted Yue's understanding of the dialectic and Hegelian philosophy in general, came to represent a negative signification for a new generation. Marxism came to be seen as deterministic, teleological, ideological—that is, not scientific. Against the dialectical mode of thinking there arrived analytical, quantitative, scientific thought, which gave rise to a neo-positivistic fetishism about facts and data. Knowledge came to be conceived of in terms of its utility. The more general concept of the good, which has been made both *material* and *materialized*, supposedly refers to the benefit of individuals in society, represented by the average man or the GDP per capita. Further along those lines of modern evolution, the National Bureau of Statistics, walking on a pavement full of old footsteps, has fully established the doctrine that works "from particulars to particulars," about which Yue's feelings were mixed.

The "particulars" have no end in themselves; instead, they always reveal something else, perhaps some sort of "scientific truth." One should not drink alcohol at all because it is not good for one's health, says one scientific *particular* truth, whereas another says that a glass of wine every night has made an average Frenchman live longer than his British counterpart. "From particulars to particulars" means an endless series of serial production and reproduction of a series of facts. In the vast continent of the People's Republic these days, a large number of particular differences are generated and produced that tend to reproduce themselves into further series of serial facts, such as the sociological reasons for divorce and suicide. These sociological observations are always built on statistical data and analysis, which, as methods for discovering scientific truth, are objective; however, the results of the analysis will often contradict each other. Underneath these particular differences there stands a unifying principle of methodology, which is formidable and coercive in the form of a law, made of iron and steel, that would allow particular facts to become scientific truths. In the new scenario in the People's Republic, the "particulars" have become particular facts, which are supposed to speak for particular truths. Truth or scientific truth is in the particulars, which are themselves also data. The specter of Marx could be eliminated only by means of this newfound love of facts and truth. But the first half of Yue's life was still entwined with an ideological past, and he wanted to bring his past into the present. Today, facts act as if they were a stripper, in the sense that Roland Barthes wrote about in his *Mythologies* (1973, 84–87). The stripping movement—peeling off one's garments, one piece after another—is not *an end* in itself but constitutes *a means* by which the effects of revealing the concealed body (of truth) can be produced. Statistical data and analysis are the garments of a scientific stripper, with all its tests and estimates, serving the purpose of revealing the concealed truth—the naked truth, if one prefers.

"The Negation of Negation"

From the 1980s onward, the idea of science has prevailed on the ruins of the Maoist revolution with a sweeping, euhemeristic force in its determination to strike down all existing myths and ideological remains such as Marxism. The defeat of the Soviet Union Theory in the field of economic statistics remained, in recollection and remembrance, as a murky signpost, pointing to a recent past that seemed to belong to a remote foreign country. The doleful discomfiture of Professor Ma's argument signified an inevitable setback for the Maoist morality and reason. In the new scientific outlook, Marxism, which used to be "the unsurpassable philosophy of our time," came to be seen as no more than one specific area of knowledge, having totally lost its epistemological status. From the other direction on the same road, positive science, for which statistical analysis came to represent its methodological model par excellence, has advanced. The methodological concern came to make up the most important question for research, leading to a new slogan: "All revolutions are revolutions in methods." This motto, popularized by Chinese intellectuals in the 1980s, came to mark the neo-positivistic spirit of a new dynasty. Subjective judgments and socialist ideologies should give way to scientific objectivity, for which statistical or quantitative analysis must constitute its essential methodology. It is in the heart of a new era that one could feel the resonance of Professor Dai's sentiment, which pointed to a global path of scientific engagement. The fight was a necessary fight, in the minds of Dai and his students, for a new page of history must be written or rewritten. If the Maoist years had *negated* the Chinese tradition through violence, the reformatory movement has wreaked exactly the same violence on the Maoist past as a "negation of negation," using Hegel's expression. It is a productive destruction, because the new came from and yet departed from the old. Life goes on, but the *cultural ideals* have altered. The ultimate inspiration, for a younger generation, has become the American dream (cf. Madsen 1995).

A distinction should be made for a clearer conception: the reform period needs to be divided into two moments. The battle between Dai and Ma in the 1980s and early 1990s, as we have described, characterizes the first moment of the reform period, during which the basic inquiry into life and knowledge remained entangled with the Maoist conception of morality and reason. From the mid-1990s onward, this inquiry has taken a different form. It has become indifferent to the Maoist past, concerning itself entirely with the question of how to choose a better transportational *means*, such as a Mercedes, rather than deciding the *direction* of the journey in which one should travel. In other words, having buried the Maoist past in the first moment, the second moment has concerned itself with the question of how to move faster on the global road of material development. On which developed country should China model its own development? Japan? Western Europe? America? This has become a fundamental question for the People's Republic today. What is happening in its vast continent is no longer a *turning away* from the Maoist years; instead, there is a *mimicking reaction* to the Other possibilities of modern development. The image of the United States, therefore, has come to play a more and more important role as the People's Republic makes sense of itself, by the way of the Other, on the road of global traveling.

Let us take a small detour in order to see more clearly the meaning of this present situation. The traditional mode of life and knowledge in China was centered on the notion of ancestor worship, in which the power of the past was an essential source for social imagination and action. The past acted as a discursive genesis or a condition of possibility for the stories of self and family, people and society, to be told and *lived* (see, e.g., Baker 1979; Freedman 1958; Hsu 1948). The Maoist power-praxis introduced a new order of things, which reversed the direction of the familial temporality away from the past and ancestor worship and reoriented toward the future, that is, toward socialism's final victory in the future. It introduced a revolutionary and epistemological break in the traditional conceptions of temporality and family that had been essential to the Confucian way of life (see, e.g., Levenson 1968). Put simply, the Maoist years destroyed the value of the past as the basis for being in society; instead, the struggle for a better tomorrow, as an emancipatory fantasy, came to reconstitute the directionality of time and history. However, despite this radical reversal, the vision of the world for both of these modes of existence was *temporal* in the sense that the chain of past-present-future was conceived of as being created by *internal* determinations (see, e.g., X. Liu 2002, 161–163). The relations of the past to the present and of the present to the future were thus *interiorized*. Life itself, as well as its essential knowledge, or "being in the world" in general, assumed a temporal directionality that was inseparable from the material engagement with the world. Time did not mean simply a few markers on a calendar; it was a directional relationality that was interiorized into the chain of yesterday-today-tomorrow. Therefore, worshiping one's ancestors is not simply a ritual in terms of performance, such as that described by Victor Turner. It is a means of enacting a particular temporality that binds oneself to the familial temporality and engages the lineage clock of the chain of past-present-future. The Maoist years made such temporality reverse its directionality, with the present being driven by the promise of utopia in the future. Although the Maoist temporality became future-oriented rather than past-oriented, the conception of life and knowledge still remained essentially *temporal*. For both moments, the notion of history played a central role in producing social discourse. Or, put another way, historical terms, temporal and internal, were intrinsic to the discourse of self and the world for both conceptions.

Today, this no longer seems to be the case for the People's Republic, whose clock is no longer a clock but has become instead a competitive game of material development with or against the Other. Other possibilities of modern development may vary, but the very conception of an Other now constitutes the basic epistemological and ethical ground upon which life and governance run their course. This is the meaning of "the negation of negation": it does not mean simply that the present age negates the Maoist ideologies but that a new basis for "being in the world" has arisen from the historical horizon of contemporary China. A different formation of the mode of life and knowledge, a different way of seeing and acting, a different mentality of governance—all these seem to have arrived on the stage of the People's Republic, which has freed itself from time and history, from family and utopia, in order to join the worldwide race for the "wealth of nations," as well as of individuals. The indefensibility of the Maoist position, using dialectical thinking or otherwise, as in the case of Professor Ma's book, simply indicates the impossibility of fighting a new battle with an old weapon. Ma did not lose his argument, as we have seen, but he lost the battle because the battleground had shifted to a place out of his reach. Terms, conditions, sites, and citations all have come to be different, being tied to the emergence of a differing conception of the world for which the directionality of time would make little relevance. The future is now spoken of in terms of growth, calculated for the purpose of comparison with other modern developments. Time has become calendric, pure and simple, like Newtonian physics, measured externally and having nothing to do with the interiorization of the past or the future into oneself as one struggles to emerge in the world.

The question for the People's Republic has become *how* to learn from the more advanced experiences of material development, not whether or not such a mode of life and knowledge should be borrowed. More specifically, in this new century, the powerful imagery of the United States, together with that of Western Europe and Japan, has constituted a model image, or an image model, for the People's Republic, whose eyes are constantly gazing across the ocean. There is a sense of tomorrow still, but it is a sense that is intrinsically tied to the fixation on the Other, who provides reasons and desires for calculating or computing various statistical figures about oneself. This is, of course, not to deny the fact that development has pluralized the People's Republic and multiplied its social fields. However, in the last analysis, in view of its *model image* as a collective illusion, which is *ideology* in the Althusserian sense or *imaginary* in the Lacanian sense, the dominant discourse on growth, capital, and marketization came to be built on the imagery of the Other. This is not to generalize about the increasingly plural material realities in and of the People's Republic. It is a statement about *the materiality* of plurality as an ideology or an imaginary, which is nothing but a refraction of oneself in the Other.

PART III

REASON AND REVOLUTION

Chapter Five

THE TAMING OF CHANCE

Change and Chance

Refracted by the positive light of the modern Other, the Chinese self-image became negative in the last moment of the previous century. This self-image was produced in *the mirror-field* of the Other and marked a significant shift in the self-representation of the People's Republic. The mirror-field, a notion borrowed from Louis Althusser, who had in turn taken it from Jacques Lacan, is *a field of mirror effects* in the production of a self-image by way of the Other. It is real in the sense that one is looking at oneself in *the mirror*, which is the Other. It is imaginary in the sense that one is not yet fully aware of the refraction in the mirror that is not simply oneself. There is more to the act of looking at or into the mirror; that is, the refraction represents more than what can be seen in the mirror because of one's desire for becoming the Other. This is, according to Althusser, a universal effect of ideology, which creates "objective truth" by means of *a subjective want*. Let us take a brief tour in the conceptual neighborhood of Althusser, which is no longer a favorite intellectual attraction (see, e.g., Žižek 1989). Althusser makes a rigid distinction between science (or theory, i.e., Marx's theory) and ideology, and maintains that all action, including socialist revolution, is carried out within the province of ideology. According to Althusser, it is ideology that gives human subjects the imaginary, provisional coherence to become practical social agents. Therefore, ideology is not simply a false consciousness that the subject misrecognizes. The misrecognition in question is a *self*-misrecognition, which is an effect of the imaginary dimension of human life. As Terry Eagleton explains (1994, 214; emphasis in original):

Imaginary here means not 'unreal' but 'pertaining to an image': the allusion is to Jacques Lacan's essay 'The Mirror-Phase as Formative of the Function of the I', in which he argues that the small infant, confronted with its own image in a mirror, has a moment of jubilant misrecognition of its own actual, physically uncoordinated state, imagining its body to be more unified than it really is. In this imaginary condition, no real distinction between subject and object has yet set in; the infant identifies with its own image, feeling itself at once within and in front of the mirror, so that subject and object glide ceaselessly in and out of each other in a sealed circuit. In the ideological sphere, similarly, the human subject transcends its true state of diffuseness or decentrement and finds a consolingly coherent image of itself reflected back in the 'mirror' of a dominant ideological discourse. Armed with this imaginary self, which for Lacan involves an 'alienation' of the subject, it is then able to act in socially appropriate ways.

Ideology can thus be summarized as 'a representation of the imaginary relationships of individuals to their real conditions of existence'. In ideology, Althusser writes, 'men do indeed express, not the relation between them and their conditions of existence: this presupposes both a real relation and an '*imaginary*', '*lived*' relation.... In ideology, the real relation is inevitably invested in the imaginary relation.

The self-image of the People's Republic represents such *an imaginary relation*, which is rooted in *a real imagination* of the Other. With the waning and disappearance of the Maoist mode of self-representation, which was temporal or teleological, the Other, materialistic and materialized in the historical experience of Western Europe, Japan, and North America, came to constitute a new foundation for the production and reproduction of self-knowledge. A radical shift has taken place, but both representations of self are *ideological* in the Althusserian sense. Their difference lies in the effectivity of the Other having functioned differently in one case from the other. The Maoist self-image, in the eyes of the People's Republic today, has become negative because the Other came to play a different role in the production of self-knowledge, which is not simply the knowledge of self.

In order for a new story to be told effectively, the old one must first be ridiculed or "falsified." The old story, in contrast to the developmentalistic one, was the Maoist tale of revolution and socialism, which had to be falsified in order for a different narration of self and the Other to be possible. The decade following the death of Mao can be described as a "liminal stage" of narrative transfer, by which I mean that *a structural rupture* in the representation of the self occurred in the People's Republic. This schism included two moments: first, the People's Republic ridiculed the Maoist mode of self-knowledge and turned it into a negative political myth; and, second, by mystifying the recent past, the People's Republic was able to tell a story about itself in terms of modern development that is dependent on a particular materialistic conception of the world and, especially, of the modern Other. The new story is not about history and values; it is about seeking commensurability and comparability with the Other in its pecuniary aggressiveness by way of a blatant materialism. For the People's Republic, the transfiguration of the Other and its role in the making of self-image and self-knowledge played an essential part in the new novel about development. In order for the figure of the Other to be reborn, according to the narrative logic in the story, the Maoist past must first be mystified. This was what happened during the initial phase of the reformatory era, especially with regard to the artistic and intellectual representations of the quickly receding past.

Let us take a closer look at how the mystification of the Maoist politics took place in the artistic and intellectual world at the time. In the late 1980s, a movie titled *Blue Kite* was released. It was not a blockbuster but rather a thoughtful, well-made, and well-received movie about the Maoist years. Like many other films at the time, this movie, which depicted an ordinary family experiencing the political struggles of the Maoist years, was intended to reflect on the irrationality of the Maoist politics. There was an intriguing scene in the movie, which was typical and representative of the general views of the time. The scene took place in an ordinary office setting, which could have been anywhere in the 1950s, partly because by then everything and everyone looked similar to each other. Similitude, as the face of the masses, made up the social surface, and as a social logic it produced its own reality of similarity in the Maoist society. The scene showed a political meeting: there was a long table around which sat a large group of people who all wore the same kind of blue jackets typical of those years and who were referred to in the same way—as a "comrade." It could have been in a factory or in a college or anywhere in the fictitious decade of the Maoist experience. But this was not an ordinary meeting. It was a meeting of the Anti-Rightist Campaign of the mid-1950s, when the Maoist government was attacking the real or alleged ideological "rightists," a special category of "bad elements" for the new society. Political movements and campaigns were nothing new, but this was the first major one that targeted almost exclusively the intellectual dissidents of the time. Most intellectuals had been enthusiastic supporters of the Maoist revolution, and this movement put their loyalty to the test. During the campaign, some officials and many intellectuals, including professors and university students, were labeled as rightists, and more than half a million across the country became rightists, an act of political death that would bring severe social and economic consequences.

The atmosphere in the office, as shown in the movie, was intense. The faces of the people in the room, who numbered about twenty-five, were serious and solemn. They were in a discussion about whether there were any rightists among themselves. Not one person dared to raise his eyebrows; instead, trembling, they all looked down at their feet or someone else's. A sudden change had come about in the life-and-death sphere of politics. A few weeks before, the government had invited people, intellectuals in particular, to examine the efficiency and sufficiency of official policies with the goal of improving them. But now the government claimed that those who had been critical were enemies of the new society. They were rightists who never tried to help and hated the Maoist order of things, which was made to benefit the masses of the people, as believed. A scary and terrifying message indeed! Some people, intellectuals in particular, had spoken out about the problems of the new society at the government's invitation and at meetings organized by the government itself. While the tone and language they employed might have been disparaging, in the majority of cases the intention was to help. From the government's angle a few weeks later, the earlier open criticism was now seen as an evil attack on the new order of things, and retaliation and repression were the official response. Anyone designated as a rightist and "an enemy of the people" would live with the consequences for the rest of his or her life. It would affect not only oneself but also one's family and one's posterity, in particular. Without a normative system of laws, the Maoist political control—which was *total*—served as a system of discipline and punishment.

This was the reason that no one in the office wanted to make a move, even to raise his eyebrows, because no one knew what would happen at the end of the meeting. The official in charge was impatiently waiting for more comments. "Has the cat got your tongue? You didn't seem to have a problem speaking up a few weeks ago." Smoking a large pipe, he looked around at everyone's poker face and sternly continued, "I thought that each of you had something to complain about. I thought that each of you had something to say about our new country. Why is there suddenly this silence?" A heavier silence was the response. "Well, if you do not wish to speak, I shall not force you, but as you all know, we have to put someone in the net, because we cannot report to our superiors that we do not have any bad elements among ourselves. Don't you think so? In our work unit, there is a rightist sentiment and there are also rightists." There was fear in the air, and everyone tried to hold his muscles and breath. The movie conveyed well the feeling of the moment, somewhat like that of an accused person waiting to be found guilty or not guilty. "Chairman Mao said that there are about 5 percent rightists in our official and intellectual groups. It is a minority group that has damaged or will damage our country. We have about twenty-five people here, and therefore we should have at least *one* rightist. Who will it be? It is our duty to seek him out, and report to our superiors that we have carried out our Anti-Rightist Campaign successfully." Despite what was being said by the official, everyone knew that it would be difficult to make such a decision, because there was nobody in the room who would be willing to name or to be named as a rightist. No one wanted to initiate an accusation in front of everyone else. The decision, even if they knew its inevitability, was a difficult one. At that moment, a gentle movement at the far end of the table drew everyone's attention. A middle-aged man stood up with apologetic embarrassment, and, pointing to the door, murmured almost to himself, "I need go to the bathroom." He left, limping awkwardly.

This was not a man who had ever complained about anything, but he had a problem with his urinary system, and the meeting had been long. When he returned to the conference room, he immediately sensed that something was wrong. There was a weird look on almost everyone's face: they had decided that this middle-aged man must be the rightist, for it was he who had not been present at the crucial moment of decision. Rather than pointing their fingers at someone around the table, it was much easier to single the man out by his temporary absence—that is, his absence filled the political requirement of a presence. The decision had been made by one and all, the masses under the leadership of the party secretary. In this way, no one could or should be blamed. One person's urinary tract infection spared the others in the work unit the embarrassment of a political struggle. In this ironic artistic statement about the Maoist mass democratic practice, the person's bladder, which resulted in an absent presence, represented the irrationality and illogicality of the Maoist ideological struggles. This is, of course, not to say that irony was the only mode of representation of the Maoist politics; on the contrary, there were, especially in the early 1980s, many artistic and novelistic portraits of its inhumanity and cruelty. Showing its irrationality and primitivity, in my view, was another dominant motif, which came to be tied more and more to the rise of a rational, materialistic, modern mode of thinking. It is China's coming of age in modern development that has made the Maoist logic of politics not only inhuman and arbitrary but also, more importantly, irrational. *Blue Kite* achieved this goal, among others, by showing that it was a bladder that determined the course of one man's political history. The man's wife, after hearing her husband explain what had happened, said to him: "I would rather you had peed in your pants, which at least could be washed out. But *now* what can we do?"

Behind the irony of this portrait lies the notion of luck and chance, which did not function effectively within the political space of the Maoist logic but instead became central for an understanding of the arrival of the market economy and its forces in the 1980s. When watching or reading such ironic portrayals of the Maoist politics, one must remember that they were made from a retrospective viewpoint after the idea of chance and luck had come to occupy a central place in the collective imagination of "getting rich first," an official slogan in the early years of the reformatory era. The notion of luck or chance seemed to help explain to a puzzled populace the arbitrary redistribution of national wealth by the invisible hand of Adam Smith. In other words, these depictions were less a revelation of the Maoist past and more a device of myth-making by a people responding to the puzzlement of marketization, which, although random and arbitrary, came to be represented as rational and scientific.

The chaotic initiation of the process of marketization resulted in two conceptual entanglements. One was the popular reaction against official corruption, which led to the student demonstration in Tiananmen Square in the spring of 1989. The other was the tendency to embrace or celebrate the notional power of chance and luck, for which modern statistics and probability theory are supposed to account scientifically. The question of corruption should be left for another treatment in its own right. The present study is concerned chiefly with the birth of scientific rationality that was also myth-making. The key point is that the way in which the Maoist past was represented resembles exactly the function of myth-making for a primitive mind, which employs myths in its search for an intellectual solution to the riddle of existence (Lévi-Strauss 1966). The idea of chance and luck belonged to the time when the new story, "the fable of the bees," was told; it did not belong to the era of the Maoist years. The Maoist past was simply an element of the myth, whose true function was to explain the intellectual problem of arbitrariness in the accumulation of wealth by individuals in the market economy, especially during the early transitional stages of reform. Although the idea of luck was not alien to the Chinese tradition, it had been largely repressed by the Maoist collective representations, which placed a greater emphasis on the power of humankind over nature. There was indeed a humanistic vision of collectivity during the years of the Maoist government that made people believe in the possibility of a total transformation of society. This should be seen as a proof of the power of symbolic domination. It is the market rationality and statistical reason of today that have, in retrospect, remade the outlook of the Maoist thought as inhuman and illogical.

Put another way, one could argue that the vocabulary of chance, luck, fortune, and misfortune returned as part of a scheme of "invention of tradition" to help the populace make sense of the new reality of marketization. The framework in which this vocabulary resurfaced is modern development, against whose scientific and materialistic self-portrait stood the darkness of the Maoist arbitrary power and politics. There was a double function for the employment of such a vocabulary: on the one hand, it provided a rationale for people to deal with the emerging socio-economic disparity, namely, by attributing their unfortunate circumstances to fate or chance; on the other hand, it relieved people from a psychological burden, largely due to the present material struggle, by shifting their attention to the extremely irrational nature of the Maoist politics. This vocabulary played a psychological function for intellectuals in particular. In order to speak of the reasoning of Adam Smith, the Maoist past must be falsified—not because it is less reasonable or less rational than the present mode of self-representation, but because it is a *different* mode of self-representation, which came to be seen as old-fashioned and obsolete. It is not our real suffering that has changed our history; it is our history that has taught us what is real suffering. It is this *difference*, which is a *choice*, between the two possibilities of envisioning that has made one inferior to the other. It is not that the discovery of a scientific view allowed the People's Republic to develop; it is because the People's Republic decided to develop that it adopted a scientific view as the justification for its course of action. The question is not whether the People's Republic is finally on the right path to modern development; rather, it is how the Maoist years have supplied the negative fuels necessary for today's collective representation, which is modernistic and developmentalistic.

A history lesson may be learned from this: despite the fact that historical materialism had been an ideological component of the Maoist outlook, it was never adopted entirely or faithfully during the Maoist political struggles. Instead, what was key to the mass campaigns of the Maoist years was a version of the idealist philosophy of "history and will" (see Wakeman 1973). There was an inherent contradiction in the "ideology and ideological state apparatuses" of the Maoist government. Historical materialism was said to be the material truth of historical development, but its ideological energy was chiefly spent on the call for constant, collective struggles of the human will. This has been reversed by the conceptual schemes of a new era: historical materialism is now viewed as a materialistic historicity that is verifiable by scientific or statistical proofs, while the will, collective or human, has been reduced to a minimum level of effectivity.

Placing these two self-representations into a conceptual contrast, we might see that during the Maoist years the ideological emphasis was given to the human will, while negligible effort was focused on the Marxist doctrine of historical materialism. A homologous reversal has come about in the present day: the materialistic notion of society in terms of market and development is now firmly established, and the schemes of science and rationality have replaced the human will as the new foundation for thought and action. In the Maoist years, the self-image was produced according to a mode of representation that was driven by the promise of a better tomorrow. In the People's Republic of today, there is no longer a tomorrow, with the real possibility of a difference in and of time. Instead of the future there has arisen the figure of the modern Other, which has become the eternal measurement of happiness. In short, in the vast continent of the People's Republic, *the future has become the Other*. Meaning depends on contrast. In shifting away from the temporal mode of self-representation, the reformatory era has prepared a mode of self-representation that is based on commensurability and comparability with the Other. The Material Reason, which is not different in its essence from historical materialism in this case, would require a scientific or statistical language for speaking in global terms. If one were to climb up and glimpse an overview of a decade in a new century, one would perhaps see a proliferation of new ideas and policies. But the principle of such a proliferation seems to have remained the same—the prescription of economic principles of cost-profit analysis in its various significations, behind which lies the neo-liberal assumption that human beings as individuals are codified by selfish genes and can be properly governed only by law and social contract. Everyone is said to have been looking for new things to happen in the new century; however, according to such a materialistic vision, nothing that has to do with human nature and society is truly perceived as *changeable*.

In one case, reality was the reality of thought and will, whose power lay in the possibilities of reconfiguring the real—that which would become but was not yet fully realized; in the other, despite the various possibilities of dressing up differently in materialistic terms, everyone seems to be tied to the reality of permanence or non-change. In one case, the future was too high in the imaginary air to be grabbed; in the other, all the truths of life are supposed to be proved by the quantity of one's own possessions. In one case, "what ought to be" became a pure fantasy that had nothing to do with reality; in the other, "what ought to be" is no longer a question but a reification of one's materiality. In one case, the socialist rebellion against the living order of things was motivated by an alternative thinking that had been forbidden by the existing ideologies and institutions; in the other, what *is* is accepted as the only real possibility, with all other modes of thinking being turned into constant permutations of the *same* on different levels of individual experiences. In other words, *what ought to be* has become merged into *what is*. Statistical variations in the motivations and desires of different individuals have become the collective representations of a new age. The impossibility of looking into other possibilities is the defining character of a new vision for the People's Republic as it follows the global path of development.

Having placed these two moments of a modern experience on the canvas of our thought, we might see that, in one case, the praise of the future produced a contradictory effect in the conception of the existing order of things, for it led to an invitation to imagine a better or a different tomorrow. Despite the Maoist failure to provide such a future, the relationship of the present to the future became one of uncertainty and changeability. It assumed a true *difference* in the temporal sense. The bitterness of the present day, according to such logic, could be changed by imagining a difference for the future. In order to change the world, life and work would have to be an act of collective and collectivized imagination. As we well know, the socialist future never showed up in history, for it was an ideology, pure and simple. Nevertheless, in the present age of the People's Republic, it seems that the future has already melted into the present order of things, which reproduces itself as a face of the future. There is no need to talk about differences in temporal terms. What is *different* is the difference among individualistic or serialistic qualities. This difference is no longer a difference in the strict sense of the term; instead, it is *repetition* or *sameness* considered as difference (see Deleuze 1994), which is calculable or computable. The process of statisticalization has constructed a pavement over the ruins of the Maoist revolution on which the present vision of the People's Republic can navigate quite comfortably.

Land and Luck

Let us return to an ethnographic experience in rural China for a reflection on the idea of luck that shows how essential it is for the peasantry to conceive of fortune as truly *fortuitous* in the advancement of market and capital, which came to sweep away the Maoist remains. That scarcity defined the relationship of the Chinese peasantry to its immediate material environment of life and survival was both an official and an intellectual conception in the history of the People's Republic. The Maoist government conceived of collectivization as a possible means to overcome scarcity and increase productivity, and it was Mao himself who gave the people's commune its name, signifying a mad moment of historical innovation in both collective representation and collective production. Peasants continued to talk about those years with admiration and bewilderment, although occasionally a bitter slice of memory might interrupt their intoxicated remembrance of past times (see X. Liu 2000). However, a couple of decades after the founding of the first people's commune, a new page of history, described and believed to be *new*, was to be written according to, in total reversal, the gospel of *de*collectivization. Just as the magic of collectivization had been held out as a solution, decollectivization was now presented as a vital means to fight scarcity in the countryside. Neither collectivization nor decollectivization is simply a history of economic facts; both are instead *histories of mentalities*, which can reveal the mentality of a history in two contrasting economic rationalities. This is *where* one may find the past in the present or vice versa. Let us take a closer look at the intrigues of decollectivization—how collective means of production, such as land and cows, were *redistributed* as a way of showing to peasants the power of the notion of luck. The following ethnographic example comes from a village, Zhaojiahe, in northwestern China, where the redistribution of collective means of production took place in the early 1980s.

This area of the countryside was neither leading the trend nor resisting it. It was, and is, the mundane location of a "typical" peasant community that simply followed the rules of the game laid out by the government. Nothing seemed spectacular in the history of this community, if viewed from the national point of view of collectivization or decollectivization. Nothing in particular would draw one's attention to a possible scholarly discussion. The village's entire significance lies in its insignificance and unimportance. In cases such as this, which represent the "normal" experience of the countryside, we have found an intriguing story of decollectivization. Officially and initially referred to as "the household responsibility system," decollectivization redistributed the collective means of production, land in particular, to each household, which became reconstituted as the elementary unit of agricultural production, as it is now. This is what William Hinton (1990) meant by "the great reversal." It was a *reversal* of collectivization; it was a *great reversal* of the intentions and policies of socialist production in agriculture; it was a *return to* an original form of agricultural production—the familial mode of agriculture. At the time, the government, preparing for the funeral of Mao, believed this to be the only righteous choice for the social organization of agricultural production. Hence, a practical question arose: how should the collective means of production, such as land, be redistributed to each household? This question could not be answered from the outside, that is, from the perspective of pure economic analysis, which applies its own rationality to the studies of the peasantry (see, e.g., Little 1989).

The problem with pure economic analysis—which involves an arithmeticization of economic choice and decision making, a dominant mode of thinking in the People's Republic today—is that it presupposes the rationality of the individual and then sets up an arithmetic analysis of his or her behavior from the end point of production. This is what I mean by a mode of analysis from the *outside*. I am not here challenging economic analysis in general. I am more concerned with *the employment* of a pseudo-economics, as both a mode of thinking and a mode of social existence, to explain the experience of decollectivization, which was not simply an economic scheme but, more importantly, a *lived* experience as both action and remembrance. For example, in this part of rural China, what was most crucial was not the result of the redistribution but the *experience* of it as a collective action whose memory continued to prevail in the socio-political domain of village life. In the village of Zhaojiahe, a decade later, the problem of land redistribution continued to trouble the minds of many families. From time to time, complaints and protests would tear off the veil of communal peace and the tranquility of village life. There was in fact a groaning dissatisfaction with the land redistribution among a considerably large number of villagers. One would note, if one were patient enough to listen to their complaints, that their criticisms and accusations were never about the initial redistribution of the collective means of production. Instead, they were worried about how to guarantee the continuation of equality and fairness, initially achieved by the land redistribution, in the face of demographic changes in the village. Whereas nobody complained about the way in which the collective land was *initially* redistributed to each household in 1981, almost everyone was grumbling about the impossibility of maintaining justice a decade later. The questions of genesis and of structure are at the crux of the matter. Here is an example of peasant rationality in thinking itself through a real problem, for which economics or even political economics could not provide a proper solution.[1]

Let us first take a look at the problem of genesis. When the villagers of this community talked about the initial period of redistribution of collective land to each household, they tended to employ the term "democratic" or "democracy" (*minzhu*) to refer to the procedures, which were guided by three major features. The first feature was the basic principle that each person was entitled to the same amount of land. A strenuous effort was made to ensure that each household received exactly the same proportion of every kind of land, such as land on the hills or land in the valley. The second feature was the democratic principle, according to which each and every step of land redistribution must be decided and agreed upon by the entire collectivity, with a representative from each household. The villagers were proud of the democratic nature of these decision-making meetings: unless a unanimous agreement was reached among all the representatives from all the families, further steps would not be taken. The third feature was the use of the random sampling technique of probabilistic reasoning. It was luck that determined the lot of each family for receiving a particular piece of land, either on the hills or in the valley. A minute and comprehensive classification of land by its quality and location had been made earlier. Parcels of land had been sorted into several categories, ranging from good to poor, according to its quality (irrigable or not) and location (distance to the village), among other factors. This classification was discussed and "voted" on by a democratic procedure that was never questioned. When it came to the point of deciding which family should be given which piece of land, the technique of gambling—or, if one prefers, random sampling—was chosen to make the determination. The use of the concept of chance, which was not alien to the Chinese tradition as a whole, was seen as rational. Thus, the final decision on the land redistribution was determined by lottery, which was, in this rural community, called *zhuazidan* (drawing the bullet).[2]

After a careful and detailed assignment of all the pieces of land into several ranks, a serial number was given to each piece of land within each rank. Each representative of a family would have to try his or her luck in picking up a piece of land that would become the family's new possession. The lottery went on for several rounds to enable each family to choose a piece of land from each rank. An important fact needs to be noted: the extreme complexity of

1. For a detailed account of the case, including its ethnographic context and historical background, see X. Liu (2000).

2. This social practice seems to be a common feature of rural China. For instance, as Chan, Madsen, and Unger (1992, 31) discussed about Chen village, the lottery was an accepted means for distributing land, either among families or between production teams during the land reform in the early 1950s. What was different about Chen village was that the cadre in charge cheated in order to benefit his own relatives and neighbors.

the topographical features of this part of rural China made it impossible for each family to possess in exact proportion the same kind of land that another might have. Even if two pieces of land were considered equally good, it was often the case that one was farther away from the residential area. Some villagers did feel unhappy about the results, but no one ever complained about the lottery as a rational procedure, despite the fact that it was no different from gambling in the traditional sense. The lottery came to represent a moment of democratic rationality, to be memorialized and talked about in the 1990s. Those who were not satisfied with their own allotment of land blamed it on bad luck. As a social notion for collective reasoning, bad luck provided a rational explanation for what occurred. During my fieldwork, it was quite common to hear people say that they were not lucky because they did not "draw a good bullet." As an old man always said, "Yes, it was so. Whatever you got, you got it by *yourself*. No complaint. You cannot complain about your own luck! Good or bad, you got it yourself."

Rationality as a conceptual requirement was essential for this kind of collective practice, which may be seen as democratic. Taken as a whole, the villagers were *rational* in the sense that the conception of random choice and the employment of democratic procedures were organically combined in their understanding of fairness and justice. But this was in *retrospection*, a recollection of the past from a moment in time ten years after the redistribution of the collective means of production in the region. The villagers' conception of their social world had changed from the previous moment, with the notion of luck being replaced a decade later with the idea of *connections* and/or *corruption*. Local people were no longer willing to employ the concept of choice and luck to explain the increasing disparity that arose as a result of social differentiation and economic development. If anyone happened to be better off than the others, he would be seen either as corrupt (particularly in the case of local cadres) or as having benefited from a superior network of social relations. A decade of reform and development set apart two modes of self-understanding. Contrary to the artistic and intellectual representation shown in the discussion of *Blue Kite*, in the view of the villagers the years of collective production and the Maoist years in general appeared, in retrospection, as an egalitarian image. On the other hand, the new trends of economic differentiation and social stratification came to be seen either in terms of having connections or in terms of corruption.

There was no objection at all to the redistribution of collective land by lottery, which was seen as rational and democratic in the sense that the collective pie was split equally among all the households.[3] When the community was still collectively organized, the rationality of the group led to its democratic

---

3. A problem came later in land adjustments. According to regulations laid out by the local government, adjustments should be made every five years due to demographic changes in each village. Families whose members left a village were expected to return a portion of their land to

praxis, which in turn generated further rational schemes of collective decisions that resulted in the transition to individual household production. For
such democratic experiences to be possible, local people acted as "common
persons" who constituted a collectivity. After additional reforms in the countryside, this common personality began to wane, which explains why it is less
possible for democratic movements to emerge today, despite greater economic
development and material accumulation. There is no longer *a common person*
whose will represents and is represented by, however partially, the collective
will. Instead, what has arrived on the scene is a pseudo-collectivity, that is, a
serial collectivity (cf. Sartre 2004) dependent on statistical surveys and opinion
polls. A person no longer shares a common will or interest with another; he or
she has become an ideological incarnation of the "naked man" in the forest of
the marketplace, with self-interest being the primary motivating factor.

The redistribution of the collective means of production took place when
"common persons" acted from the viewpoint of a *common personality* defined
by a common will or a common project. Today, local people continue to live in
the same village, but they no longer envision a common project among themselves. Their existence has become *serial* in the sense that they live next door to
each other but have no shared understanding of themselves in life. The *seriality*
of their existence, constantly surveyed and polled by governmental statistics,
is an *impotent collectivity* that is a collective impotence. I would argue that
there was a genuine democratic and communal moment that characterized
the initiation rite of decollectivization. Almost every night, villagers gathered
in an overcrowded room, listening to each other and debating about how to
redistribute the collective properties. This image is an ethnographic portrait
of the lived experience of collectivity and rationality, for which the notion of
chance was indispensable. In this part of rural China, the redistribution of the
collective pie and today's accumulation of wealth consist of two contrastable
moments of the reformatory era: one moment was conceived as rational by
way of luck and chance, and the other as irrational by way of corruption and
connections. A more general ethnographic point is that democracy and rationality are organic elements of particular historical conjunctures; they are not
fixed qualities of general institutional arrangements (cf. Wilson 1970).

In the village of Zhaojiahe, the past required the notion of luck or chance
to render it *rational*. However, the point is that despite its different employment, the idea of luck or chance itself, in a new context of modern development, came back to establish an important mechanism for social and historical
interpretation. In the coarse hands of the peasants, it was used to portray "the

---

the village, so that it could be given to those families with newborn babies. But in practice, this
policy never worked well. Typically, this was a battlefield for disputes and fights in the village.

pleasure of the past" as a nostalgic egalitarianism. In contrast with the artistic and intellectual representation of the Maoist years, the peasants' use of the notion of luck and chance moved in a thoroughly opposite direction. Those divergent viewpoints were reflections of different social positions in a new world of power and wealth. They were both indications of the return of a powerful concept, which had little significance for the Maoist discursive formation. After modern development was initiated and the official slogan of "getting rich first" was heralded, it was inevitable that the idea of luck would be used to explain the economic disparities that began to emerge. This particular case of peasantry is simply *a reversed employment* of the notion of luck, which once again has become popular in the People's Republic, for interpreting the Maoist past as an egalitarian dream. What must be noted is the re-emergence of such a conception of self and the world for the People's Republic.

Today, one can employ the same idea of luck or chance to explicate fortune or misfortune in various situations and according to different social interests. However, misfortune and fortune were not supposed to be explained by luck or chance during the Maoist years. Everything was to be interpreted according to a certain deterministic logic that would result in a necessary progression to the utopian emancipation. According to the Maoist ideologies, the goal of social development was to overcome, by human will and action, all the inequalities in society. When the Maoist imaginary failed, crashing on its own materiality, its deterministic and utopian mode of reasoning was replaced by the notions of chance and statistics, which have played an important role in making a new form of life and knowledge in China. In this view, society does not have to be responsible for the suffering of individuals; rather, it is luck or chance that determines whether individuals will face a fate of economic hardship. The relationship of the social to the individual has thus been given a different conceptualization, for which statistical reasoning is indispensable. This is the *truth* of statistical analysis or, rather, the power of large numbers governed by the law of probabilistic theory—which has become a new fantasy for the People's Republic.

Fortune and Fate

The world of China is a *plural* one consisting of several spheres, each being both quantitatively and *qualitatively* different in its composition. The rural and the urban worlds, for example, represent *two different orders of things* within the world of China. By no means can their different modes of sociality and politics be considered *similar*. They are now, in their essentially different ways, integrated into the global system of production and consumption. This is a *plural* plurality in the sense that each of these worlds consists of a multiple field of socio-economic struggles. And this plurality is pluralized by the multiplicity of such worlds. For ethnography to account for this, it must not generalize, for the plurality itself cannot be entirely grasped by the ethnographic experience. However, this does not mean that ethnography cannot or should not be employed as a possible means to comprehend the emergent ideological currents of a changing reality, which has become more and more statisticalized.

The entrepreneurial world was a recent addition to the plural world of China. For a new generation of businessmen, a fast accumulation of wealth in the past two decades or so gave rise to the return of chance and luck as invisible yet palpable forces of the marketplace. Let us relate an illustrative anecdote that became popular in South China at the turn of the millennium, appearing frequently in local newspapers and other forms of media. The story was about a poor peasant who became wealthy by accident. As the narrative goes, he had grown up in a distant mountainous area in the north and had never left his village until he decided to find his friend in Hainan province in the south. His quest represented a touching image of economic freedom and social experiment for the country in the 1990s, which was also a time when "the stock fever" (Hertz 1998) was generating a lot of interest among ordinary people. After arriving in Haikou, a major city in the province, this poor peasant, who could not read and write well, could not find a job for days and had no place to stay. Then one night he happened to take shelter in a doorway. To him, it was an ordinary, plain doorway—nothing about it seemed unusual. However, when he awoke the next morning at dawn, he saw a long queue of people standing behind him. As he was about to leave, a policeman came over and handed him a number on a slip of blue paper, which puzzled him even more. Had a fat man not come up to him, he would have thrown away the number. The greasy man said to him in a coarse voice, "Hi, kid, would you like to give me your number in exchange for ten thousand dollars?"[4] Our hero did not even have a chance to react. The man snatched the slip of paper and gave him an envelope in return, pushing him out of the doorway. The peasant looked around and saw more people accumulating around the door area. He shrugged and left. Had he known what was happening, he might have reacted differently. A few minutes later, he opened the envelope and saw a bundle of cash that was more than he had ever dreamed of seeing.

Why did people want this number so badly? What was it for? Why were people lining up in front of this small, ordinary door, one not dissimilar to many others in the city? When the stock markets were being established in the People's Republic, there was an incredible demand for shares from public and individual buyers. Since the quantity of shares and of companies chosen by the state to be listed was limited—far less than the demand on the streets, where

4. Somewhere around $1,200 in US currency.

wild dreams of becoming rich came to be associated with the possession of those shares—the local authority had to institute a lottery system for the share purchase demands. This meant that whoever wished to buy shares had to go through the lottery system to obtain a certificate that would enable one to purchase stock shares. These certificates were supposed to be given out randomly to those who came for the lottery. However, because of this complication, these certificates themselves became extremely valuable. One could sell one's certificate for a good price, and, as a result, standing in line for other people also became a profession. Our hero, an innocent peasant whose ignorance of the situation was misunderstood, had slept in front of a doorway where the local authority had decided to produce the lottery. The number that he was given was the number to secure his place in the line. Only with such a number could one get a certificate for purchasing stock shares.

In a Chinese novel titled *Yaoshi* (The Key), the author, Q.-H. Wang (1997), told a similar story in which the peasant-hero left the crowd, planning to return home to show off his quick money to his family and relatives. With the cash in hand, he first went to have a haircut and took a bath. Wandering around the city without purpose, he passed by a men's clothing shop and could not refuse the temptation to get some new clothes for himself. Finally, he chose a decent place for a good meal and decided to stay in an inn for his last night in town. Having taken a nap in his room in the late afternoon, he was on the street again in the evening and walked into an enormous building. He had been in the city for a couple of weeks, but he had never felt so relaxed. No sooner had he entered the building than a young woman grabbed his arms. She was a salesgirl in charge of selling office space in several new buildings. In fact, a real estate festival was taking place in the exhibition hall, and many businessmen and companies had come to buy or sell new and old buildings in the city. The peasant was brought to a big desk and asked whether he wanted to buy some office space in a new building, which looked extremely grandiose and beautiful in a showy picture. The salesgirl was very friendly and told him that he did not need to pay anything right now. As long as the funds were transferred into their bank account within three days, everything should be fine. He was totally out of his depth and did not know exactly what she was offering. He simply nodded his head, without being able to utter a word properly, while smiling with a widely opened mouth. The salesgirl, eager to fulfill her daily quota, helped him sign a contract to buy the entire two floors of this new building, which would cost millions of dollars.

When it was time to sign the contract, the peasant-hero began to realize what had been going on, but he did not exhibit any reluctance. He pressed his thumb on the contract to make it official. The salesgirl kept saying that the contract would be finalized within three days when the money was transferred from his company's bank account. But he did not have a company or even a bank account. He had nothing except for this big contract. He decided he would leave the city tomorrow and go back to his own world in the north. The cash that he got from the fat man was enough for him to marry three times locally. Who cared about signing or not signing a big contract? Just take it as a joke, a bit of fun, made on behalf of a lovely young woman who smelled good. However, in the morning the salesgirl came to his hotel with a middle-aged, serious-looking man. This was an official who had some government funds to play the game of real estate in Hainan. Because everyone believed that the price for the building that the salesgirl had just sold would go up soon, they had come to see whether the peasant-hero would like to sell it to this official for a good price. Everything was negotiated by the salesgirl. The peasant-hero sold what he had bought—without having paid for it—to the official for twice as much. The difference was split among the three, and each made a fortune, including the official, who had bought it at a much higher price, using government funds, in order to receive a kickback from the seller. In the end, the biggest beneficiary of this transaction was our hero, who made a couple of million dollars out of nothing from this deal.

The key component of this story is its reliance on the idea of fate for its narrative emplotment. The person involved clearly did not understand what was going on—and that did not even matter. He would get rich anyway if he were lucky enough to be in the right place at the right time. This is the message of the story. It is also the general meaning of the Chinese developmental story, according to which there are two basic ways of "getting rich first": one by power or corruption, the other by luck or chance. The notion of fate is in opposition to that of will. It is the idea of fate and luck—forces that are external to human determination—that have become a main theme of the new developmental stories. Even among officials, talking about fate and misfortune was often meant to provide a "rational" explanation of those external forces. Following is an interview, conducted in South China in 1999, in which an official talked about the reason for having a pair of stone lions placed in front of the city hall in which his own office was located.

> You know why? Let me tell you. You must have seen the new building across the street. It's the new building of our finance department. They have money, and therefore they built this amazing building, big and modern. Good perhaps for them, but not for us. They have taken up this spot and blocked our wind of fortune. It was a good *fengshui* [geomancy] spot, but their building is too high. You know, they blocked our way to the wind of fortune. Soon after their building was finished, one of our chiefs—the guy in charge of fishery and agriculture—died all of a sudden, for no reason, at only fifty. He had been a very healthy man, but he suddenly died of a stroke, some sort of a brain break. Who would have thought of his dying? He had been eating all these good foods for his health. He could get all the shrimp he wanted for free, and he used to run every morning. We used to joke about him, saying that

he would live longer than the president of the United States. And then he died just like that. A week later, another chief passed away exactly in the same way. A stroke, for no obvious reason. Both of them were relatively young.

What was happening? The building across the street had brought us *misfortune*. Everyone was in a bit of a panic after we realized this. We talked about it nervously and wondered what we should do. The mayor—you know him, Lao Wang—truly understood what was going on, and he suggested that we should have a pair of stone lions put in front of our gate to protect us from losing more people. So we ordered those lions from Guangzhou and placed them right by our entrance. And then no more strokes. Can you believe it? The lions have suppressed the evil spirits and brought back our good fortunes. It was a scary time, and at one point we were talking about who would be the next to disappear from our office. Whatever one believes, one can't afford *not* to believe in one's fate and fortunes. The stone lions can do a lot more than one believes. The whole building is safe now. This is life. There's always something that we can't completely control. We can make policies to change the city, but we can't change our own fate, you know. Without the lions, I don't know how many of us would die soon.

This official was a serious man in his late thirties. Perhaps not everyone in the business or the official world would believe that the erection of the stone lions had fended off the evil spirits from the building across the street. However, the message is clear: in accounting for particular causes, there is an irreducible need for thinking of fate or fortune in terms of uncontrollable—perhaps even supernatural—forces that are beyond the human will. This certainly does not mean that people did not try hard to search for a better or a more secure business environment, for example, by building a stronger or a more effective network of social relations. Instead, it means that they were not able to make sense out of the fact that some people could not avoid misfortune or failure in business or life, whereas others could. Once again, this example demonstrates, although somewhat differently, that the idea of fate and luck or fortune and misfortune, while external to "being in the world," has been internalized in the stories about Chinese development.

It is not a contradiction to accept the idea of science and modern development in *general* terms but, in *specific* instances, to rely on the notion of luck or fate to explain personal success or misfortune. Such notions are close to how chance is employed in statistical and probabilistic usage. Exemplified in the statistical table of random digits, the idea of chance has a double quality: on the one hand, it is deterministic and necessary as a general scheme, and, on the other, it is arbitrary and almost mystical when a singular instance of random figures is generated. This is what happened in the People's Republic. The logic of "random choice," dependent on probabilistic theories of large numbers, came to function as an essential social logic. It accounts for China's tremendous material progress—which is seen as inevitable or deterministic, proved or provable by statistical data and analysis—*as well as* the incredible disparity among its people in terms of individual shares of the collective pie of wealth.[5] This double phenomenon of economic development can be explained by one mechanism—the probabilistic theory of large numbers in statistical terms. In such a case as this, statistical analysis is not simply a tool for a different mode of governance, as several studies on the rise of statistics in modern societies have suggested (see, e.g., Cole 2000). It is instead a form of thinking, or a mode of reasoning, that points to an important innovation in a history of mentality for the People's Republic today. The employment of statistical reasoning is not simply an official attempt to mystify the social world: it is the social world remade anew.

When we talk about an official view, we do not mean that it is simply a viewpoint of or made by the official world. An official view tends to be a generalizing or generalizable outlook that shapes a social world. An ordinary person could adopt such an outlook to defend, for example, China's economic growth, which is a *general* fact that is statistically verifiable. However, the same person would perhaps not use the same official view with regard to his or her relatives' success in business or life. In specific cases of success or failure, he or she would most likely employ the notion of fate or luck as an explanation. In the vast continent of the People's Republic, which constitutes a plurality of difference, one can get a glimpse at its enormous diversity by understanding the powerful resurrection of "statistical reason," which has functioned far more than a tool for effective governance over the population. The process of statisticalization in this instance must be understood as an "epistemological break" from the Maoist morality and reason. Key to such a break is embracing totally and implicitly the statistical law of *deterministic indeterminacy*: *deterministic* in the sense that it is inevitable in general, as proved by the probabilistic theories of large numbers; *indeterminacy* in the sense that individual fate would have to be explained in terms of chance, based on the simple idea of random choice theory. Luck is an idea, an image, an index, an aspect, or an element in various stories about development and wealth. But above all, it is *a sign*, that is, a relation of the world or a function of the truth effect, which could bring the objective world into one's own world of perception and understanding.

5. If an Azande were to visit the People's Republic today, he would be not surprised by the mystique of statistical reasoning. The belief in witchcraft, described by British anthropologist E. E. Evans-Pritchard (1937), would allow the Azande to approach the statistical reasoning in today's China with little difficulty. From the Azande's viewpoint, there are two causes for a happening—a general cause and a specific cause—neither of which can be understood without the other. For example, as Evans-Pritchard showed, no Azande would deny that a falling tree had killed the man underneath it. However, the Azande would turn to witchcraft to explain why this *particular* man went to take shelter under that *particular* tree at the *particular* moment when it fell down. The general or the first cause cannot explain the *particularity* of a specific event or experience. The incident must thus be explained in terms of magic or witchcraft.

As a sign, luck signifies the replacement of the Maoist discursive formation by the probabilistic vision of deterministic indeterminacy: it has taken up the language of the sign as a sign language to speak about the coming of age in the marketization of a social world.

This is a local affair, occurring in a hoary neighborhood of the globe, which is now unable to resist paying attention to its own noisy reconstruction. In such parochial scenery as this, if viewed as a provincial episode, it might appear, once again in the history of the world, as a partial march toward the completion of the old Enlightenment project, which had inaugurated a particular mode of rationality and reason. However, on its way of becoming what it will be, the People's Republic has sown a history of interiority that cannot be objectified by statistical analysis, which, as a scientific means of objectification, has only made up its redesigned street scenes. Looking at this new city of the world, which is conveniently called "China," one might wonder whether one should proclaim any acquaintance with its inhabitants. Who are these people? Capable of running all kinds of computer programs and enjoying the same kind of pleasures that are characteristic of modern development, are they similar inhabitants of the same globe—are they like everyone else?

When the Maoist years became past times, there was almost a sudden collapse of the country's interior design, which was averted when a new one was brought into existence. It is not the destiny of the trip but the feeling on the way that has tickled our intellectual curiosity. Our scholarship on such a new social entity tends to be blinded by its own pride and prejudice. History has informed us that both the Maoist past and the present age claimed to have found the final truth. The difference is that *this time* we believe that we have *really* found the truth, according to which the past is now seen as a nightmare in history. In the next round, change will come under another name, perhaps neither revolution nor reform. To get closer to what needs to be known or to feel how it would feel in a new era of modern development, one should step away from the images of the present day in order to take a longer view, which will allow one to see the shape of the current sentiment in a slightly clearer way. For it is against the old design that the new ideas of decoration and adornment have fallen into place.

Chapter Six

INTERIORIZATION

❖

So far we have made the Maoist experience sit at an analytical distance in a conceptual backbench, for our attention has been focused on the more recent happenings that have given rise to the current age. Now that it is time to analyze the present sentiment itself, we should invite the backbencher to appear on center stage. The world of China is no longer what it was, especially after the late 1990s. The present moment, in the strict sense of the term, differs *in kind* even from the 1980s, which were still entangled with the Maoist morality and reason. That is, the Maoist past was not *truly* a past during the 1980s for the reason that the decade was running through the same platform, only in an opposite direction. This is no longer the case today. The train of the People's Republic now runs on a new track built by an altogether different technology of self and a dissimilar mentality. It is as if the 1980s represented a decade of painful contractions before the birth of a new outlook on the world, whereas today the experience is one of growing up in the cradle of global materiality and productivity. The pain and contractions have so far taken up our analytical attention.

Now let us go back a bit further in time to bring the Maoist morality and reason in direct contact with the present structure of feelings in order to show what is happening. In doing so, we must introduce the problematics of *power* and *subject* as two key conceptualizations underlying our previous and entire discussion. These two notional areas must be rendered explicit in order for us to reach a more general understanding of the contemporary world, of which the present-day People's Republic is a most fitting image. The Maoist years represent a disparate configuration of power and subject, in contradistinction to which we shall examine the sentiments of those struggling on the ruins of it. I will use a sociological study by Fang Huirong (1997) as a guidebook for traveling in the Maoist past. Fang's work, which is about how the Maoist years were remembered in a rural community, was part of a larger project, the Oral History Project, directed by Professor Sun Liping, a well-known sociologist in China.[1]

Reflections on the Maoist experience have been an important area of inquiry in fields such as history and literature, but this has not often been the case with sociology. Re-established as an academic discipline in the 1980s, sociology has focused most of its attention on the emerging social problems—economic disparity, unemployment, prostitution, etc.—that had been brought about by the economic reforms. Sociology, in short, has played a chiefly intellectual role by helping the state diagnose what went wrong in society and how to cure those social injuries. The Oral History Project, in contrast, is a serious sociological attempt to determine the significance of the Maoist experience and to assess its impact on China today. This intriguing project, outside the mainstream of sociological inquiry, hopes to provide a historical understanding of the current age. Fang's work was part of this general effort. The spirit of the Oral History Project, which no longer exists in any active form, is the spirit of my conceptual exploration here. More specifically, there is an immediate impetus for sustaining the Project, for apart from what can be found in official documents and archives, little is known about the everyday struggles in the Maoist years. A *moment* of the recent past has become *invisible* from the present stance, if guided by the official view. The Oral History Project has attempted to find a different path to the past. Based on oral stories rather than official written records, the Project focuses on the mechanisms of remembrance and forgetfulness as revealed in accounts told by and about ordinary people. The empirical object was the vast countryside, where there existed a massive population and a great diversity of local experiences. What made the quotidian life-world different when it was preoccupied with endless mass campaigns and political struggles? This is one of the basic questions of the Project. The entire problematic of the Project is to question a set of naive assumptions that have simplified the Maoist experience, which should be understood today as an absent presence of history.[2]

1. Professor Sun, who used to work for Peking University, has joined the Department of Sociology, Tsinghua University, in Beijing.

2. There is a general introduction regarding the intention and purpose of the Oral History Project, which is printed on the first page of each research paper published under it. The Chinese version of this introduction is much better phrased than the English translation below, in which there are many grammatical errors. Still, the powerful message delivered by this declaration is unmistakable

Our project is to collect daily life materials by using oral-history methods, to search for and research into the Chinese rural area's social change in the latter half of this century.

This century has seen China a particularly unusual century. In and through the intersection of turbulence and revolutions, which reflected in various levels and areas, some profound and lasting

The Project originally targeted several rural communities in the vast countryside, and its principal method involved fieldwork and interviews, during which life stories told by ordinary villagers were recorded. In the early 1990s, the Project produced a number of "working papers" that, intentionally or not, paved a different intellectual trajectory in which a number of unusual questions were given powerful, intellectual articulations. These working papers, written by either graduate students or their professors, derive their intellectual energies from a different theoretical source, built on a systematic reading of contemporary social thought. This approach has given these papers an original and powerful style. Although they are not widely read, either inside or outside the People's Republic, some of them have since been republished in academic journals.[3] One of them is Fang Huirong's paper, whose theoretical focus is on memory in the countryside. Fang's intention is to show how a different mode of social existence was made possible by the Maoist power-practice. The question of memory is central to her discussion: if the Maoist government was effective, the reason was that it succeeded in reshaping the relationship of the present (as well as the future) to the past. It is how people remember—or,

---

changes have taken place in China. Thus the traditional, rural society has stepped into the modern one. To record and study the history of period in detail contains no doubt far-reaching importance.

As we know, so many official written materials are available today, however, we find it is almost no oral data from grass-roots level, which is fundamental to study more concretely (and authentically, even the meaning of "truth" is increasingly open to question) on the transformation of Chinese Peasants' daily life. To fill the gap and open up the new respective, we hope this project will bring the true life and "history" back in. And the oral history is the best (of course not the only) framework for us to fulfill the plan and achieve the aim.

This project has two concrete aims: (1) Materials' collecting and collating. We want to lay a firm foundation for oral-history research on Chinese rural areas and peasants' daily life. Our project would produce several-thousand-hour tape recordings and written materials. (2) Describe and analysis the social life in Chinese rural areas during the latter half of this century. And we can reveal and interpret the cause of these transformation.

We plan to select six villages as our cases. They locate respectively in the Northeast, North, Northwest, Southeast, South and Central South of China. Our principal task is to interview deeply with the ordinary peasants and local grass-roots cadre, who have the personal experience of this period of transformation. In the meantime, we will collect extensively other related documents, photographs and material objects.

The span of period of our project's object as long as half a century. And the transformation of Chinese rural society undergoes several distinct phases during such a long time. Our project will be accordingly divided into six stages. The material-collecting work of every stage would be last for about three years. To say concretely, these stages are Land Reform, Collectivization. People's Commune and Great Leap Forward, Socialist Education Movement, Great Cultural Revolution, and Reform and Open. It is estimated that the whole project be last for twenty years.

3. Most research was done by a group of then graduate students at the Department of Sociology, Peking University. I have read some of these working papers. The first issue of the recently established journal, *Tsinghua Sociological Review*, reflects their intellectual taste (http://tsinghua. sociology.org.cn/Default.aspx?tabid=522).

more accurately, how they *remember to forget*—that made the Maoist political struggles inevitable and even desirable.[4]

Some clarifications are necessary. Firstly, the question of memory in this treatment is not simply about "remembrance of things past"; it is concerned with social existence in and as a temporal form. It is a form of temporality by which one could live his or her life according to the internal clock of a collective order. To problematize this collective clock is to reconceptualize social existence in today's world. Secondly, the notion of power-practice is central to the concerns of Fang and her colleagues. Their approach allows us to view the shift in life as closely related to a certain mode of governing. The effectivity of the Maoist power-practice, as Fang seems to suggest, lay in its action, that is, in the political struggles and mass movements that were making—and being made by—a new mode of remembrance and forgetting. The Maoist political struggles introduced a new vision for life, which in turn made the life of those struggles desirable. Thirdly, Fang's approach was empirically based, focusing on a particular rural community. Her study invites us to think about how the Maoist ideologies were absorbed into the practice of everyday life, becoming a new "practico-inert" (Sartre 2004) or a new social inertia. Unless something became routinized and naturalized as a social habit, life could not become "normal" or "comfortable." This process of habituation presents an interesting problem for us when considering the effectivity of the Maoist power-practice.

Stories and Memories

Fang's text begins with an interesting observation. When going to the village to collect what she calls "oral texts"—stories told by and interviews with local residents—Fang found that she and her colleagues were often mistaken for cadres or local officials sent down by the government. Her case involved the people of Xicun, a rural community in Hebei province, not too far from Beijing. This misrecognition, as Fang later points out, is a reflection of the Maoist

---

4. The following is the abstract of the work in English, written by Fang (1997), in which there are again some obvious grammatical and spelling mistakes, although the meaning is quite clear and consistent. This is an exact copy of the original, with all of the errors intact.

> This thesis tends to analysis the profound and complex transformation of Chinese rural social life during the latter half of 20th century, attempting to make use of a somewhat new perspective, namely mentality.
> The main presumption is that, in traditional rural communities, the dominant type of memory about events can be called as memory in "non-event state". For the occurrence of events is rather highly repetitive, and for events there is lack of the precise location by institutional time, various events pile up and mix together without any specificable order, chronological sequels or intervals. In other words, all kinds of details or components of event(s) intersect and interpose one another

inertia produced by the endless mass campaigns and political inquisitions. In the Maoist years, whenever there was a political movement, cadres or officials would come to the village to inspect the organization of the movement. The mention of this misrecognition, as a textual strategy, is meant to direct the reader's attention to a central argument in Fang's work: this misrecognition implies a way of remembrance that does not or is unable to organize actual happenings or events coherently in a steady flow of temporal sequence. As Fang (1997, 5) says, the villagers "could not establish comparable relations among different events, that is, it is impossible for them to locate a local event in the historical process that is larger than what happened in their own community."[5] This means that when she and her colleagues went to the village, local residents, chiefly the elderly, got confused and returned to past experiences to explain the coming of the sociological students. Their research was conducted in the late 1980s, and the reminiscences of cadres being sent to the village referred to a time more than two decades earlier. This is the opening of Fang's inquiry: why did there exist such a gap in understanding? It seems that local people did not take the economic reform as a radical break, and the senior members of this community continued to think of sociological visitors in terms of cadres and officials, an experience that was typical during the Maoist years.

---

in and(or) between event(s). Living in this state of memory, villagers would not "intentionally" specify a clearly discernible limits of event and identify a "true" event in some modern sense. To them the "truth" or "reality" is precisely those intersected and interposed events. In chapter 3 we try to discover the characteristics of memory in "non-event state" by analyzing "pouring out grievance" oral texts. Our conclusion is that it is the particular living circumstances in rural communities, which hardly need any condition to link several events and set up comparable relation (sequel and interval), that constitute this peculiar state of memory.

A significant change during the latter half of this century is the increasingly common occurrence of events which beyond local level in rural communities. Then comes the demand to set up the comparable relations between so many ever incomparable events. Meanwhile, the setting up of relations should be closely connected with two simultaneous courses: to achieve the ideological education on villagers by State, and to locate villagers in the new social classification. These processes are conspicuously reflected through two means taken by State to permeate its authority and power into village, which were all invented in the period of Land Reform. In chapter 5 we define the power of "investigate and research", the first means. And in chapter 3 we redefine the limits of latitudes of the second means, say "pouring out grievance". This thesis will take pain in discussing this two practices implying power, to reveal the fundamental dilemma faced by these power-practices when they encounter rural communities (and, of course, not limit to the period of Land Reform). To say concretely, one side is the "event sense" in modern sense and correspondently "fact-reality", while the other side is the above-mentioned "non-event state" and its "truth" or "reality" in rural communities. And we should study the effect of this dilemma on rural communities' everyday life and mentality.

The materials are mainly based on our field work in Xi Village, Zunhua, Hebei Province. Apart from the oral texts, we have collected a lot of related documents in Zunhua Achieves. Using concepts from narrative analysis, we want to grasp the change of mentality in rural communities, which usually hard to study directly, by analyzing oral texts.

5. All translations of this text are mine.

Fang's inquiry then proceeds with the problem of memory. For example, as Fang continued her questioning, it was revealed that once there had been more than 30 cows in this village. However, a difficulty arose when Fang and her colleagues wished to document the years in which the villagers had those cows: no one could be specific in his or her answer. Whenever local people talked about the cows, they tended to employ terms such as "a long way back in time" or "prior to collectivization," etc. Having collected different accounts of the same event, Fang and her colleagues still could not figure out the specific years or even the decades in which villagers possessed the cows. Local people could only say that they had them before the collectivization took place in the 1950s. Hence, Fang suggests that, in such a case as this, the lineal time reference in the calendric sense has little to do with the remembrance of the past. Local people could recall only that *once upon a time*, a time before collectivization, they had 30 cows. From a retrospective point of view, this means that the possession had crucial social significance in telling the story of collectivization, but the temporal register, in and of itself, had little importance for the villagers. Fang was dealing chiefly with the elderly, who had the most extensive experience of the Maoist years. Young people might have had a different reaction, to be sure.

Fang later found out from another source that there were still 13 cows in the village in 1953. However, to her disappointment and dissatisfaction, she could not verify what had happened to the other cows prior to that year, for all the stories and interviews regarding this important and yet simple fact, a material fact of history and life, consisted only of contradictory and confusing statements. The sociological rationality with which Fang seems to have begun her inquiry is that one should know what the villagers had owned prior to the land reform and the subsequent collectivization in the 1950s in order to be able to evaluate the impact of these measures on the lives of the people. However, accurate information about material possessions of productive means could not be obtained by interviews because local people did not respond to the chronology of the sociologist. It seems, as Fang has suggested, that the relations between events are far more important than the correlations of those events to a calendric time reference. Therefore, the question of "being and time," that is, the problematic of social existence and temporality, must be raised.

This is the beginning of Fang's inquiry, which is an excellent starting point. The sociologist came to the village with a different conception of events and time, which was not the *time lived* by the peasants. As a result, Fang's research diverged from its original course, which had hoped to focus on the material possessions of each family before and after collectivization. It is a rare case of a sociology student turning to an anthropological mode of questioning due to an ethnographic encounter with another way of life. Behind Fang's confounding experience lies the *scholarly* assumption that time should be *an external reference* by which a sequence of events can be established as objective and comparable.

Somewhat curiously, Fang makes a brief reference to Nobert Elias's study of social time in setting up her own conceptual framework of analysis. Her point is that by establishing an external, objective temporal sequence, an event can be defined as an event because it becomes a happening in time. In other words, the status of an event or the event-ness of an event is due to its possible fixation in a lineal flow of temporal units represented, for example, by a calendar or a clock. In this modern conception, the status of an event or its event-ness is secured by its locatability *in* time: by definition and by virtue, an event *must happen in time*. This rational assumption of the sociologist, an "event-in-time assumption," was contradicted by an ethnographic experience. If the idea of event-in-time is modern and sociological, as Fang suggests, in such a case as Xicun, one must draw a distinction between events and "non-events" or a "non-event state," for the sequence of certain happenings, such as the possession of cows, was never made clear with reference to calendric time. Neither externally nor sociologically verifiable, these events were not defined according to the lineal progression of time but were instead measured in relational terms to other events in the telling of a particular story. Fang saw this "non-event state" as the state of everyday memory in Xicun.

Xicun, one of a few selected sites for the Oral History Project, is a unique place in that it was famous in the 1950s. At that time, Zhao Xiguo, a poor villager, initiated and organized a village cooperative known as "the commune of the poor," which brought the peasants together to perform collaborative and collective agricultural work. This attempt was encouraged and praised by the government. Mao himself once said that "the commune of the poor should be the image of our entire nation." By this he meant that China as a new nation should be able to achieve modern development by following the example of "the commune of the poor," which had created its own means of production in a few years, starting from a ground-zero level of accumulation. Xicun thus came to be regarded as an exemplary model for all the villagers, due to its key message—that the peasantry could improve their material environment through will power and collective labor. By studying this village, Fang had hoped to find certain general characteristics of the Maoist morality and reasoning, and to determine how the Maoist power-practice had transformed the countryside and introduced a different mode of social existence.

In the second chapter of her work, Fang cites a short text about Xicun. This popular booklet, which chronicles the village's exemplary history, was written by the Department of Literature of Beijing Normal University. Published in 1976, the year of Mao's death, 220,000 copies were printed on the first impression alone. The text opens with a famous quotation from Mao. Referring to the poor peasants in Xicun, who owned only three legs of a donkey to start their collective labor, called themselves "the commune of the poor," struggled for three years entirely on their own, and ended by producing initial wealth and accumulating a significant amount of necessary productive means, Mao ended: "This must become the image of our entire nation; and is it not possible for China, consisting of six hundred millions of such poor people, to become a prosperous and strong socialist country in a few decades if we work collectively and cooperatively?"[6] This last sentence produces a double signification, to which Fang hopes to draw the reader's attention: "the commune of the poor" should be an image of the entire nation, and the entire nation ought to be able to achieve what this particular rural community achieved by collective will and agency alone. This is *not* redundancy. It is a strategy of the Maoist political preaching that introduces a vision of a new relationality: each and every person is an organic part of the entire nation as *a national whole* that determines, in its final and entire signification, the significance of each and every person.

One could perhaps take from Fang's reading of the booklet the following messages: such a mode of political sermon making contains a strategy of epitomizing, in which the situation of the entire nation is reduced to the vivid image of one rural community, and also employs a strategy of amplifying, in which a partial image of a village is magnified to represent the visible future of the entire nation as a whole. This is a powerful means of political preaching, although perhaps not entirely new. On the one hand, it situates the specific history of a local community in the greater picture of national development, and, on the other, it uses a local history as a metonymy for the hope of national achievement for an entire people. Fang suggests that the booklet is an excellent example of the Maoist attempt to build an imagery and/or imaginary bridge between the local and the national, the personal and the social. The Maoist political strategy contained an epistemological tactic, which meant to reconstruct the relationship of oneself to both the past and the nation.

Fang's illuminating reading of the booklet poses the question of whether such a political strategy succeeded. How could local histories be rewritten according to the time map of a larger, innovative conception of the nation? In the Maoist view, every event and happening—regional, local, or trivial—should be rearranged according to the successive stages of national socialist victory in the People's Republic. Official history, therefore, should concern itself not simply with the hierarchization of events and the identification of heroes and villains. It was, first of all, a reworking of people's interior clocks, both *personal and social*, in order to reorganize their relations to the past and the future. The story of Xicun, a poor village, was not a national story; however, its referential temporality—the interior clock of its plot—was neither regional nor local. Instead, it was national and nationalistic. The era of the People's Republic gave the Xicun story its narrative coherence and intelligibility. In such a booklet, as

6. This translation of Mao's speech, which had been made much earlier than the publication of this booklet, is also mine.

Fang observes, an event that happened in Xicun could become meaningful only if it fit into the Maoist calendar of socialist victory and national development. If a specific local event did not fit into the national calendar, its occurrence would be described as "one day" or "a while ago" or "some time in the past." For example, sufferings of poor peasants should not have occurred after the national socialist victory according to the necessary logic of the government's official history, whose narrativity depended on the ideology of emancipating poor peasants from such sufferings. Those who complained about the new socialist order of things must be its enemies, and this is the other side of the same reasoning. The internal logic of the national story required local events to be told in a particular way and their chronology to be set up in such a way as to make the story a story. If this was the case, would it not have been easier for the officials simply to write a national history of the Maoist victory? Why did they bother to write such a village history? As Fang rightly points out, this is not a history book; instead, it is *a textual embodiment* of the Maoist mode of power-practice, whose aim was not to record the Maoist victory but *to transform* the habituation of peasant memory. It was not simply a text to be read. It was an ideological script to be believed, to be practiced, to be lived. Fang's reading of this booklet inspired me to take her approach seriously as a way to get into the ideological struggles of the time, although my theoretical concerns and arguments are different from hers.

In my view, Fang's work has made the question of narrative an essential problematic for thinking about social existence. In reading her paper, one cannot help but reflect on the nature of the Maoist power-practice as a more general intellectual question about life and knowledge. From today's aspect, the Maoist revolution is seen as a total disaster, and this is both a scholarly and an official assessment. If the irrationality and insanity of the Maoist political struggles are so evident, how can one explain the effectiveness of its exercise only a few decades earlier? Simply say that everyone had been bewitched by socialist witchcraft? How can one explain the Great Leap Forward or the Cultural Revolution in its own terms? These are seen as mad political movements that are unintelligible to a younger generation today. Should one say that at the time everyone was fooled by an ideological magic? I believe that such an interpretation would simplify the complicated problematic of human existence, which is *narrative* in nature. Any social existence can exist only in and as *a story*, whose emplotment would invoke a particular conception of time or temporality. Capitalism is a story about life and history, just as socialism was and is a similar but different story. Fang's analysis has made us think about how the Maoist revolution could be understood *as a story*, which was not entirely indigenous or new, and how it became a powerful narrative for the Chinese peasantry. A story could become effective for the peasants only when it was told and lived by them.

A most interesting element of Fang's study is her suggestion to examine how a new story came to grasp the hearts of the peasantry. Fang describes this mode of storytelling—which was enacted by the Maoist power-practice and usually referred to as "speaking bitterness" (see, e.g., Wolf 1985)—as "pouring out grievance." Numerous studies on the Maoist political campaigns have been piling up on our bookshelves; however, Fang's approach, which deals with the effectiveness of the Maoist revolution in terms of the narrative restructuring of collective experiences, is innovative and provocative. Her focus is not on the reworking of a national story; it is about how such a story came to be effective in colonizing the hearts and minds of ordinary people in the vast countryside of the People's Republic. The ritual that allowed the Maoist power-practice to make its socialist ideology become a living reality was "speaking bitterness," an essential part of the Maoist mass campaigns in the early 1950s. Bringing poor peasants together and instructing them to talk about their sufferings under the old regime constituted the essence of such a political technology. After the peasants had been mobilized to speak out against their class enemies—the rich peasants and landlords—the next step would be to confiscate the private properties of these enemies and redistribute them to the poor and suffering peasants. Given the traditional structure of village life, in which kinship identities and family ties predominated, the initial step of "pouring out grievance" held the key for such a political campaign to succeed. There was an essential need for the poor peasants to stand up and speak out, because the new ideological machine sought to locate the problem of disparity and suffering in the old society. A key objective was to make the peasants aware that their sufferings were not of their own making but rather were due to the oppressive nature of the old regime, which would be overthrown by themselves under Mao's leadership.[7]

It is therefore not a coincidence that the booklet was written collectively by the Department of Literature instead of by a historian. It was meant to be a political metaphor. Apart from certain important official dates, such as the Maoist national victory in 1949, there is little reference to the actual dates of any happenings in Xicun. The general textual strategy was to tell a story about personal suffering, such as someone starving during the war against Japan. This person would eventually be saved by the Maoist troops, and the new government would give him land and everything else that he needed. He would then become happy and content—and grateful to the new society. In using one person's experience as a means to release all the pain and suffering for the entire countryside, the text would produce its metonymical politics. As the collective author would ask, "Is it not true that many of us, the poor and the oppressed, had a similar experience of suffering under the brutal rule of the Japanese troops?" Or, "Is it not true that, like Lao Wang, we have become the

---

7. To make it clear, this is *my reading* of Fang's work, not necessarily what she has argued.

masters of our own country by possessing land and other means of production?" Such a textual strategy would make one person's experience of suffering and emancipation *an individuation* of the collective experience of everyone else. The rhetorical questions at the end of these individual portrayals of collective suffering were intended to lead to a revelation for the reader—that a change of society must be made. This textual strategy was an ideological praxis that strove to connect personal need and suffering with the general condition of life in society and the national necessity for a Maoist revolution. Such a form of "collective representation" drew its ideological energy from, as Fang puts it, a rhetorical move "from the singular to the plural." This narrative strategy, exemplified in and by this booklet, made up the core of the mass campaign for "pouring out grievance" whose goal was to introduce the individual to the social, to adhere the personal to the national, to fasten the "I" to the "We."

Genealogy of History I

The Maoist epistemology placed a tremendous emphasis on the collective will and agency of the people taken as a whole. As an ideological notion for collective action and political struggle, this whole is not a *static* one. It is conceived as a conceptual ensemble that would require constant articulation and rearticulation based on the changing situations of real struggles at different historical moments, which are themselves dependent on such articulations. If one wished to rationalize the Maoist past, one could point to the material fact that the Maoist revolution occurred in the environment of a fierce national struggle for independence, in the environment of World War II and the subsequent Cold War, when the People's Republic stood in almost total isolation from the outside world. Where or what else could the Maoist shamanism turn to for its mythical power and material energy? The foundational force of the Maoist revolution was invested in the Chinese peasantry, who fought with bare fists and bent teeth to establish the People's Republic. To rationalize the Maoist past, one could say that its maximization of human power or of the power of the human will constituted an essential means for its truth and virility. For its energy, this shamanism drew on the *male organism*, phallic and penetrating, almost brutal, if seen from the eyes of those being or having been injured. A distant observer, either in space or in time, might have found it inhuman or inhumane. However, it was *intended* to be so, as a means of awakening and penetration, forcing itself into the feminine body of the Chinese peasantry, who would later embody the true spirit of such a penetration. The Maoist epistemology was shamanistic, and its magical power consisted in making people believe the powerful magic of their own will and agency.

Not every element of this shamanistic epistemology came from its Marxist affinity. A large portion of it was indeed traditional or indigenous. Peasant revolts had been familiar scenarios throughout China's long dynastic history. This time, however, a crucial element was added, one that was truly foreign or alien to indigenous Chinese thought. This was the innovation of the Maoist shamanism in which a particular ailment of the Chinese peasantry was characterized as a symptom of a *universal illness*, diagnosed by Marx as the capitalistic-imperialistic oppression of the working-class people of the world. Thus, the suffering of the peasants was no longer seen as being inflicted by a bad emperor or as a particular disease of a particular element of society. Instead, it was looked on as a sign of a structural and universal oppression of all poor peoples *generally*. Fighting the evil forces, immediate and Chinese, was no longer limited to emancipating the peasantry; it became a necessary part of revolutionary action for the *universal emancipation* of humankind in history. For those under the Maoist spell, the concept of "the people" or "the masses of the people" transcended the traditional notions of "family" and "state" and came to represent a collectivistic moral obligation for each and every human being. This was no longer a personal fight against one's wealthy and malicious brothers; rather, the challenge was to accept the moral obligation to be or become what one *ought* to be. The entire tradition of ethical orientation, deeply embedded in Chinese thought, Confucian or otherwise, acquired a renewed and refreshing refurbishment through its association with the Marxist philosophy.

The logic of the Maoist power-praxis elevated the particular struggle of the Chinese peasantry to a higher platform of moral necessity. This powerful calling was magical and yet effective for a major part of the twentieth century. Marx's effort to put Hegel's head on its feet—that is, Marx's historical *materialism*—was adopted into the Maoist epistemology only as its *vocabulary*. What became its *grammar* was Marx's universal categories, which were also Hegelian and even Christian (see, e.g., MacIntyre 1968). This *self-elevation* had little to do with the immediate and the particular, which was sensuous; it was instead a spiritual or ideological call for revolution and salvation for all. The Maoist epistemology made this mode of relating oneself to the whole, the masses of the people, a most effective socialist strategy that few could resist. The moral power of this Marxist affinity came from and made use of a collective and humanistic conception of the world. In the apt hand of a great poet, Mao himself, the masses of the people, an indigenous remaking of the Marxist category, came to signify the collective agency of all. It is the people, only the people, and nothing but the people who have made and will make history, as Mao himself once proclaimed. Based upon such a vision of the world, and surviving in an isolated political environment, the Maoist power-praxis achieved political hegemony through its universalistic appeal. Aided by its shamanistic ideology, the People's Republic was born, after having won a series of extremely savage political and military struggles. It was hoped that its mode of discursive practice would continue to work well in achieving social and economic development for the People's Republic in its adolescence. However, after gaining sovereignty the Maoist government did not succeed in accomplishing its goals. Therefore, after the death of Mao in 1976, the government launched its reform plan, which led the People's Republic into a different lane of modern development. Now in the next century, with the country well under way on its progressive, materialistic journey, global and globalizing, one can grasp a better view of the Maoist past as a form of collective humanism whose intention was to make the masses of the people a *real* force for transforming society. Under this new light of a hindsight reflection, one may realize that it is not Marxism that can explain the reason and logic of the Maoist revolution; it is the Maoist power-praxis, in its concrete historical vitality, that will explain the Marxist thought and influence in the twentieth century.

The Maoist power-praxis aimed at producing a momentary unity, however phantasmal, by enacting the collective will of the masses of the people in order to achieve its political and economic efficacy. That is to say, as a political signifier for the entirety of the people, the word "we" needed to be articulated as a collective unity or identity so that it could function as an effective force in transforming society. The notions of the people and the masses of the people made up the rudimentary building blocks of the Maoist conception of politics and history, which were thought of and portrayed as the perpetual revolutionary struggle of the people against their enemies. Achieving a collective unity was therefore essential to the Maoist conception of victory and a first step toward its accomplishment.

Secondly, according to the Maoist epistemology, there was no natural or pre-existing collective unity, ready-made and handy for such struggles. The peasants were by no means united—naturally or even willingly—by the Maoist project that would change their life-world. By definition and inclination, they were backward and asleep, unaware of their role in the socialist struggle and their own historical mission for human emancipation. They needed to be awakened by the Maoist vision of the world, to see themselves transformed into a new figure by a different story. This awakening consisted essentially of transforming peasants into "common individuals" and, in the process, making them realize the power of their collective will and agency to reshape social reality. The masses of the people therefore became a powerful political signifier for the entire Maoist epoch, allowing peasants, who had been bound almost entirely by familial or kinship ties, to experience a commonality greater than their own immediate experiences in their villages. The Maoist power-praxis made it possible for them to envision themselves as *common individuals* whose power could be far greater than had ever been imagined. This commonality, articulated quite successfully during the Maoist years, was the commonality of their project.

Thirdly, throughout the Maoist years, the conceptual boundaries of this collective identity, represented by the masses of the people, were often redrawn according to the revolutionary need of a particular moment. The articulatory strategy remained, but the inclusion or exclusion of individuals or groups at different moments of the struggle varied greatly. This is an important feature of the Maoist epistemology: both the telling and the content of the story made social reality a battleground for political struggles. The story was always told at a specific moment for a particular political reason. Therefore, the question of *who*, *when*, and *how* was always part of the telling: "Who are our enemies? Who are our friends? This is a question of the first importance for the revolution. The basic reason why all previous revolutionary struggles in China achieved so little was their failure to unite with real friends in order to attack real enemies" (Mao 2001, 11). This was written by Mao in 1926 before the seed of the People's Republic had been germinated. However, as we understand it now, this message defined the spirit of the political struggles throughout the Maoist years. The notion of the masses of the people remained unchanged as a powerful political signifier, but who ought to be included in such a category depended on the revolutionary needs of particular moments. It is important for us to view the Maoist epistemology as an innovative form of power-praxis. That is, the Maoist story about human emancipation and socialist transformation might not be new, but the way in which the story was *told* was indeed original.

The grand narrative of human emancipation was only half of the Maoist story. Its efficacy and effectiveness were rooted in its revolutionary political praxis, which transformed the relationship of oneself to history and society. It made peasants realize their common project, for which they were willing to sacrifice. The masses of the people could be seen as a categorical signifier, constituting a condition of possibility for the Maoist discursive praxis. But the practical efficacy of this concept always depended on how it was articulated *in* and *for* a particular political task, which was always specific and circumstantial. "Who are our enemies? Who are our friends?" These questions had to be asked continually during different moments of social development. From an outside perspective, one could view the Maoist political struggles as insane because the ritual of inclusion was not predefined or predetermined. No one could be entirely certain that he or she would not be criticized and excluded in the next round of political campaigns. It was in the articulation—that is, in the practice itself—that enemies and friends were to be decided. Participation was therefore an important feature of this power-praxis. The categorical signifiers must be kept alive by collectively living their reality, which is of course ideological. In other words, inclusion or exclusion was *internal* to the articulatory practice, not outside it.

"Who are our enemies? Who are our friends?" These questions could not be answered from an entirely outside perspective; their possible answers existed *within* the articulatory practice. The question of objectivity, from a naturalistic or a positivistic perspective, would be meaningless for such a form of power-praxis, which denied the naturalistic or positivistic notion of objectivity without human will. According to such a conception of the real and the objective, historical moments were partially the effects of such articulatory practices: the objectivity of reality existed only in and as power-praxis, which would enact the human will as an essential source of transformative power. From hindsight—that is, from the sight or site of a materialistic conception of the global economy—the Maoist epistemology should be no more than a fantasy, an ideology that failed its own reality. However, a similar intellectual dilemma made Louis Althusser (1970) proclaim that ideology is *an objective social reality*, for ideology constitutes *a living relationship* of the real to the imaginary or the phantasmagoric. We believe in what we believe today precisely because we are able to deny the objective reality of a passing ideology, which is, in this case, the Maoist epistemology. By embracing or engendering a different imaginary relationship to the world, we have created another fantasy.

The Maoist power-praxis drew a tremendous practical or political energy from its incessant ideological (re)production of the will of the people as the historical genesis of power and vitality. It was an *ideological* production in that it generated a collective fantasy that would in turn effect social and material changes. Its power lay not in the technical improvement of each individual's life but in the organization of their collective energy into a momentary whole to work on various national projects. The whole is bigger than the parts put together, and this was the truth of the Maoist world. Many national projects were carried out by simply pooling together a great collective force. The economic and material development of the Maoist years was also impressive, especially considering the primitive conditions under which progress was achieved. In a sense, the Maoist government had to bring about national development from a zero-degree grounding. Human will was therefore taken as the essential machinery for socio-economic development. Socialism was a story in the sense that it was a story of human will and collective agency. It was humanistic in its peculiar collectivistic conviction. During the Maoist moment, it was believed that material development depended on making the masses of the people realize their true potential. An active ideology, it hoped to make a socialist reality by *awakening* the people into action. Therefore, telling a new story came to constitute an important task for the Maoist years. The material reality was recognized—China was poor and backward. But according to the Maoist conception, this reality should and could be changed.

The possibility of change required or demanded an *interior* revolution more than an exterior one. Put another way, it required a "revolution of consciousness" more than anything else. This interior revolution meant to awaken the collective agent that was the masses of the people, who had been put into a deep slumber by the old society. To begin with, the peasantry must be awakened by telling them a different story, one in which they would be given an important role. To get into the interior space of the peasantry, to tickle their drowsy consciousness, would be a starting point for a real revolutionary movement, according to the Maoist epistemology. The intention was to remake their world from *within*, which would give rise to changes in the external material world. The articulatory practice, which was interiorizing, was the necessary fuel for the Maoist engine to work effectively. Contrary to the essential point of the Marxist teaching, which prioritized the decisive significance of infrastructure or economic base as the motor of history "in the last analysis," the Maoist power-praxis focused on the discursive power in remaking the social world. Historical materialism might have been part of the official language, part of the vocabulary, part of the signifying practice; yet in its practice, the Maoist epistemology was *humanistic* in essence. A form of collective humanism, it rested its feet on the ground of human will and collective agency. In this conception, real or imaginary, the human will was prioritized over the materialistic conception of the world. The phantasmagoric power of the Maoist ideology, which encouraged people to believe in their ability to transform social and material worlds, was therefore *real* in its effectivity.

The Maoist experience constituted a rationality of a peculiar kind, although it is usually thought to be irrational when looked at under the light of a materialistic lamp, both within and outside the People's Republic. It was perfectly *rational* in its execution and design—a fanatic rationality. It was fanaticism of a peculiar kind, which meant to bind all the peasants into One, viewed as a concrete revolutionary *whole* symbolizing and symbolized by the image of Mao himself. Mao's image initially functioned as no more than that of an effective leader. Later, his image came to signify the people as a whole and was defended, especially during the Cultural Revolution (1966–1976), as the unity and essence of the People's Republic. Never has such a fervor performed greater deeds. In dynastic histories, peasant revolts against the terror and tyranny of imperial rulers had always been limited to specific objectives. The enthusiasm of the Republic of China, in its revolutionary struggle to get rid of the imperial monarchy, was bloody and violent, but it had its finite aim, which cannot be compared with that of the Maoist revolution. An all-comprehensive and all-inclusive zeal—restrained by nothing and absolutely indifferent to obstacles of all kinds, at least in its conception and ideology—characterized the Maoist power-praxis. It was *not* a limited force, despite the fact that it always worked on a particular problem at a time. The concept of the masses of the people was not, according to the Maoist fanaticism, a local notion; rather, it was a *global* one, for revolution would recognize no regional or national boundaries.

Temporality and Subjectivity

Let us return to the Xicun story. Intriguing as well as revealing, Fang's telling of the account seems to invoke an exceptional historical sensitivity to the Maoist past. In the subsequent two chapters of Fang's work, her attention is given to how the notions of class and class struggle were made essential elements of the Maoist articulatory practice. Her analytical focus is on *how* such notions were brought into the life-world of everyday existence in the countryside. Her concern is not formal but socio-historical. Fang wants to show how an alien notion, Marxist in origin, came to be domesticated and how it became a self-identity that was essential to the political struggles of the time. In her analysis, Fang concentrates on the land reform period of the early 1950s, especially on the mass campaign known as "pouring out grievance" or "speaking bitterness." Interestingly, she begins, once again, with an ethnographic observation. In Xicun as well as other rural communities, she observed, daily events tended to overlap in memory. That is, to remember was to produce a *memory-impression*, a chunk of impressionistic images so jammed together in recollection as to defy any externalizable calendric chronologization. For example, when a peasant woman was asked about her difficulty in life, she would most likely present such a memory-impression, which would not correspond to any particular happening at any given date or month or year. Instead, the account of her experience, full of bitter images of suffering, would be a cluster of stories and images that could not be organized into a meaningful sequence in time. As Fang observes, what the peasant woman was able to present would be *an impression* of her life-world rather than a meaningful chain of events according to a sociological or historical chronology. Fang notes that peasant recollections of everyday experiences tended to be impressionistic in the strict sense of the term, and that the Maoist power-praxis made a positive use of this tendency in remembrance, turning it into a chronological hierarchy of suffering in favor of the Maoist revolutionary strategy.

Herein lies a general theoretical concern of the Oral History Project: how could the bitterness or grievance or suffering of everyday life, which is still a factor for many people in the countryside, be reorganized into a hierarchy of historical significance as an effective means for revolution in society? This was the aim of the mass campaign known as "pouring out grievance." As Fang seems to suggest, the Maoist power-praxis was more than simply a political movement. It was *an epistemological revolution,* for it redesigned the interior space of everyday life by producing an entirely different conception of time and history. The suffering, both past and present, was given a different interpretation that allowed a new possibility for social action. Then the question of memory arose as a central conceptual problematic. Memory is not simply recollection; it is a mode of existence or a form of life, that is, a way of relating oneself to things past, a vehicle by which we are able to travel in history (cf. Nora 1989). Therefore, the mass campaign of "pouring out grievance" that accompanied the land reform must be seen as *an epistemological movement* that remade a form of life by establishing a new mode of remembrance of things past. The victory of the Maoist politics could be explained not only by the material benefits it afforded the peasantry but also by its imaginative power in transforming the peasants' existence into a new way of being in history.

"Speaking bitterness" or "pouring out grievance" entailed a double aspect: something that was waiting to be expressed, on the one hand, and a performative aspect of telling or speaking it, on the other. The message depended on the power of "speech act" in order to become socially productive and recognizable. As hinted by Fang, it was the performance that drove the message into social significance—that made oneself and others *feel* the bitterness, which otherwise would have remained a trivial, mundane experience of everyday life. For the Maoist power-practice, the task became how to channel such bitterness of life and grievances toward certain social groups, such as landlords or rich peasants. This was its political strategy: poor peasants were carefully guided to systematize their pain and suffering in such a way as to reorganize their trivial daily experiences into a grander scheme of social meaning that was essential to the Maoist revolutionary attempt. There had been class differences and antagonisms in the countryside prior to the Maoist years, although they had occurred chiefly along those lines of descent groups or segments of lineage organizations (Baker 1979; Freedman 1958). The predominant image of struggles in the countryside had been tied to consanguineous and affinal concerns. Social relations had been always relations of kinship (Fei 1992). Even if they had not entirely been understood as outcomes of luck or fate, everyday suffering and pain had never before been explained in terms of exploitation and repression, which was an interpretive novelty introduced by the Maoist political machine. The Maoist challenge was to make peasants realize that their hardships and condition in life had nothing to do with bad luck but were instead a material effect of class inequality inflicted by society. The question was not simply about *what* to believe; it was about *how* to make the belief into praxis, that is, a habituation of what must be. The key concern for the Maoist political struggle in its early phase was to lift up the peasants' consciousness and, through a mass campaign, reshape their understanding of social inequality. The starting point was to recognize the fact that some people were better off than others. After this, the peasants would be guided by the Maoist work teams to realize that revolution was necessary. In this mass movement, the Maoist power-practice took up the remembrance of things past as its initial moment of a radical transformation.

Fang's inquiry is historical in the sense that it penetrated the past through a simulation of the actual life of the Maoist power-practice. At least, her text could be *read* in this way, since the relationship of memory to history and vice versa came to constitute the essence of her inquiry. It was a social fact that some peasants were better off than others. It was also true that everyday life in the countryside was full of pain and suffering. To make a connection between the remembrance of suffering and the idea of exploitation would be an entirely different story, which was the Maoist story. How could a new story then become habitualized in the life-world of peasantry? As suggested by Fang, the Maoist power-practice aimed to reorganize the memory-impressions of everyday life—those of suffering and pain in particular—into a new temporality, which made up a particular historical consciousness essential to the socialist victory. In this way, the peasants' sufferings obtained a historical meaning. Society itself was at fault, the past became unbearable, and a socialist revolution came to be seen as a historical necessity.

The life-world of everyday existence in the countryside was recalled by the peasants as an experiential chaos of memory-impressions that were highly repetitive and anti-calendric. In the process of conducting interviews and collecting oral histories, Fang realized that many events, real happenings in the village past, could not be verified accurately according to a calendric chronologization. This is why she identifies the life-world of Xicun as a "non-event state." An external, analytical view of an event, by definition, presupposes a happening in time. This was not the case with Xicun. The peasants remembered painful stories and recalled images of suffering, but it was hard for them to specify those happenings in a temporal order of sequence in order to make sense of the sufferings as a whole. For example, a poor peasant might say, "Once upon a time, my wife was sick. I tried to borrow money from this guy, a rich brother, who refused to lend me anything. Instead, someone tried to take away my daughter for his concubine." Upon further inquiry, the sociologist could not find any connection of those happenings in time. The year in which someone tried to marry his daughter perhaps had nothing to do with his hope of borrowing money from someone else. From an analytical point of view, without a temporal fixation of the eventness of an event, cause and effect between happenings cannot be conjectured. This is what puzzled Fang and her colleagues initially.

There is a particular kind of event that Fang focuses on in her analysis. These events, such as marriages or harvests, are what Fang calls "as if [they were] events" (it is a difficult term to translate, although Fang's meaning is clear). It refers to a category of events different from both a "non-event" and a real event. It is a kind of event that lies between the memory-impressions of everyday life and real happenings locatable in calendric time. The analysis of these "as-if events," divided into three subcategories, composes an intriguing part of Fang's work. The A-type is supposed to mark a shift in life for an individual. For example, getting married, which is significant, particularly for women, will be remembered by the person involved. However, as Fang insists, this kind of shift does not change one's relationship to the life-world, although it might involve a transition from one "non-event state" to another. In the case of a woman, marriage involves a transfer from her natal family's "non-event state" to a new one of her husband's family. This transition does not change her way of remembering things past; it simply provides a new ground for continuing the same mechanism of memory. The implication is that an individual goes through a number of "rites of passages" in life (see Gennep 1960), but that his or her relationship to the life-world usually does not change. Seasonal returns, another kind of A-type "as-if events," do have a "semi-event" character because they mark the temporal changes of an annual cycle. However, villagers tended to confuse one annual cycle with another. The return of seasons, which corresponded to the time reckoning of agricultural production, produced less a sense of physical time than a rhythm of collective life. This obvious temporal change, one may argue, was simply an element *external* to the peasants' life-world, which was made of memory-impressions. The B-type of "as-if events," according to Fang, consist of extraordinary moments of social life, such as a good harvest in a year of drought. This kind of event is different from the non-event because it is extraordinary and unusual. The C-type is similar to the B-type in nature, but different in character. This type is socially or historically distinctive, such as the Japanese invasion of the region.

The discussion of "as-if events" has paved the way for Fang's introduction of the concept of "narrative transfer," a mechanism that transfigures an "as-if event" into a "non-event state," allowing it to become a living part of the life-world. "As-if events" are significant because they tend to break the social inertia of everyday life. However, in order for them to be truly meaningful, they would have to be incorporated into the life-world by a narrative habituation or routinization. This means to say that these extraordinary moments must go through a "narrative transfer" in order to be *made* a living part of the life-world. An unusual occurrence is not significant in and of itself; instead, its significance for the life-world lies in the telling or retelling of it in a particular "non-event" fashion. By now, an attentive reader might go further than Fang in suggesting that the "non-event state" of quotidian life is not a social fact in the Durkheimian sense; it is instead a *narrative* condition of everyday experience. Put another way, it is not the happenings themselves that are significant; it is the *narration* of those happenings that gives them extraordinariness and distinctiveness. A crucial implication is that an important event could grab one's heart only if it were narrated in a certain way. As Fang observes, a villager who had suffered an accident might not be able to convey his experience very well to other people. A listener from the audience would stand up and take over the task of narrating the story. Later on, after more telling and retelling, people would forget who had originally experienced the accident. They were interested only in hearing about it again as told by a superior storyteller. In the end, the person who had initiated the story would become simply a listener in the audience. The crowd, gathered in the village square, could be seen as an embodiment of the life-world that would carry on the narrations of everyday experiences, with the chronology and original truthfulness being secondary in importance. If the question of authenticity were to be raised here, one might say that it was the authenticity of *narration* rather than the authenticity of *experience* that made up the foundation of a life-world of everyday experience.

Fang relates that there are a number of narrative strategies that a superior storyteller tends to adopt or employ. The first is the strategy of *repetition* of a chosen set of features or details. Here is an excerpt from Fang's work that gives us a sense of what she means by repetition as a narrative strategy. She and her colleague were interviewing an old man in Xicun, hoping to figure out his life in the past, that is, prior to the establishment of the People's Republic.

> *Question:* Your family life used to be fine, wasn't it?
> *Answer:* Family condition, well, nothing, nothing but not starved. He lost all on gambling, playing around, let's say.
> *Question:* All lost in gambling?
> *Answer:* Well, my sister found a mother-in-law for sixty dollars, all lost in Xinyemiao in the east, not a cent left; my mother saw nothing of it, not a single cent. My sister nineteen years younger than my brother-in-law. Haya! He did this good thing! Not that I did not think of him well. Nineteen years older, my brother-in-law than my sister, like selling her for a price, to Chenjiapu in the east.[8]

Fang uses this example to show how "immediate reasons" for an "as-if event," which was an extraordinary event for this old man's family, are not important. It is the repetition of certain details, such as money lost in gambling or the improper marriage of his sister, that makes the "as-if event" worth narrating. The conversation was supposed to be about the marriage of the old villager's sister, but there was no sequential account for the reasons that she was married to someone far-away. Matters such as matchmaking, engagement, bride price, etc., were impossible to be organized into a proper chain of causal relations, which was what the sociologist had hoped for. Instead, the old man repeatedly emphasized the age of the bridegroom and the loss of the family's fortune due to his father's gambling. As Fang argues, this narrative strategy allows an experience to become, through transferral, a memory-impression, that is, a living part of the narrator's life-world. According to Fang's analysis, the cause-effect model of reasoning, based upon the sociological assumption that an event always happens in time, should not be presumed to be the model of the peasants' everyday experience.

The narrative strategy of repetition served another important function in the telling of such stories by bringing into focus the image of suffering, which was—and to a large extent still is—the reality of peasant life in China. In such

---

8. This is a literal translation of the example provided by Fang. I have tried as much as possible to keep its oral character.

cases as this, cause and effect or event and time were far less significant than the repetition of a painful truth of life, especially when such stories were told to an outsider, sociologist or not. This was where the Maoist political machine started its work in the 1950s: instead of alleviating peasant sufferings, it encouraged them to speak bitterness or pour out grievances. One should note that although suffering was only one aspect of everyday life in the countryside, it was picked out by the Maoist political machine as a predominant theme for everyday narration. Other topics, such as dirty jokes, were shunted aside as insignificant and lacking in meaning. But in terms of *how* to speak, the Maoist political machine took up the peasant narrative strategy, with its essential tactic of repetition. The success of the Maoist story can be found in its emphasis on a particular theme of experience *and* its dependence on a peasant mode of narrativity. A chief task at the time was confiscating private properties from the landlords and rich peasants and redistributing them among the families of poor peasants. This had to be done by the poor peasants themselves under the guidance of a Maoist work team consisting of cadres or party members. The task of the mass campaign was to awaken class consciousness. The work team came to each village, organized poor peasants into groups, and encouraged them to speak about their bitterness in life. It is true that the material gains from the land reform made up an important incentive for poor peasants to get involved, but the justification for a new order of society would have to come from a different source that would vindicate the violent confiscation actions.

The second narrative strategy, as Fang shows, is one of absorption and combination of different descriptive elements from other sources into one storytelling. For the Xicun peasants, telling a story well was to give it color and vivacity. To *tell* a story was not simply to report a series of events that had happened in time; it was a *performative act* that established a milieu in which intended effects and effective intentions would intercept or interrupt each other. In telling a story about one's experience in the past, one would appropriate a cluster of seemingly (or actually) irrelevant elements, persons, or events, taken from other stories or hearsay, into the present telling in order to make it lively. Thus, the present telling of one's own story would always be entangled with an intricate web of different stories or happenings at other times. In Xicun, no story was told as a story in and for itself. Every story would constitute a plural field of meaning and signification, past and present, that was oriented toward an intended audience. An outsider—a sincere sociologist or a naive ethnographer, for example—would often misrecognize the intended effect of the telling because of the intricacy of a plural motif. In answering a simple question in Xicun, a cluster of details regarding seemingly irrelevant persons or events would be given. For example, when a peasant woman talked about her brother's death, which would be an "as-if event," she would also mention how she had gone to enjoy a local opera, a popular form of entertainment in the region. Going to see an opera, to the mind of an outside researcher, might appear *irrelevant* to the telling of her brother's death. The point that Fang tries to make, according to *my* reading, is that everyday remembrances of things past germinate and thrive on an enveloped plurality of meaning and signifi-cance. The materiality of everyday memory is *chaotic* and perhaps *illogical*, yet also vivacious and spirited precisely because of this messiness.

Fang's text, to my mind, discloses the problematic nature of the life-world of everyday existence in the countryside. Almost every question of hers was a problematization of a naive ethnographic attitude, full of presumptions about the villagers' lives. The reality was not what Fang and her colleagues had imag-ined it would be when they sat down, with their notebooks in hand, carefully listening to stories about the Maoist past, which was neither plainly unbearable nor gratefully cherished. Fang gradually brings the reader to the key point of her inquiry: the way in which the peasant life-world was *refurbished* by the Maoist power-practice. In order to make an effective change in that world, the Maoist political machine engaged with it and made use of its inertia. Moving in this lane of thought, one could read Fang's treatment of peasant narrative strategies as the strategies of the Maoist power-practice, which remade every-day experiences toward a revolutionary goal. In the life-world of everyday life, relational qualities of things, persons, and events are not predetermined by a categorical logic, sociological or historical. They exist only in the narrations of such relations in the form of memory-impressions, which have structured daily experiences. In such a world, identities or identifications among people or things are not the result of logical or sociological classifications; they are the effects of performative acts, narrative in nature, entreating or entrapping an irreducible audience. The Maoist political machine rightly understood the nar-rative nature of such a life-world, made use of its habits, and guided it toward a revolutionary direction.

The third narrative strategy, which Fang touches upon only briefly, is one of coloring or image making. As a good narrator knows, the use of figurative language is a necessary requirement for effective storytelling. The vividness needed to engross an audience depends on creating a lively pictorial narration, for which proverbs, aphorisms, poetic images, obscenities, etc., are of crucial importance. In particular, in Xicun, local people created and accumulated a large onomatopoetic vocabulary, with which they were able to produce extra effects during the telling.[9] These onomatopoetic words did not add more infor-mation to what was being told. Their employment simply induced or enhanced the expected impression, as vividly as possible, on the audience. On this strategy

---

9. It is quite difficult to translate this kind of oral text from Chinese to English. One also needs to note that there is a great deal of regional and local variation in terms of what kind of onomato-poetic words may be used in different rural areas of China.

of "image production," one should note that Mao himself was an excellent image maker; put another way, Mao, as a brilliant poet, knew very well how "to think in images" (see, e.g., Wakeman 1973).

In Fang's research, the "non-event state" of everyday life is properly identified as an existing social inertia, with which one had to engage in order to facilitate any true revolutionary movement. This holds a key to understanding the Maoist politics, which set itself to work on the inertia of the peasant life-world and succeeded in transforming it into a revolutionary force. The socialist ideology would have to be installed into the hardware of the peasant mentality by reshaping its habitual interior space with a different sociality. In this way, the Maoist power-praxis made its ideologies part of the peasants' inertia, and their hearts began to respond to the revolutionary movement. In achieving this, the mass campaign should not be seen simply as a power that came from outside the village to exert influence on the peasantry. It was an interiorizing force that not only raised the peasants' class consciousness but also restructured the way in which they told stories about themselves and others. A revolutionary way of seeing and narrating got *habitualized* by making use of the peasants' own habits.

Let us sharpen our thought a bit before moving on. Firstly, repetition is a narrative feature of the peasant life-world in its structural inertia. In order to become an integral part of the life-world, an event would have to obtain a narrative character in its repetitiveness. This implies that a "real" event, one that could be marked in a calendar, should lose some of its phenomenal quality in order to be truly integrated into the life-world. In other words, the extraordinariness of an event must to some degree lose its unusualness in the repeated narration of it in order to gain its significance for the peasant life-world. And the telling of those stories, in the repetitive and impressionistic manner of everyday life, would allow local people to live in their own world. Temporality in calendric time or physical linearity does not belong to the experiential world of the peasants; it belongs to an external measurement. This is a key point. The official story was and still is, to a large extent, an *outside* story.

Secondly, for an outside story to work, it would have to be told in the way in which the peasants tell their stories, at least at the beginning. To change the way in which stories about the world are told should be an excellent entry point for a revolutionary attempt, and this was what the Maoist power-practice achieved. The Maoist mass campaign made use of such a habitual feature of the peasant life-world by inducing the villagers to "speak bitterness" first. This campaign picked just one feature of the peasants' life—suffering and pain— and reinforced it to an extreme extent. The official ideological indoctrination followed after the images of pain and suffering became predominant in their life-world. Later on, the pain and suffering would become transformed into rage against the villagers' own brothers—the landlords and rich peasants. The identification and use of the structural inertia of the peasant life-world gave rise to the Maoist success in transforming the countryside.

Thirdly, both the narrators of pain and suffering and the audience in the mass campaign were guided into an ideologically designed social space. In the process of telling and retelling their painful experiences in life, peasants habitualized a mental transference from the singular to the plural. This is what Fang terms as "narrative transfer." Either hearing or telling a story of hard life in the singular mode at the outset would end in a collective resonance, guided by the work team. In telling stories of suffering, there were indeed blurred boundaries; time or specific calendric marks were never clearly indicated. However, this was exactly what was needed for the Maoist power-practice, for it wanted to project this blurred narration, singular to begin with, onto a collective temporality. The existing order of things was not right. It came from the past, which was the old society, and must be demolished.

Fourthly, the pluralization of personal sufferings into a collective feeling was an essential task for the mass campaign. In this way, individuals could find a *direction* to pour out their grievances, and this directionality, brought into the village from outside, was essentially the calendar or clock of official history. The Maoist change was not simply a change in the reorganization of society, no longer based on kinship ties. It also effected a change in the directionality of the peasants' anger, which became collectivized against the old society, a past that was still present during the land reform. Revolution was equated with changing the old society into a new one, the Maoist one. This change would require a change in the inertia of everyday life, its way of remembrance and narration. Since commonality in individuals is a *narrative* commonality, an effective change would require a revolution of individuals' narrative habits. The Maoist power-praxis was a historical innovation that was both practical and epistemological.

That every farmer should have his own land sounded more traditional than Marxist, at least to the ears of poor peasants. However, to elevate class consciousness to the level at which poor peasants would slap the faces of their rich brothers in public was altogether another thing. The Maoist story was a combination of traditional sentiments and Marxist gospels, and what was innovative and indeed powerful was its *implementation*, the extensive and intensive *care* given to the ideological seeds on the peasant soil. It was successful in its *praxis*, and this is why we must see it as a mode of "power-praxis." It was not simply "an order of things"; it was *an ordering of things in practice*. It was not simply a habitualization that came into its own existence; it was a revolution that changed the existing habits. In other words, the Maoist power-practice altered the structural functions of the peasants' social inertia, reorienting their bitter and painful memories against a common enemy, the old society, which was exemplified by the existence of land inequality. Everyday stories came to be represented in collective terms, which gave the life-world its directionality. This was the promise of the Maoist story, which, by denouncing the old and the past, proclaimed its discovery of a socialist future in the present struggles—and in so doing helped to win the hearts of the Chinese peasantry. In the new temporality, it did not matter whether the official calendar was remembered clearly or not. What was important was to associate the past and the old society with pain and suffering and to eliminate the veneration and reverence associated with them. "Pouring out grievance" was a mass movement to remake the discursive function of the past by telling a new story, the Maoist story, which was future-oriented and yet present-focused. The Maoist machinery altered the relationship of the past to the present, of the present to the future, by transforming the social inertia of the peasant life-world. Thus, the Maoist power-praxis was not entirely an external force, military or political, forcibly imposed on the villages from outside; rather, it was an internal force that, by means of the mass campaigns, refurbished the interior space of *being* in history.

Fang's discussion of the peasant life-world, although limited to Xicun, would remind the reader of Alfred Schutz's *The Phenomenology of the Social World* (1967). Not to confuse it with the anthropological debates on rationality or primitive mentality (see, e.g., Hallpike 1979), Fang's study seems to have brought us back to a number of features characteristic of societies of oral communication in which a clear registration of events in time is difficult if not impossible (see Goody 1968, 1977). One might extend Fang's observations for a consideration of some general attributes distinguishing oral communication from written communication (see, e.g., Ong 1982). To be sure, Fang and her colleagues did not mean to generalize; what they hoped for was to find out how the Maoist political machine operated. In Xicun, life seems to have run in accordance with a narrative clock of everyday experience. The vivification of an image or the unwilling affinity of one event with another, rather than its chronology, was more memorable for Xicun villagers. Scarcity, for example, was a powerful image, and it had always been remembered and recited in public squares. But it became a collective source of hatred only *after* the Maoist power-praxis penetrated the village. When Fang asked the villagers to pinpoint *when* the Maoist work team arrived in the village or *when* they bought or lost a cow, etc., both the obstinate researcher and the hearty peasants came to realize that they were different species. A stubborn economist or some other positive social scientist might have insisted that, like primitive tribal people, Xicun peasants were wrong in their views about events and time. However, our sociological student from Beijing, awakened by an ethnographic encounter, realized the importance of researching the problem of the *habitualization* of narrative habits. The secret of the Maoist revolutionary success could be found in its ability to change the way in which peasants' stories about themselves and others were told.

Genealogy of History II

Ushered into the habits of heart for an enormous population by the Maoist machinery was a "narrative transfer," which allowed for the stories of "myself" *and* "ourselves" to be told in a new light, the light of socialist revolution and its promised final victory. In view of the habitualization of a new mode of life and knowledge, the mass campaign of "pouring out grievance" was not only an innovation of political praxis but also a materialization of a different system of ideological signification. The Maoist order of things was *a system of signs*—in the strict sense of the term—both politically real and ideologically imaginative. Its political potentiality was already implicated in its sign system as a system of ideological signification. It is the reciprocity between a *real* production of the *ideological* forces and an *ideological* production of the *real* struggles that marked the physiognomy of the Maoist power-praxis. This process was truly reciprocal—a double force producing its political practice under specific conditions while, simultaneously and exactly on the same ground, reproducing its own practicable ideologies. This could be made possible only by a transfiguration, that is, a rehabitualization of a new conception into an old mode of life and knowledge. Thus, "narrative transfer" means *a transference or transfiguration of everyday narrativity* understood as the way in which the life-world of everyday life is or is able to be experienced as knowledge. The Maoist power-praxis did not impose itself on its subjects; it *induced* them into a grandiose lyric whose mode of telling was earthy and worldly, aspects familiar to Chinese peasantry.

Several points may now be made. First, contrary to the common view of seeing the land reform more as a material transformation of productive means and social relations in the countryside, we should see the Maoist power-praxis as an ideological production of social reality, for it worked on and transfigured the mode of memory in the peasant life-world. In and through the mass campaigns, an enormous population came to feel their pain as a *different* kind of pain—one that became recognized as curable and momentary or temporal. Suffering, or remembrance of the past in general, was no longer viewed as a chronic ill or seen in terms of good or bad luck tied to one's ancestral influence through the web of kinship; instead, it came to be understood as the fault of society, a disease of the old society. Contrary to the aged Confucian or orthodox ideology centered on the notion of fate in life, the Maoist power-praxis provided a collective hope for a total cure of every kind of suffering, which was indeed attractive and enlightening. The innovative prescription offered by the Maoist sermon making brightened the mundane, dark world of the peasants' everyday life. Second, in the Maoist strategy, the symptom of pain was dislocated and relocated by means of a different diagnosis. This dislocation was a *relocation* in diagnosis. The pain remained painful, but its treatment would be different, according to the Maoist interpretation, whose effectiveness lay in a remodeling of the remembrance of the past. The notion of the *real* was not a real notion: in telling a story about everyday experience, as we have seen, real reference to time was always added to the story that had been told. Time and eventness were not naturally given; they were made into a certain correlation. The mass campaign made a great reversal of the temporality in the country-side; it gave the peasantry a different directionality for knowing and living. Suffering remained to be suffered, but it was identified as a social evil inherited from the old society. The materiality of the life-world continued to be what it always had been, but the *understanding* of it became altogether different in the hands of the Maoist work-team magicians. The issue is therefore not whether materiality can be objectively measured in quantitative means; it is a question of how and why the Maoist power-praxis could grab the hearts of the peasants and make them subject to the law of collective will and agency.

From today's materialistic point of view, the Maoist political machine stands in the shadow of history as a failure. In the eyes of another generation yet to come or from a future retrospection, a rupture would appear in today's China: the Maoist morality and reasoning have been totally negated. Precisely because of this emergent abyss, if standing on a new balcony of the present age, with a lofty and panoramic or paranoiac view, one would feel the irony of history or its madness. The Maoist storm came with such force and inevitability and then was itself blown away by yet another conception of force and inevitability. Claiming to be a child of the Marxist tribe—with its faith in historical materialism—the Maoist subject instead lived a firm belief in the power of human will and agency. This fantastic fantasy created an illusory unity known as the masses of the people, which was *narrative* in nature and made a *temporal* and *directional* or teleological demand for life and knowledge. As we have seen, this subject formation required an endless articulation of its phantasmal whole, a real fiction that produced a fictional reality. There is no doubt that the Maoist subject was a phantasmal subject, produced by and also producing a mystique about itself. The Maoist revolution is no less than a story or a super-story, just as historical materialism is a story; it is an illusionary story, just as Bernard Mandeville's *The Fable of the Bees* is illusionary. Perhaps not every proponent of Adam Smith, both inside and outside the People's Republic today, would realize that "the invisible hand" is also a phantom, a livable or living system of signs that is currently objectified by the material development of a global system of production and consumption.

The Maoist subject was a *historicalized* subject because its struggles were defined in terms of time, that is, in terms of a better tomorrow—and this tomorrow could only be a tomorrow of the *we*. Yesterday, today, and tomorrow were conceptualized as an organic whole, which was understood as a chain of *temporal* relations that were truly changeable. Becoming different was inevitable because the human will *could* and *would* effect a change on material reality. Narrativity rather than measurability structured the identity of the subject, whose life was dependent on the telling of the Maoist super-story. Telling it was not an external requirement but was made *internal* to the very nature of the mass struggle; it was part of the condition of possibility for being in the world. It was almost impossible for the mass movements to take a break during the Maoist era, for the life of the masses of the people had become defined as a perpetual political exercise of its subjectivity. "Speaking bitterness" or "pouring out grievance" was not an external requirement imposed on anyone from outside; it came from within as a need to enlighten oneself by one's own experience. The Maoist work team only guided and assisted the process, which produced a self-knowledge that would make a *being* into a *becoming*.

The historicalized subject was dependent for its existence on the making of a temporalized interior space. An inward-looking attitude defined the Maoist subject, which unrelentingly examined itself in the historical mirror internally set up by and against itself. That mirror for and against oneself was transindividualistic in nature, and this transindividuality was not simply a "collective solidarity," as defined in the Durkheimian sociology, for the *we*, the author of the Maoist super-story, was by definition and logicality *the effectivity* of its praxis. The *we* was not a social totality definable in *external* terms; instead, it was a form of life, or *praxis*, that oriented itself toward the illusionary effect of such an authorship. In terms of its function, the *we* was a phantom, a *real* phantom, which derived its power from the unrelenting practices oriented toward the *reality* of a fantasy. This fantasy was *real* in that its effect was affecting the material world. The Maoist super-story was supposedly authored by a *transcendental* subject, the masses of the people, which made time and will an essential social gravitation. The future, a promised utopian tomorrow that would perhaps never arrive, became the soul of this directional or teleological gravitation. Life and change, which was possible and yet *necessary*, therefore became future-oriented. The condition of becoming, as a new possibility for experience and self-comprehension, came to be lived as a real phantom. The Xicun peasants, among many others, were absorbed into this gravitation of socialism. The idea of development was not appealing; rather, the appeal was in the notion of revolution to bring about real and genuine changes, as authored by the masses of the people. Their *tomorrow* was seen as a perpetual struggle against various kinds of social evils.

Class and Classification

In the remaining part of her work, Fang examines how the Maoist work team carried out its mission in Xicun. An attentive reader will have realized by now the existence of a scheme in Fang's writing. It started with an ethnographic dilemma that introduced a sociological inquiry into the Maoist power-praxis, which has remained a historical puzzlement. Could we really go back to the Maoist past as *a* past, pure and simple? Could the Oral History Project be carried out as originally planned, without a necessary problematization of the condition of life on the ruins of the Maoist struggles? Is it not true that today's remembrance of the past has already been affected by the Maoist experience? Thus and then, a *real* question emerged from this sociological scenario: to what extent has the Maoist power-praxis affected the way in which Xicun peasants were able to reach or retain their past? Did the Maoist revolution transmute the mode of memory in the countryside? Put in Fang's words, how did a "narrative transfer," introduced by the Maoist power-praxis, alter the peasants' remembrance of things past? A crucial assumption here is that memory is not recollection; it is a way of our being in the world in the present tense. Now at last, in the final part of her work, Fang is willing to move on to discuss what was then known as "class struggles" in Xicun—which directly involved the mission of the work team. Fang's work would make a careful reader feel as if she intends to let the mystique of the Maoist machinery reveal itself through its own praxis.

How to make poor peasants become part of a revolutionary force was the first and primary question for the Maoist political machine to address. This question of *how* constituted both the practical and the ideological core of the Maoist problematic for socialist revolution in China. Now let us take a closer look at what happened in the countryside. The Maoist work team came to Xicun during the land reform in order to awaken the poor peasants from their historical slumber—to bring them back to a social status that would truly represent their power in society. In order to arouse their class consciousness, the work team, consisting of several cadres or party members, visited poor households and engaged their hosts in intimate dialogues. In particular, at the beginning, they encouraged the peasants to complain about their living conditions, that is, "to speak bitterness." After becoming better acquainted with the villagers, and having solicited numerous complaints, the work team tried to induce and/or enforce a certain pattern of telling or retelling of the peasants' life stories, helping them focus on everyday bitterness as an unbearable fact of life. From time to time, a hint was given in order to guide the peasants' attention in a particular direction, letting them know that their suffering was representative of the suffering of all the poor people in the entire nation. The cadres did not need or intend to talk much, merely to channel the peasants' focus in a prepared direction. As a result, a pattern of remembrance of things past was born: a singular experience of suffering came to be understood as a representative symptom of the *manifold* ordeal of the masses of the people.

At the beginning, local people could not see anything beyond their immediate concerns in their own village. Later they began to feel the pulse of the masses of the people, who were suffering an acute pain that was not of their own infliction.

One's own suffering became a *sign* of the suffering of all the poor people. Having worked the singular into the plural, the work team then introduced the notion of class classification, which divided peasants into five categories: landlord, rich peasants, middle peasants, poor peasants, and pure laborers. The first two categories were considered "bad classes," and the last two, which made up a large majority in the countryside, were "good classes." The category of middle peasants, which could be further divided into upper middle and lower middle peasants, was considered a middle layer of social reality. The Marxist story was taken up and applied here in a simplistic way: those who owned the means of production, land in particular, did not labor; hence, they exploited the labor of others. For poor peasants, it was the other way around: they labored very hard but owned neither land nor other means of production. Poor peasants had not rebelled against their rich brothers because they did not realize the true condition and power of their own life. They lived their lives under "a false consciousness" based on the familial or kinship ideology. This must be changed. Marx's theory was secondary in importance to the Maoist powerful reading of it into a particular situation of the Chinese peasantry.

This was the general practice of the land reform in the countryside. Curiously, Fang does not pay much attention to the collective violence, allegedly an essential attribute of the mass movement at the time, during which poor peasants, after pouring out their grievances, beat up their class enemies—their rich brothers. Instead, Fang directs the reader's attention to the interesting problem of how to assign everyone a class label. The five categories were not difficult to define, but it is altogether another matter to assign them to each person. A tremendous difficulty arose when considering how to draw a distinction between a rich peasant and a middle peasant. The former was considered a class enemy, while the latter was viewed as still part of the masses. Both categories consisted of people who owned some amount of land and were supposed to hire others to work for them, for example, during the harvests. The countryside was enormous and unevenly developed. How could a clear or clean line be drawn between the people and their enemies? The instruction given to the work team was that the category of rich peasants indicated those who *hardly* worked themselves and *chiefly* relied on the labor of others. How was one to interpret the terms "hardly" and "chiefly"? The political result of class classification would be fatal: a rich peasant's possessions, such as land, would be confiscated entirely, while a middle peasant would be able to keep what he had for the moment. How to define the term "chiefly" therefore became a decisive political game in Xicun. "Did I *chiefly* exploit others or *chiefly* work on my own land?" By asking such a question, the real quantity of one's possession of land or other productive means became a secondary question, for it was not only how much one possessed but also how much one labored on one's possession that would make one what he was.

Village life in traditional China had always been a life of family or kinship connections, and mutual help among members of an extended family was looked on as a virtue and would not have been considered exploitative. The classification of peasants into categories introduced an unprecedented problem, for one would have to behave according to new rules that ran against consanguineous or affinal ties. Let us take another example for further illustration. Some poor peasants worked hard throughout their lives in order to purchase a piece of land, and they might have done so just before the land reform began. As Fang shows, it was difficult to set up a proper framework for the categorization of peasants. If a landlord had just sold his land to his brother, would he still be considered a landlord? A family disease could easily turn a landlord into a poor peasant over the course of a few months. In order to carry out the classification, some arbitrary standards would have to be made in the first place. In Xicun, as in other places, a set of quantitative criteria had been provided and was utilized. For example, it was decided that if 50 percent of a peasant's total income came from hiring others to work for him, he would be classified as a rich peasant. If the figure was less than 50 percent, he would be considered a middle peasant, whose land and other productive means were not supposed to be confiscated during the land reform. It was also decided that the category of landlord would be given to those who owned their lands and had stopped laboring for more than three years prior to the land reform. Considering the enormous size of the countryside and its uneven development, the task of categorizing peasants remained an extremely difficult one. The National Day was designated as 1 October 1949, but in different regions the work teams were sent down according to the gradual progress of the Maoist military victory over the entire mainland. How to calculate three years prior to the land reform therefore became a serious problem in practice. If going by the day when the work team arrived in a village, there might be a great discrepancy between two neighboring villages because, due to various reasons, they might not have had a similar schedule for the land reform.

The practical difficulty of categorizing peasants into classes, which makes up Fang's central concern, generated social struggles of another kind. While trying hard to obtain or reserve a good seat in the new social hierarchy, Xicun villagers attempted to remove from their memories some unfavorable temporal markers regarding their own possessions to avoid being drawn into a wrong category. It was a battle fought on two fronts at the same time: on the one side, they fought together with the work team in order to gain benefits for themselves; on the other side, they tried hard not to remember clearly what had become of their own possessions. One should note that this classificatory effort, which would have set up a concrete and solid foundation for political struggles, became an endless struggle in and for itself. In the course of more than a decade, there were several rounds of rechecking of the initial classification in the countryside.

For example, Fang shows that as late as 1963–1964, when the Socialist Education Movement was carried out, 10 percent of the class labels in Xicun, which had been given in the early 1950s, were changed by a reclassification. Whenever the work team came to the village, efforts were made among the peasants themselves to gain social and political capital with the endless use and abuse of memories and stories in producing truth effects. A crucial observation can be drawn from the above discussion: while the Maoist power-praxis redefined the meaning of the peasants' pain or suffering in life, *at the same time* it also reinforced their mode of memory as a way of being in the life-world. In terms of introducing a new story into the heart of the peasantry, the Maoist power-praxis indeed revolutionized the countryside; however, on the other side, the same force also reinforced the peasantry's inertia, its remembrance of things past, its way of being in society.

In Xicun, as Fang shows, the relationship of the work team to local people later changed. In the beginning, the poor peasants were the storytellers who poured out grievances, and the work team was the listener. Even during the mass meetings, the work team played only a secondary role of encouragement and inducement. When the land reform progressed into its second phase, the work team came to assume a different role. Instead of being simply a listener, it became the authority in making final decisions regarding the classification of peasants into categories. After the masses were mobilized and everyone was ready, the work team members performed the role of inquisitor, questioning and investigating everyone's past and possessions. Who worked for whom? When or in which year? For how long? Under what circumstances? How much was one compensated for one's work? What percentage of income came from hiring others to do the work? As we have seen, these were difficult questions because they demanded a logicality *external* to the peasants' life-world. Apart from the impossibility of framing everyday happenings in a calendric chronology, the exchange of labor in rural communities had never been thought of in terms of *quantity*. Instead, this common practice had been conceived in terms of *social qualities* such as family cooperation and neighborhood help.

Let us provide some further background for the problem. Mao himself once proclaimed that although the class of landlords and rich peasants consisted of no more than 10 percent of the population, they owned 70 to 80 percent of the agricultural or arable lands. This was a chief source of social inequality and exploitation and a reason for the mercilessness and cruelty experienced by the poor and middle peasants, laborers, and other exploited classes. This inequality must be overthrown, for it not only made poor people suffer but also was the cause of the poverty and backwardness of the entire nation, which had been invaded by the Western powers over and over again since the Opium War (1839–1842). The idea that each peasant should have his own land was not a new concept, but the notion of class struggle was. The Maoist victory was by then envisaged as a step in the advancement of *total* human emancipation. The struggle in each village was therefore considered not simply a struggle *within* but also a struggle *outside* the village toward a national or global goal. This articulation of the Maoist story, which was Marxist in some respects, would guide the work team to grind their figures of class categorization in the villages to approximate the national proportions. Thus, the notion of class enemies composing roughly 10 percent of the population—a national figure mentioned by Mao without any verifiable calculation—would become a workable scheme of calculation for each specific location. The logic of proportionality played an intrinsic role in the Maoist political struggles and provided a national justification for interpreting local battles.

Life in the countryside had never been measured in this way. Mao was not a mathematician, and this proportion itself was not very accurate. Nevertheless, it became an underlying basis for social classification, resulting in a great deal of confusion and frustration during the land reform and afterward. Accuracy was impossible, although the politics of calculation became the fact of life. The "weapon of the weak" in this case was to produce further memory-impressions in order to refute or deny the official attempt to classify neatly or cleanly. No one could be entirely certain about the result; everyone was in a constant state of defensiveness and apprehension with regard to being assigned a classification. The inaccuracy of political calculation gave rise to its constant recalculation in and for an approximation. As Fang shows, some crude quantitative criteria, usually in the form of *percentage or ratio*, were introduced in the early years of the Maoist struggles in order to designate a class position for each person. However, these efforts became tedious and tiresome, for a minimum understanding of time as a linear progression from days to months to years constituted an essential condition for the implementation of such quantitative calculations, but, as we have seen, the peasant life-world, with its impressionistic memories, registered no such form of temporality.

As Fang suggests, the Maoist work team was trying to find out the truth about each person by attempting to reconstruct his or her life experience *in time*. Instead, the team received many confusing—if not entirely contradictory—accounts either from the same person at different times or from different people who had experienced a similar happening. This was not because the villagers *lied* to the officials; it was because it was *impossible* for them to make sense in the way in which they were requested to be truthful. Put simply, there existed, in such cases as this, two *relations of truth* to time: one was repetitive and impressionistic and did not assume the lineal progression of time with regard to specific happenings; the other was built on the modern conception of lineal time and its relationship to events. The former belonged to the life-world of Chinese peasantry, the latter to the sociologist and the official world.

However, the key point is not to ascertain the existence of two modalities of temporality; rather, it is to recognize that the Maoist power-praxis was a self-contradictory practice. On the one hand, it could gain its vitality only by correctly identifying the nature of the peasants' life-world and making use of it. On the other hand, its own modernistic ambitions and political strategies ran counter to the structural inertia of the peasant world. Therefore, the Maoist mass campaigns were by definition *self-struggles*, only trying to break through their own contradictions and impossibilities. As a result, the "non-event state" of the peasant life-world was strengthened rather than weakened, unlike what happened to the peasantry in other modern experiences of industrial development. Despite the great collective energy generated by the Maoist appeals, which indeed changed the material conditions of life in the countryside, the inertial impulse of memory reinforced itself into a stronger one, which continued to allow the peasants to live in their own world. That is, the Maoist power-praxis changed the content of the villagers' life-world but kept its form.

During the course of the Maoist power penetration, a habit of everyday life in the countryside—"speaking bitterness"—was turned into a habit of heart, which produced and signified social existence itself. This habit became a form of social inertia, a real driving force in defining and identifying oneself as being allied with the masses of the people, the alleged master and author of the People's Republic. This process of the habitualization of a habit into social inertia, which defined and made possible the revolutionary sentiments of the Maoist struggles, was an unexpected result of the endless mass campaigns. "Speaking bitterness" later became the inertial or habitualized identity politics of the Maoist brand. That is why Fang and her colleagues, when they went to Xicun, were misrecognized as cadres sent down by the government to conduct another round of political inquisition. The Maoist inertial power continues to grasp the hearts of many people of this older generation, whose identity politics of "speaking bitterness" was—and still *is*—the means for making sense of oneself and others. Social relations were to be produced by "pouring out grievances" to and against others. For some, this became *a form of life*, interiorized as a collective narrative experience nurtured by the Maoist mass campaigns. What confronted the sociologists in Xicun, hoping to collect "oral texts," was precisely the residue of this *inertial* force. The Maoist power-praxis had prioritized the present and oriented itself toward the future. The extreme success of its early years in denouncing the past and the country's semi-colonized and semi-feudal old society took on its own inertia in running a new course. Memory was made full of bitterness in order to carry out the Maoist mission of transforming the countryside. Nevertheless, although the mission was completed, the inertial force seems to have continued to this day. Memory is always a memory of *something*; one should hope that it will not always be of pain and suffering.

Genealogy of History III

The Maoist epistemology was not only teleological but also *interiorizing*, for it required an inward-looking attitude that encompassed self-criticism and self-examination. The outward battles against the class enemies would have to rely on a correct political self-scrutiny that was understood as the genesis of power and force originating from the human will alone. Social existence, according to this view, consisted in and of essential contradictions, of which class struggle was the societal form. The masses of the people constituted a majority, not a totality, and it was the majority who had suffered at the hands of an undeserving minority. There was a double movement in the Maoist call for revolutionary struggles: on the one hand, the poor people had to be united into a predominating majority in order to fight the battles against their enemies, and, on the other hand, the possibility of arriving at a united front depended on an unrelenting self-scrutinization that would *make* oneself part of the predominating majority named as the masses of the people. Although the Maoist work team came from outside as an external force, imposing itself on a rural community, the possibility of its success came from this interiorizing practice, by which segmented or fragmented individuality was made into a common individuality, a powerful political vitality. The energy of *subjective politics* derived entirely from the interiorization of the political subjectivity into a phantasmal unity. The phantasmal subjectivity thus achieved was *new* to the Chinese peasants, who saw themselves for the first time as *a living force*—however phantasmagoric and hallucinating—that could remake life in its chosen way.

Viewed from a Marxist perspective, the chief task for the Maoist subject was to check oneself, unrelentingly and continuously, in the phantasmal mirror of the Maoist super-story. There was no certainty guaranteed from outside the practice of this subjectivity; its reason and logic came from within itself *as* and *in* praxis. The masses of the people—the means of making oneself interiorized or internalized—existed nowhere but in the practice of such a predominating majority. From the official point of view, an order of things should not be established based on external regulations or rules of punishment. In this sense, and considered historically, the Maoist politics was *a politics of practice* in the strict sense of the term. Suffice it to say that it was *qualitative* and *confessional*. Some scholars might argue that the Maoist politics achieved its power by means of force, and one cannot deny the fact that different forms of extreme violence against individuals occurred throughout the Maoist years. But more often than not, raptures or ruptures of mass violence were not directly ordered by the government; instead, they tended to be the result of certain collective rites of passage that lost control on the way to ecstasy. In its style, the Maoist politics was a form of *confessional politics*, for it was through confession (to the party or its representatives) that the political subject came to interiorize itself to the satisfaction of the masses. In order to purify or aggrandize oneself, one needed to step forward and speak out about oneself to the masses of the people, sometimes symbolized by Mao himself. In this instance, the liturgical institution for such practices was not the church but rather the mass movements led by the party.

The Maoist subject was therefore an ethical subject, questioning itself unrelentingly in search for the greater good. A super-story was given from the outside, and it was a super-moral story that required the practice of subjection to its ethical demands. This made the Maoist self both an inward-looking and an intensively sensitive social being. The super-moral story was external to oneself, but one had to internalize it in order to become a revolutionary subject for the masses of the people. Key to the Maoist subjection was the appropriation of oneself to the greater good, but the realization of such a movement within oneself was carried out before the eyes of other people, neighbors and comrades, who showed up at the same mass meetings, acting as a grand jury for the testimony of oneself. The eyes of the masses were sharp and observant, far more effective than any security cameras, and no interior error or betrayal would have been missed by their inspecting panopticon (cf. Foucault 1977). It was this double movement—the struggle of an interiorizing self through the court of the masses of the people in both the metaphysical and literary senses—that characterized the Maoist mode of self-identification and made life what it was. For both the inward-looking self and the outward social being, every distinction for the subject was a *qualitative* distinction, a moral one, an ethical judgment of value, rather than a quantitative evaluation. In responding to the Maoist requirement to participate in the mass movements, one had to subject oneself to the inspecting eyes of others, the masses of the people, a reified entirety of an ideological phantom.

Vigorous and vigilant, this double movement derived its vital force from within and outside oneself, germinating both an inward-looking attitude and an outward-looking hyper-concern about one's position in society. The Maoist political innovation lay in its form of political praxis known as "mass line," in which each individual was made a habitual subject of confessional solidarity. The peasants' social life was then dominated by unending mass campaigns that grew more and more serious or severe in their demands for loyalty and reverence for the state and its ideologies. To take the Cultural Revolution as an example, life at the time was not lived or possessed by an individual; instead, it was part of a zealous, vital, and vibrant force of collectivity, an illusion of a tragic kind, driving itself toward an encompassing totalization that was not achievable as an end in and for itself. In its final vision, the Maoist epistemology was not individualistic but rather humanistic; in contrast, today's ideology and state ideological apparatus have made life too cellular, too materialistic, too individualistic to be humanistic. It is true that inequality and injustice continue to exist everywhere, as it did in the Maoist society, but a sharp and agonizing difference is that today the existence of inequality or injustice, insofar as the People's Republic is concerned, is seen as an *inevitable result* of development. The idea of exploitation is gone, as is the notion of class struggle and social contradiction. Society is no longer viewed in terms of an inherent historical struggle for a better tomorrow. In the vast continent of the People's Republic today, there is no comfortable lodge that would allow the masses of the people to reside there unless they could obtain their share value on the market. An enormous material force, measurable and justifiable only by means of statistical data and analysis, has swept aside the dilapidated remains of an outmoded ideological apparatus.

For the Maoist subject, the question of objectivity could not have arisen outside the interiorized site of self-scrutiny or from a purely external or externalized standpoint, whether scientific or not. If it had been raised during the Maoist years, it would have been a question of *whose* objectivity and whether or not it was objective from the point of view of the masses of the people, who, as a gravitational notion, constituted both *subject* and *object* of the revolutionary history. This point of view, which was believed to be truly *objective*, should outstrip other claims of objectivity, such as those made in the name of statistical science. The ethical concern, central to *being* in the Maoist world, was regulated around the notion of *positionality* rather than that of objectivity. The concern was always about how to adopt or adapt oneself to the right view, the objective view of the people, who were stepping onto a new path in history. To raise the question of objectivity from a supposedly objective point of view, according to the Maoist epistemology, would have been an entirely false question, if not reactionary, for there could be no objective view without a position from which such a view was projected; and the objectivity of the social world was its positionality, defined in terms of social positions or class struggles. There was no *neutral* stance—no position without positionality, no perspective without perspectivity—for the Maoist subject, who had to decide whether to stay aligned with the masses of the people. This could well have been the most difficult fact of life for many at the time, as it provided no individualistic space, no study or closet, for anyone to hide in. Every closet was interiorized as a place for self-criticism, which penetrated the deepest layers of subjectivity.

In this way, the good—that is, the value and reason for revolutionary struggles—was made *a total quality* that could not be measured by any means but could be only articulated or narrated in and as positionality or perspectivity. Participation was to be total. No one could or should be excused when a mass movement arrived in a village, for the political subject was realizable only in the production of such political subjectivity. The mass movement was truly *a movement*, a force that lived its life, with all its energy and vitality, in and by the influence that it exercised on the masses. Contrary to the normal political scientific sentiment (e.g., Townsend 1969), the Maoist "mass line" was less a political strategy than an *existential politics*, embedded in a particular version—whether adequate or not—of *a Marxist phenomenology of the social world*, which created life, sense, and meaning out of a peculiar conception of time, narrative, and history (see Carr 1986). Confessional collectivity could or should have no end, becoming a perpetual struggle against the possible falling or failing as long as one lives. It was a tiresome life in some ways, and the Maoist politics of subjection allowed no stopover, not even a brief nap, for anyone who wished to be good—to be with the masses of the people. Such a form of political subjection presupposed a peculiar social attitude and demanded a lifelong commitment. In practice, it required a constant engagement in self-criticism and self-improvement, which would never arrive at a final station, if seen from an individualistic point of view. According to the Maoist epistemology, life was a commitment to unending social struggles within which one must struggle against oneself in order to become other than oneself. Change, which was always possible, would have to be produced from within oneself.

Chapter Seven

EXTERIORIZATION

❖

Epistemology I: Anti-humanism and Narcissism

Our "ethnographic present" is painted on the canvas of the Maoist years as an eclipsing background for meditation and reflection. The immediate object, the central figure of the portrait, is not the background tincture of the painting; however, it is necessary for the image to be painted on a canvas of analytical distanciation. The mirror effect of the recent past is both historically real and conceptually made, with each aspect being intrinsically dependent on the other. The posturing model of the picture is sketched on a particular choice of conceptual coloring so as to make the modeling gesture *visible*. This visibility is not a given or inherent historical fact; instead, it has to be produced as an effect of our drawing and perception. The ethnographic strategy of my writing intends to *construct*, with the conceptual tool of deconstruction, a double structural rupture of recent origin in order to bring into focus an abrupt family division in the lineage of the People's Republic. If the picture were to be placed in a global framework, it would be hard for one *not* to think of "the mirage of China" as a mirror effect. On the one hand, the sign of "global China" is an effective image-sign for the country's ongoing *global* transformation; on the other hand, it is also a sign-image for the People's Republic to think of itself in terms of modern development modeled especially on North America. Yet a mirage is a mirror that exists only in the mind of the mirror-*looking* person, with the word "looking" standing here for both "looking at" and "looking for." In other words, the mirror, which is a mirage in this case, serves a *double function*—as a global image for what China wishes to be, and as a freakish looking glass for the world to comprehend itself in relation to China. Thus, this mirage functions as a mirror both for the world to look *at* itself and for the People's Republic to look *into* the mirage, partially of its own making, in order to conceptualize the world through its imaginary relationship to the Other.

However, one should note that since the mid-1990s a new countenance seems to have crept onto the face of the People's Republic as it turned its attention to the global world rather than its own past, marking an important shift in its *addressive referentiality*. Referentiality and addressivity, considered here as *analytical* rather than linguistic notions, would introduce the question of *who* is speaking or *whom* one is speaking to, rather than simply what has been said. The Maoist discourse, as well as that of the 1980s, was essentially delivered to the world of China from an insider's perspective; it was speaking to itself as a new historical emergence. This is no longer the case: the modern Other has now become the super-addressee for the People's Republic. In the 1980s, despite everyone pouring out his or her grievances against the Maoist inhumanity, the official discourse continued to address itself to itself; today, the official eye has focused on the charm of the modern Other—a contemporaneous, competitive, and yet more advanced existence in space—as its fundamental referentiality. The question of time or temporality, so essential to the Maoist conception of socialist struggles, has given way to the politics of power and wealth composed in spatial terms and geopolitical representations. This does not imply just an alteration in the message of the speech; that is, one could continue to talk about the backwardness of the Maoist years or the advancement of modern America. Nevertheless, it signals a change in the *intended direction* of the conversation. The *directionality* of a speech, which is also formed by the assumed addressee, is as significant as its message (see Bakhtin 1986; Volosinov 1973).

Within a decade or so, the Maoist mode of life and knowledge came to be seen, gradually and yet inevitably, as an irrational, superstitious (or perhaps romantic), and subjectivistic abuse of reality. The collective conscience and consciousness of the People's Republic could no longer bear the ideological remains of the Maoist years, which had to be removed entirely. This was not simply *removal* in the sense of storing something in an old drawer, along with other out-of-fashion items; it was instead a demolition, just as a high-rise building might be demolished in the very center of a large city. This removal was a collapse, a sudden collapse of self-demolition, a sudden collapse into itself as non-existence or nothingness. It was gone with one blow. The dynamite was set off from *inside* the center of the Maoist utopian city, crushing its balance of gravity and destroying its structure of architectural support, forcing it to disappear—an entire multiple-storey mansion collapsed onto the ground.

Let us start, once again, with the notion of historical materialism to illustrate how this came to be. Although it had played an important role in the official discursive formation at the time, historical materialism was then used, in its chief employment, only as an abstract signification for the official view on human emancipation as a material process. In the hands of Mao's explication, such a notion principally came to mean the inevitability of Chinese revolution, which would liberate the masses from the oppression of a semi-colonized and semi-feudal society. In this way of reading Marx as well as Lenin, the emphasis was placed on the historical inevitability of peasant revolt or revolutionary action, while the *material aspect* of historical development, in terms of the actual improvement of the material conditions of daily life, was never properly addressed. During the Cultural Revolution (1966–1976), for example, revolutionizing the superstructural realm of society became almost the only concern for a peculiar mode of governance, which, with the greater intensification of its mass campaigns, further slighted the need for any material improvement of daily life. In the course of a couple of decades, a small interstice, already implicated in the Maoist power-praxis during the land reform, grew into a prodigious rift that totally divorced theory from its practice. Historical materialism did not realize itself as a true historical force but instead became, in the hands of the Maoist government, a skeleton or a mummy of pure ideological signification. As we have shown, this mummification was indeed powerful and effective, although at the same time it inevitably introduced a self-contradiction, one inherent to all the alleged socialist revolutions in the twentieth century: it impregnated and nourished a gigantic rift between its theoretical vision of human emancipation and the actual practice of such a vision. On one side of the rift stood the ideological mummy, refracted in the glittering pyramid symbolizing the Maoist political achievements in the past; on the other side gathered the increasingly anxious and dissatisfied masses, whose life conditions had changed very little during the years of strenuous revolutionary struggles.

The reformatory era, starting in the late 1970s, was indeed an attempt to build a bridge over the prodigious rift, in order for both the government and its people to travel from one side to another. This approach reflected the new ideology of Deng's government: "It is practice, and practice alone, that can testify to the truthfulness of a theory." With this reorientation toward practice, the idea of historical materialism was given a new connotation by the government: it signified the official urge for economic development, rather than continuing the mass political campaigns, in order to improve the material conditions of life for the country. In this way, the Maoist power-praxis was "proved" to be wrong, because it had departed from the essence of historical materialism, which must be *materialistic* in terms of real development. The infrastructure or the economic base now became the official primary occupation and focus of attention. This was not a total abandonment of a mummified ideology but rather a reorientation to bring it in touch with the materiality of its own mummification. The masses had little difficulty accepting this renewed materialistic understanding of history, which would be credited or discredited based on whether there was a resultant increase of national wealth and personal earnings. The Maoist understanding of historical necessity and revolutionary inevitability was thus remade into a fatalistic metaphysic of a materialistic interpretation of history.

This materialistic conception of humankind and society, against the fading image of the Maoist call to mobilize human power and collective will, has become the new doctrine of the People's Republic. A metaphysical materialism and a materialistic comparativism have paved a new ground for its official discourse. Attention is now fixated on economic markers, such as GDP growth and salary increases, and there is a focus on comparing one's own material gains to those of others. In the mirror of this materialistic metaphysic, the Maoist years seem not only unrealistic and romanticized but indeed insane and phantasmal, for the Maoist reality could not be verified in terms of econometrical indexes, by which the world is seen as essentially quantitative and analytically statistical. This new attitude toward life has bid a historical farewell to the Maoist sentiment. The mirror is still in hand, but it has less relevance for a younger generation born after the infamous one-child policy of 1979 (see, e.g., Banister 1987), for the metaphysic needs no longer to be proved but simply to be *lived* as both knowledge and governance.

It was the birth of a materialistic metaphysic that, in conjunction with the initiation of a pragmatic attitude toward life, doomed the Maoist mode of existence. The Maoist subject could dwell only in the shadow of the masses; he could have had no individualistic life of his own, for he was only and yet always a partial author of a *we*. Likewise, the Maoist subject could not hide himself away from those collective demands at the time, for the human will, represented by the masses of the people as its author, is by definition and in nature transindividualistic. The power of this transindividualistic signification proved itself in the struggles of the time, with people willing to die for the Maoist cause. If this is taken as a different kind of humanism, defined by its collective authorship and by its ultimate goal for the hope of a total human emancipation, then the reformatory initiation ritual could be equated to an epistemological circumcision on human will and potency. No longer a powerful signification, the masses of the people became "a lonely crowd" (e.g., Riesman 1961) to be fed and clothed, or were bundled in statistical yearbooks as a taxonomical collection of quantifiable individuals. The government's attention shifted to the lives of individuals as "citizens" in a material world. This individualistic outlook in life is now called "humanistic" because the material conditions of daily life came to be a central concern for the government.

The grounding of the social world, which used to bear the weight of the masses of the people, has shifted to one in favor of a modern, individualistic self-apprehension. If one could say that in the Maoist world it was the *political* that predominated over its discursive field, one would have to say that it is the *sociological* that has constituted the primary official concern today. Unlike anthropology, the academic fields of applied sociology, social welfare, and social policies are booming in a way that is astonishing and yet somewhat disproportional. Implicitly, the practical orientation in sociology, and the social sciences in general, demonstrates a tendency that is similar to what has been shown in the statistical yearbooks. Contrary to the Maoist years, if there is any commonality among individuals that can be measured from the outside by means of statistical analysis and tabulation, it will be the material desire that each is struggling with. That is, there is no commonality among individuals except for their preoccupation with their salaries or drinking patterns or preference for luxury cars. It is *sameness*, rather than difference, that has come to represent the commonality of individuals today, which is a commonality external to the individuals in consideration.

Contrary to the Maoist appeal to the human will for organizing individual differences into a totalizing power, individuals today seem only to *resemble* each other. Their differences are seen as purely external in terms of salaries and other material possessions. In the vast world of the People's Republic, individuals have become exactly the *same individual*, despite a proliferation of statistical differences. Although during the Maoist years almost everyone presented an identical physical appearance, each person was thought of as different in his or her essential qualities. Today, one may look entirely different in appearance, but, in the fundamental definition of a person, everyone is thought of as a bee in the hive of society. There is no essential or qualitative difference from one bee to another, except for his luck or position in the hive. It is this sameness that has paved the way for a great amount of external individual differences—all of which make up the *same man*. This man, a new man in an old coat, who escaped the imprisonment of the Maoist power-praxis, is now drawn to an irresistible force of *narcissism*, reflected by and refracted in his burning material desires and eager egocentric concerns. With bitter collective struggles still lingering in the background of his memory, he has now obtained a sharp vision and a pair of quick eyes that are prone to turning red either for shortage of sound sleep or for envying his neighbors and colleagues who are surpassing him in the race for wealth. Whatever profession he is engaged in, he tends to keep his heart close to that of an accountant, who will calculate everything possible for selling or purchasing according to the best available price on the market, which nowadays is a global market. He may not be a businessman, but he is far better than one; he is a super-entrepreneur by birth and in his essentials. He may not be charitable, but he is very competitive—the living embodiment of "the Chinese spirit of capitalism" (Redding 1990)—and perhaps has not yet been affected by Protestant ethics (Weber 1958).

This new man, as a reincarnation of an old spirit, keeps his eyes wide open, both at work and at home, checking and examining how everyone around him—his neighbors, colleagues, and friends—*manage* their lives. Life has become a management of material things, comparable to and measurable in terms of other people's possessions. It is no wonder that an MBA degree is now seen in the popular imagination as a great achievement in life, for it has become the best means for acquiring knowledge of what a man needs for material success. In a sense, this man does not concern himself with the mechanism of the solar system or a world of concerns beyond his immediate material interests; he tends to care more about whether Newton's apple will fall into *his* garden. Far more close to the worms and insects of the earth in his mode of thinking, he is thus indeed a man "from the soil" (cf. Fei 1992). Being a realist of a different kind, his life orientation is earthy and worldly, that is, materialistic and narcissistic. He is materialistic because he is narcissistic; he is narcissistic because he is materialistic. He reads the financial news more carefully than anything else and checks the stock market on the Internet every few hours. He often looks at himself in a huge mirror, well situated in his bedroom, in order to see how he appears in the eyes of others, who are now thought of as universally the same as himself in both mind and character. In a nutshell, the center of his world is focused on himself as its gravitational core, from which the material world and its interests are to be perceived and understood. Thus, with the assistance of official statistics, his world has become one of minute calculations for the sake of competition and material gain, whether foreseeable or not.

The administration of this earthy and worldly creature has come to be understood by the government as *analogous* to the management of things in the material world. That is, the transformative transition from the Maoist years to the present age may be understood as one from the *management of people* to the *administration of things*, which has required a statisticalization of society. This is what has happened: in "the long march" of a parochial modern development, the People's Republic has been statisticalized to the extent that data, analysis, and tabulations have come to constitute a *necessary* means for the administration of things, including the enormous population. It is certain that the human will should *not* be given a significant office in this emergent *managerial* government, which believes in modern technology and objective social sciences that attempt to reduce meaning, whether socio-historical or politio-cultural, to its material effectuality. The effect of power, according to this conception, is nothing but a powerful effect, measured and measurable by statistical means from an end point of view. This is, of course, a totally different conception of man and his world from the Maoist mode of life and knowledge, which built itself on a life horizon of intentionality and human will. The People's Republic, having departed from the Maoist years, now walks on a path trod already by many others, past and present. A number of old and obvious Anglo-Saxon signposts, such as Thomas Hobbes, John Locke, David Hume, Adam Smith, Jeremy Bentham, James Mill, and John Stuart Mill, could well indicate the itinerary—utilitarian in its vision—of such a journey. What is *new* is not the pavement being trod upon once again by a clumsy new leviathan; instead, what is refreshing is the renovation of an old sentiment. Not only will this new crowd on the path make a difference to the scene itself, which may be called "globalization," but also, and perhaps more importantly, it will redefine the meaning of such a journey as *becoming*. A historically unprecedented renovation of the *interiority of being* has come about, and this has made the People's Republic a global spectacle and a mirage—*the mirage of China*.[1]

Along with the emergence of a different mentality of governance, in and for the People's Republic, there also came a redesigned or renovated "structure of feelings" in the life-world of everyday experience. If a history of the present may be written as *a history of mentality*, it must also be, simultaneously, *a history of sentimentality*, for which, in the case of China, a narcissistic selfhood and a materialistic metaphysic have supplied the life vitamins for the present moment. Against the Maoist sentimentality, which was humanistic in its own way, the delivery of a new sentiment was made, on the ruins of the Maoist revolution, as an immediate reaction or rebellion.

A Silicon Valley entrepreneur once spoke at a dinner gathering about his experience of leaving China to study law at Northwestern University. After graduating in the mid-1990s, he decided to join a group of young men and set up a computer company to work on software design. They succeeded in selling the start-up for a large profit a couple of years later, and the entrepreneur, whom we will call Brad, went to work for other big corporations in Silicon Valley. With the rapid rise of China's economy at the time, he made himself a significant figure in the consulting business and built up his connections all over the world, advising on investment in China's new economic zones. With earnest admiration and almost envious eyes, several guests, chiefly Chinese, whose experiences of the Maoist years made them a perfect audience, could not help but be amazed. Brad turned the conversation in an unexpected direction, as if he were responding to the puzzled faces of his guests, and proclaimed: "Well, as you know, history is a material struggle. Marx himself taught us this very fact. The Maoist revolution was a total failure because it did not pay attention to *material* development. The focus was on violence and fights, not on gaining wealth and material power. Human emancipation means to take everyone out of his poverty, doesn't it?" His house, which was huge and newly decorated, was brightened by a row of beautifully arranged ceiling lights and had a shining bathroom resembling the presidential suites of a five-star

---

1. This study can be seen as a *prosopographic* study—that is, a study of individual traits—by means of genealogizing genetic connections with regard to socio-political origins and historio-geological locations. In such an enormous assemblage, these aspects have made up the modern family of "difference and repetition" (see, e.g., Deleuze 1994).

hotel in Saudi Arabia. Brad continued: "Well, as you all know, even Marx said that in order to save the people, the majority of the people, you have to save yourself first. That is, until one emancipates oneself from poverty, one will not be able to emancipate any other man, let alone the majority of the people. I think that Marx was right and that Mao was wrong when he urged everyone to serve the people. It is a most stupid idea to say that one has to help all other people before one can look after oneself properly. Unfortunately, we lived in the past according to such an ignorant idea for so many years."

His confidence and eloquence excited a momentary silence. Then a timid and slightly trembling voice was heard from the far end of the dining table: "I think you made a mistake, and Marx said just the opposite—that the proletarian can emancipate himself *if and only if* he emancipates the entire world. Is it not so?" Indeed, this is what Marx had said, and several guests knew it—but not Brad. According to Marx, one's freedom is conditioned by the freedom of everyone else. The flush on Brad's face was due only to the best Napa wine, and he continued: "That means exactly the same as what I have just said. History is material, and this is what Marx taught us. How can you help anyone else if you yourself need help? If you do not have a lot of things in the first place, how can you give anything to other people?" Brad did not feel the need to respond to the Marxist challenge, which concerned moral rather than material wealth. The key to this exchange, which resembled many similar dinner conversations in and about the People's Republic, was Brad's abuse of Marx's aphorism casting the proletarian as the historical agent for the emancipation of humanity. There is nothing wrong with presenting a different approach to understanding man and his destiny, but it was troubling to hear a dialogue in which Marx was being used to argue against his own doctrines. Brad's generation is that of the Maoist children, but their memory has been reformulated by a narcissistic materialism that has been nurtured by transnational capital and digital capitalism. It was against such materialism that Marx took a stand almost two centuries ago, yet he was now being half-preserved as a materialist and half-reversed into a supporter of the individualistic or narcissistic sentiment of the new man in and of the People's Republic.

Of course, Marx was not what Brad said he was. One's eyes tend to be blinded from within oneself, and it seems as if a new faith has obscured Brad's vision, leading him to see only things he wants to see, even in Marx. Brad's memory appears to have been remade by his new desires, which have little to do with his remembrance of Marx's ideology. The point is that the new man arising from the horizon of the People's Republic cannot believe in any truth other than what he sees with his own eyes. The gravity of his world is the world of himself as a gravitational force, both centrifugal and centripetal at once: centrifugal when he thinks of other people in terms of himself; centripetal when he thinks of himself in terms of other people. It is a dual-dimensional psyche that, either way, is attracted to the gravitational hub of one's own struggle in life. This is by no means a *humanistic* reorientation, as has been thought. In the mirror of today's China, which is a mirage, one can get a glimpse of this diploid personality: a narcissistic self standing on the emerging skyline of a new world tries to speak a humanistic sort of language that is no longer refreshing to the inflamed ears of an old man known as Europe. This is indeed different from the Maoist conception of self and the world. The spirit of the present age (cf. Kierkegaard 1962), both within and outside the People's Republic, has come to reside in the body of "the selfish gene" (e.g., Dawkins 1989), in which a demystifying mystification has allegedly demonstrated that life, far richer than human existence alone, is universally determined by the law of irresistible narcissistic gravitation.[2]

Epistemology II: Objectivity and Corporeality

A delightful discovery is that sociology has ferreted out the formation of a middle class, on the debris of the Maoist revolution, as a positive sign of modern development for the People's Republic. From the mid-1990s onward, the idea of "middle class" has become a tedious obsession of the discipline of sociology, a redecorated temple of social sciences in China. On the other end of the same ideological spectrum of this socio-*logical* operation stand the various marginalized groups, such as laid-off workers and rural migrant laborers, who have experienced the entirely opposite effects of China's economic growth. The cohabitation of such differences in the actual experience of reform should be understood as an effect of the double development in the vast province of the People's Republic, where there has existed a *dual-organization* of its social world. "One country, two systems," a political slogan referring to China's official policy toward regaining ruling power over Hong Kong and Macao, is an excellent characterization of the dual production of reality within the People's Republic. There are two, if not more, worlds of social experience, but they are no longer viewed as antagonistic or contradictory forces in society. In the trembling hand of an eager, perhaps good-willed, sociologist who believes in universal science, this reality of *differences in kind* could always be reduced to *differences in degree*, that is, a kind of difference measured or measurable in statistical or quantitative terms. To the sociological mind, which officiates reality, difference should always be *calculable* and *computable*—the new dogma of an old faith.

The underlying quantitative unification has arranged everyone according to a matrix of statistical differences, such as the percentage of income or salary increases, and has redrawn a map of social positions, according to which people

---

2. For an anthropological critique of sociobiology, see Sahlins (1977).

can see themselves as "objective" social beings. To "the happy consciousness" of the sociologist, whose power and influence has come to be recognized by the state, statistical classification or calculation is no longer understood as a purely analytical tool; it is now an instrument for objectification of both reality and self. Hence, statistical analysis, with all its power to synthesize and serialize, has become the scientific cradle for a new sense of self by which individuals may be related to each other through quantitative comparison and classification. For example, peasants are no longer poor or rich, good or bad; they are instead processed as tabulations according to, for instance, their annual incomes and are placed in the tiny grids of a statistical yearbook. This new sense of self, insofar as the People's Republic is concerned, has allowed the birth of an objectifiable subject whose material condition of life has become a man-measurement for life in general.

Such is the transformation taking place in the People's Republic today. The rise of statistical reasoning, in the name of a universal science and sealed by the governmental stamp, has begun to refurbish the interior space of a subject who has come to see his or her family members, neighbors, friends, and colleagues in materialistic and objectifiable terms. There is no longer essential difference, that is, *difference in kind*, such as in class struggle or social contradiction; instead, social cleavages or political gaps are now taken as calculated or calculable *differences in degree*. It appears that even intimacy and moral value may also be made into their material equivalences by means of statistical or econometric reductions. It is on the devastating ruins of the Maoist years that this new mode of mentality and sentimentality has come into being, and it is the delivery of itself as a "second occurrence" that demands our attention. The notion of the *secondary* is important here. All of the statistical means and formulas of analysis are not new in themselves; however, the refurbishment of a subjective interiority has made an *authentic* difference. The authenticity of this experience is neither "other modernity" nor "alternative modernity" (see, e.g., Feenberg 1995); it is instead "Time and the Other" (cf. Fabian 1983) as *secondary modernity*, which is renovation *in and as* innovation. This must be what globalization means: simulacrum *as and in* an authentic production (see, e.g., Baudrillard 1983).

Statistical analysis totalizes, although in a way that is different from that of the Maoist power-praxis. The Maoist machinery totalized through a mystical appeal to a collective imaginary, made of a hegemonic *we*, demanding endless mass campaigns as "totalizing totalizations," to borrow a term from Jean-Paul Sartre (2004); today, in contrast, it is a *totalized* totalization that defines and analyzes the conditions of life from an external or externalizing point of view, requiring no interior praxis as a precondition for this objectified or objectifiable subjectivity. In the Maoist years, it was the political appropriation of the *we* that defined or created the interiority of the subject; today, in contrast, totalization is made from a subjective *outside* that has been statisticalized. The relationship of a person to the whole in the Maoist years required interiorization of the subject in the name of the masses of the people; today, in contrast, it has become a calculation of one's possession *in relation* to other possessions, statistical and comparative. In the Maoist years, to live was to experience the politics of subjection, relational and total, defined in terms of a common goal; today, in contrast, life has become a battle for "the survival of the fittest" in terms of material gains and concerns. The Maoist politics of subjection demanded a constant articulation of the "I" to the "We"; today, in contrast, statistical tabulation or analysis has allowed the "I" to be related to other such "I's" in indifferently quantifiable terms. In the Maoist years, no one could entirely escape from the political demand to interiorize the collective good under the common pronoun of the *we*; today, in contrast, there is no way for one to be truly part of anyone else *except* through statistical tabulation. In other words, the Maoist politics of subjection started from the collective whole in order to shape each individual into a person who was greater than him- or herself; today, in contrast, the technology of the self begins with the person as an individual in order to collect assemblages of his or her social traits.

Thus, solidarity, which is ideological and imaginary, has become an assemblage, that is, a togetherness achieved by physical or material accumulation, like piling up a stack of potatoes. In such a conception, an individual is no longer a person. The subject has been objectified by means of this assembling technique, and statistical analysis, with its efficiency and effectivity, has created an individualistic grounding for being in the world. These days, the saying goes that the individual makes up society, not the other way around. The "I" is not—and should not be—made or conditioned by an interiorizing force derived from a "we." Individuals should not be asked to sacrifice themselves for the imaginary phantom of the totalizing project, be it for the benefit of the nation or the world. Today's logicality asserts that it must be the other way around; the state or the government must accept each individual as a natural and biological existence in and for its own right. This is the *reverse* of the Maoist self, whose life was defined by and in "serving the people." Ironically, the highest value of life was death for a worthy cause. "The Chinese people are suffering; it is our duty to save them, and we must exert ourselves in struggle. Wherever there is struggle, there is sacrifice, and death is a common occurrence. But we have the interests of the people and the sufferings of the great majority at heart, and when we die for the people, it is a worthy death. Nevertheless, we should do our best to avoid unnecessary sacrifices. Our cadres must show concern for every soldier, and all the people in the revolutionary ranks must care for each other, must love and help each other" (Mao 2001, 311). Recited by everyone during the Cultural Revolution, this message clearly stated the importance of death in the service of a good cause. "Serving the people" was not considered a given quality of any individual; rather, it was looked on as a *required praxis* for being or becoming good in the Maoist society. It was a goal, internalized and yet internalizing, to be achieved by means of practice. It has been against this Maoist conception of life as a struggle that the naturalistic and utilitarian mode of life and knowledge has fought its battles.

Few social scientists in the People's Republic would have read John Locke's *Treatises on Government*, but the idea of natural law (see, e.g., Russell 1945, 624) seems to have been accepted by the generation of scholars growing up on the rubble of the Maoist revolution. John Locke and other utilitarian philosophers might not even be relevant here, but it is true that implicit meanings, embodied or embedded in popular media such as Internet novels or Hollywood dramas, have been sought after by an audience eager to find a way out of the Maoist prison house. The vocabulary of humanism has therefore become current, but its language is more individualistic in character. For example, to define life in terms of death, no matter how worthy it might be, is now seen as anti-humanistic, for it is said to be against human nature. To an outsider's ear, today's opinion, which views natural laws as laws of nature that are meant to be a guidebook for understanding human nature, seems to sound like a remote echo from a distant past. There is, of course, a faltering history of conceptual development of the European notion of nature and its humanization (see, e.g., Collingwood 1960), but this has not gained much attention in the People's Republic. The essential scheme of the present age is to turn all things upside down through a reversal of the Maoist morality and reason, to burn the Maoist past down to its ashes in order to allow modern life—narcissistic and individualistic—to be seen as evidence of a global arrival.

Statistical analysis also exteriorizes. On the ruins of the Maoist revolution arrived a proud fellow of statistical science, professing objectivity and neutrality. The Maoist self, at least in its idealistic form, was so interiorized as to be visible only in an unrelenting struggle against itself for the hope of achieving the greater good, which was *invisible*. The "man-measurement" in this case was measurable only by means of a greater man, a *we*, a phantasmal figure or monster produced by the Maoist super-story. Such a conception presupposed the contradictory nature of social existence: *to be* was to struggle, and this struggle was not only endless—captured by the Maoist term "perpetual revolution"— but also *internal*. The visibility of the means, which made up the self and social struggles for the common good, was produced by the invisibility of a phantasmal end, which, although it was never achieved by the Maoist government, provided the incentive for continuing the struggles that required a perpetual effort in deepening the well inside oneself. That well, from which the spring of life originated, is now perhaps gone forever, as the People's Republic has begun to walk at the global pace. Quetelet's notion of "the average man," celebrated as an epistemological revolution in the 1980s, has required of a person no internal depth; it is simply a man measured from outside himself. The Maoist self, seen in the eyes of the average man, is a madman, a lunatic in the strict sense of the term. In his place has come the average man—of a second or a third birth, perhaps—delivered and taken care of by the midwife of statistical reasoning. The leveling effect, understood by the average man as scientific objectivity and neutrality, is to externalize or exteriorize the self according to a numerical seriality. The notion of the masses of the people therefore represented, in a historical aporia, a real opposition to the idea of the average man, a person who can examine himself only from an external perspective. This new man, the average man, does not believe in the spring of life from within himself; instead, he sees the world of wealth and development with a comparative mind.

The average man represents an exteriorization of the self, whose image is now more like a storehouse than a well. To his mind, development has become a race in the field of wealth. Hence it is that economic indexes such as the GDP per capita have become an important measurement of developmental distance, from one individual to another, from one neighborhood to another, from one province to another, from one country to another—namely, from one storehouse to another. The average man is no longer a living self, for his life has been exteriorized by the numerical seriality whose visibility has become the definitional criterion for self identity or identification. The rational average man could be a consumer, a share-holder, a factory worker, a scholar, or anyone else defined from outside himself; but he can no longer drink the water from within himself as a source of becoming. The feeling of the average man may resemble aspects of Einstein's theory of relativity, according to which time could be turned into space or, in the sociological mind of the present age, morality into materiality, or difference in *kind* into difference in *degree*. It is no wonder that social scientists of the People's Republic keenly search for every new computerized tool of statistical or quantitative analysis. Only now can such an eager interest, coming out of the Maoist apoplexy, be understood as a technology of self that strives to see oneself in terms of quantitative equivalences and permutations of materialistic others. "The Other is a Hell" only if one cannot endure such a systematization of equivalence and permutation, if one cannot see a way out of the trap of materialistic competition. From the governmental point of view, nothing is invisible if the systematization of materialistic comparability is properly established. The average man, from the sovereign viewpoint, is no more than an ant in the anthill.

In retrospection, the Maoist years never achieved what the government claimed, while in contrast the present age has accomplished far more than it is aware of. From the vantage point of the present time, the Maoist man was like a drunk who believed that he could climb up to the clouds, whereas today's individual is more practical, believing only in what is palpable and visible. The Maoist man's heart was chiefly touched or touchable by a super-story, whereas today's individual is an observant man who attentively watches everything happening around him. He will resort to his own "participant observation" to verify and confirm whether the grass in his neighbor's yard is greener than his. It is therefore not surprising that in various kinds of media there has been a growing interest in comparing living costs across regional and national boundaries, for it is a way of determining where one stands in the "great chain of developmental being."

The adventure of statistical reasoning has infiltrated almost every corner of an elephantine world, resulting in a gradual and persistent systematization of quantitative classification and analysis. Statistical yearbooks, as a symbolic and synoptic representation, allegedly scientific and objective, of economic development, are viewed as mathematical evidence of national achievement. Statistical figures seem to have gained a family life by producing their own posterities and descendants, generating more numbers as hard facts. It is difficult to see whether the facts or the numbers representing them came first, for they seem to make up a promiscuous, polygamous lineage whose children, after a few generations, are identifiable only by a totemic claim of scientific objectivity. There is no way to establish parentage because promiscuity and polygamy have muddled the genetic connections. This totemism, not unlike that described by Claude Lévi-Strauss (1966) in his anthropological critique of the Freudian theory of totem and taboo, represents a peculiar mode of thinking that is *universal* if not global. In this totemic belief, no distinction is made between a man and his totem, say, a lion. Similarly, there is no difference between materialization and statisticalization of social reality, which is now seen purely as the work of development. Analogous to the totemic system that exemplifies the savage mind, no distinction is made between the objectified and the objectifying; both are representable only by the statistical datum. The world of the People's Republic, in its mind and reality, has become a material externality that can be captured by itself only in terms of a numerical seriality. The reality and *its representation* have melded into one process of statisticalization rather than being separated or even separable. In this new, totemic politics, *true growth* has come to mean the *growth of truth*. Both are supposed to be handled by the magicians of the state, whose offices are comfortably located in the enormous building of the National Bureau of Statistics. That is, materiality, which is the key word for a new age, is nothing but a numerical seriality, statisticalized and yet statisticalizing.

The parochial visit of a global agent has reified statistical reasoning in and for the People's Republic, in whose province a "lonely crowd" has eagerly joined the Olympic race for power and wealth. The materialistic and quantitative configuration of reality has helped construct an "objective" platform for the masses to wait, patiently or not, for the developmental train to arrive. For those ahead of others in line, the distance from China to America is no more than a few thousand dollars, statistically measured in their respective GDP per capita and other quantifiable categories. The statistical yearbook has come to function, for those waiting on the platform, as a real Yahoo map for the global world. Seeing, in this case, means to calculate. Shown in the statistical yearbook are not two national geographies separated by the Pacific Ocean but a *developmental map*, a distance in terms of growth and resources that are quantifiable and statisticalized. To shorten the distance—that is, to travel faster on the global path of growth—has become a predominant concern for both the government and its subjects.

The emergence of statistical reasoning in the vast continent of the People's Republic has also made its social world *corporealized*. This is not simply because national, international, and transnational corporations have become a predominant force in policy making and development, but also because the spirit of life has become *corporeal*—in the sense that life has become nothing but a *regurgitation* of itself. Today, if one were to question the corporeality of our world, one would be seen, from an "objective" point of view, as a Don Quixote attempting to fight against the monstrous windmills, which are supposed to be real and natural. In this way, the reality of the People's Republic has become a *corporeality*, tangible and palpable. Statistical objectification or quantification in general has constituted a means for ordinary people to live such a reality of the corporeal: corporeality is the reality of *homo œconomicus*; corporeality is the reality of growth and its meticulous calculations; corporeality is the reality of self-interests and its materialistic manifestations; corporeality is the reality of "the wealth of the nations" on a global stage. The term "corporealization," exemplified in a case like this, has a double signification: *corporationalization* of a national economy, on the one hand, and *corporealization* of its life-world of everyday life, on the other hand. As soon as one sees how new models of cars have been produced and purchased, adding extra burdens to the already congested cities, one would perhaps understand the reality of the corporeal, which has made itself visible everywhere in the materialistic world of today's China. With the assistance of statistical analysis, this reality of the corporeal has been made comparable to other similar realities.

The comparability of such different social realities comes from its corporeal assumption of the basic equivalence of all social worlds. It is therefore no surprise that government officials of the People's Republic nowadays wish to demonstrate their knowledge or memory of national or regional statistical figures as proof of their capabilities. An official's ability to recite certain precise figures of economic performance might indeed impress the CEOs of Boeing or Microsoft. Seen from the historical horizon of contemporary China, a topographical change has allowed the immigration of a different mentality of governance and a different mode of knowledge, although the sentiment avowed may not be historically innovative if one were to look further back in time. As Arthur Lyon

Bowley stated: "As economists and statisticians, we are not concerned with palliatives or expedients (for reducing poverty), but are concerned with correct knowledge and an exact diagnosis of the extent of these evils, for which reasoned and permanent remedies can then be developed" (quoted in Desrosières 1998, 224). This was, in fact, Bowley's presidential address to the economic section of the Royal Statistical Society at the beginning of the twentieth century. After a long political struggle over the problem of measuring poverty in England, a social division of labor seems to have been firmly established. At roughly the same time, Max Weber made the known distinction between "the scholar and the politician" (see, e.g., Aron 1970, 185–193). What was said by Bowley is not new to us, since we live in the contemporary world where statistical knowledge plays a crucial role. But what is interesting to note is that at the end of the twentieth century, in another part of the world, it seemed as if Bowley had been reincarnated and Weber brought back to life—but with a difference: the governmental officials themselves had become the most ardent statisticians.

In order for statisticians to function in society as "objective scientists," there should be a distinction between the scholar and the politician. The complication in this case is that scholars became officials of the state, which saw itself as battling against the Maoist irrationality. For the intellectual who suffered under the Maoist regime, nothing is more desirable these days than becoming an official. The scientific scholar, it is believed, should be responsible for making decisions about development. If history is always *written* (see, e.g., White 1973), then the writing must be a *rewriting*. Rewriting is an innovation insofar as it is a production of new feelings or sentiments and not simply a replication or repetition in the normal sense of the term. The taming of chance in the world of China should therefore be seen as an innovative replication, because it has produced a new leviathan. "Probability has two aspects. It is connected with the degree of belief warranted by evidence, and it is connected with the tendency, displayed by some chance devices, to produce stable relative frequencies" (Hacking 1975, 1). It is such a twin birth—of both evidence and the power of large numbers—that has given rise to a new sentimentalization in the People's Republic. The statisticalization has produced, in this gigantic social world, an objectifying discourse, constituting a form of political reasoning that is essential for the ongoing economic development. The Maoist claims came to be seen as teleological and deterministic due to such an epistemological rupture. Today, almost a decade into a new century, when the specter of Marx, both within and outside the People's Republic, has sunk into oblivion, one cannot help but notice another deterministic tone, one that is statisticalistic and comparativistic. It is, however, a different kind of determinism, necessity in a new mask, that has come into existence.

If one may say of the Maoist years that they were brutal, one would have to say of the present age that it is pitiful. While "speaking bitterness" is no longer an officially sanctioned mass sentiment, "groaning and moaning" have arrived on the predominantly televised stage of public performance. Today's elephantine world of the People's Republic, transformed by mass media of various kinds, has turned itself into an enormous performance platform, where groaning and moaning have characterized its comic as well as tragic scenarios. These performances are so well done that it is hard to distinguish narcissism from nausea. Of the two, the latter tends to register an actual pain, either physiological or social, whereas the former reflects egocentrism. With or without reference to the Lacanian theory, we know too well that in today's world the real is a phantom. However, it is perhaps harder to think of the suffering of a dying patient as his just deserts simply because he lacks sufficient competitiveness in a neo-Malthusian world. There is, or should be, a clear difference between a Peking University professor who complains that his salary (ranging from a few thousand to a few hundred thousand Chinese dollars) is too low and insufficient for his research and a poor Henan peasant who is inflicted with the AIDS virus as a result of selling his blood to earn money and who cannot manage his medical bills. The real is not rational in such cases as these; nor is the real entirely phantasmal. The performative world into which we are drawn nowadays, exemplified in and by the world of China, has blurred the necessary boundaries between narcissistic and nauseous pains, whether social or personal, pathological or physiological, material or metaphysical.

From the vantage point of the CCTV, the equivalent of the CNN or the BBC, diluting the pupils of the audience and making their hearts pump heavily should and must be the priority of the performative purpose: the phantom must be *produced* from the real, and vice versa. The CCTV seems to have come to play the role of a Lacanian analyst, who, holding *Les écrits techniques de Freud* firmly in hand, hopes to transform the real into the imaginary in the minds of the mass audience, who in turn recognize nothing but their own *real* imaginaries. The disjuncture—or rather the conjuncture of a postmodern vision of reality with the emergence of a neo-Malthusian world—became a real historical existence that was possible *only* because of the mediation of the mass media; that is, its logicality is totally made of performativity, pure and simple. It should be no surprise that in such a conjuncture of historical influence, the masses of the people, once a collective author, have been turned into various kinds and degrees of mass audiences. Having been stripped off their authorship and agency, they have become a massive recipient of the performative effectivity.

If one may say of the Maoist years that they were ferocious, one would have to say of the present age that it is ruthless. The masses are no longer called on to take part in various kinds of political campaigns, and individuals are allowed greater freedom with regard to personal choices and preferences (see, e.g., Davis 1995). The "street corner society" of any urban center in the People's Republic now resembles that of other cosmopolitan regions of the world.

Instead of an enormous bicycling horde, so emblematic and characteristic of the Maoist urban space, nowadays a dreadful multitude of cars make up the scene of congested rush hour traffic in most major cities. Sitting comfortably in the leather seat of a brand new car, one might not be able to resist the temptation of checking oneself in the rearview mirror, where a plastic smile or a quiver of pretentious anxiety might be visible. The street scene is a good place to observe history; memories may come up, unexpectedly or unwillingly, to disturb pleasant ruminations on the present day. Let us take a turn and dwell on an ethnographic observation of what is happening on today's streets of a prosperous city in South China.

The street was spectacular. It was elegantly guarded by two beautiful lines of fine trees on both sides of the pavement, behind which were marvelous skyscrapers. Cars of different sizes and shapes were moving slowly on the wide, newly paved avenue. When I arrived, my first sensation was one of intense curiosity and excitement. The city was colorful, lively, dynamic, modern, and green. Walking around as an ethnographer who was working on a project in another southern city, my pleasant meditation was interrupted by an urban scene. In front of a luxurious seafood restaurant, a mother, holding a small baby in her arms, was trying to grab things to eat from a waste bin by the road. The woman was young—perhaps in her mid-twenties or even younger—clean, and fair-skinned, and was dressed in a white shirt and blue jeans. She was sitting on the pavement with her legs crossed and had placed her baby between her knees. The waste bin, which looked heavy, was sure to contain some edible items because of its location. With one hand reaching out, revealing a rusty stubble under her armpit, and holding the waste bin toward herself, the mother took out refuse and ate it. She must have been very hungry. Pawing at the mother's nipples with little hands, the baby was also eager to have its share.

By standing a little bit away from the scene, one could observe the street life better. There were chiefly five kinds of people on the street. People of the first kind were men, who were the most fully represented and also the most varied within their kind. Some were bald, usually well-dressed in ties and suits, holding briefcases in their hands; some were younger, dressed perhaps not so well, but with a similar kind of countenance. Some went where they had to go in a self-effacing and gingery shuffle, paying no attention to anyone else on the street; some moved steadily with their jaws jutting out, as if to tell the world that they were the true masters of the city; still others were almost running, as if they were about to miss their trains or flights. Most people of the first kind did not pay attention to the young mother and her baby on the pavement, or if they did, it was only with indifference and haste. Their reactions seemed to be saying that such a scene should be taken as nothing but a usual disturbing inconvenience of urban life in a new era. People of the second kind were cheerful, a mixture of men and women, often in pairs or small groups; their heads turned around restlessly when they were walking; they were joyful, quite loud but not threatening. They were the kind of people who tended to whirl about with a fluttery, directionless verve. A couple of them almost stepped on the foot of the young mother, but they bounced away immediately, still laughing and seemingly determined not to be disturbed by anything unpleasant. People of the third kind resembled the first in some respects, but they were predominantly young females. They were also quite gay and joyful but in a much less noisy way. When they walked, they tended to chat with each other, holding in their hands small plastic boxes that probably contained their lunches. Several of them were in a uniform of a dark blue color. Their countenance demonstrated a slight weariness, and when they saw the young mother and her child, they seemed to show a quick sympathy but then walked away. People of the fourth kind were men, often quite young, and their clothing seemed to indicate their rural origins. They stood apart on corners or edged their way sideways through the parting crowds; they did not talk like other people; they either muttered to themselves or attentively watched those who passed by. From time to time, they would make an effort to speak to a passerby. They looked around carefully but paid no attention at all to the scene of the mother and her child. People of the fifth kind were young, always in skirts or tights or jeans. It seemed as if they were not entirely sure who they were supposed to be or where they were heading; they seemed to be idling around without any particular purpose. They stood there motionless for a minute and walked again for another, but they often only circled around within a circumscribed area. When they saw the young mother by the waste bin, they stared at the scene with disgust and abhorrence.

This was Shenzhen at the turn of a new century, a famous city symbolizing "the South China miracle" of a great economic boom (see, e.g., C.-K. Lee 1998). Almost a twin birth, the booming economy arrived together with a new structure of inequality and disparity in the People's Republic. The official slogan of the 1980s—"to get rich is glorious"—was an expression of the belief that economic differentiation is a necessary condition for any primary accumulation of wealth. Behind such a shift in the moral outlook of a new leviathan facing economic transformation lies the pain of development. Once again, beggars have become a common phenomenon in Chinese cities. Poverty itself is far less a problem than the attitude toward it: hardly any attention was paid to the young mother in this case. The intention is not to point out a tiny mole on the shining skin of a stunningly beautiful model, but it seems, at least to myself, an extreme difficulty to avoid such an ethnographic encumbrance, which has come to symbolize a crucial feature of the corporeality in the People's Republic today. The government is now paying attention to problems such as this with its new policies and hopes for developing "a harmonious society," and different kinds of philanthropic institutions of official and non-official organizations have been attempted.

However, "a structure of feelings," to borrow a phrase from Raymond Williams, has prevailed in the vast continent of the People's Republic. In contrast to the Maoist years of collective violence and political struggles, this new structure of feelings may be seen as the emergence of narcissistic *indifference*, the growth of an intense and excessive egocentric concern with one's own well-being coupled with minimal attention to the sufferings of others. The attitude of indifference came at the same time when the narcissistic selfhood was born. There are benign individuals who help other people today, just as individuals did during the Maoist years. However, if a historical contrast were to be drawn, it would be impossible to avoid the impression of *a rupture* of sentiment: the Maoist madness of group or collective entanglement has been replaced by a narcissistic individualism. If we were to return to the street scene in Shenzhen, we would see the stunning contrast: inside the seafood restaurant was a noisy crowd, gulping down delicious seafood while being attended to by uniformed waitresses; outside, a young mother, holding a baby on her knees, swallowed the dirty leftovers. And yet hardly anyone paid attention to the contrast, which was perhaps already a common scene in the city. Businessmen, tourists, female factory workers, various kinds of street corner people, working girls on the street—all seemed to share a similar attitude of indifference.

Indifference also implies a certain sort of *tolerance*. The Maoist government had forbidden begging, which was viewed as a criminal act and was punished severely. Nowadays, begging has almost become a profession, and this does not seem to bother either the government or its citizens. This is indeed a "transvaluation of values," following Nietzsche in his use of the term. "We know what transmutation or transvaluation means for Nietzsche: not a change of values, but a change in the element from which the value of values derives" (Deleuze 1983, 171). It is a double change: a change in the structure of feelings, on the one hand, and a change in the authorship and its essential interests, on the other; it is a change of personhood, on the one hand, and a change of the order of things in the worldliness of the world, on the other. As if it were an old man wishing to walk on a new path in order to become a new leviathan, statistical or quantitative analysis as a mode of life and governance has made itself a beloved and needed crane, which has helped the new leviathan to objectify the objectivity of the world. The corporeality that has developed on the ruins of the Maoist revolution is also a reality of indifference.

Epistemology III: Mass and Massification

With the Maoist mass campaigns no longer a factor, another kind of *massification* has arrived. Statistical measurements and tabulations have come to play an important role for such a new and yet different mode of massification. Either to be massified or to massify, that is, either to be objectified or to objectify in this new fashion, it is inevitable to be statisticalized in the first place. Probability theory, regression analysis, sampling survey, and many other aspects of statistical knowledge are not only a necessary means for government administration but have also become a decisive instrument for self-comprehension. Statistical tools have always been, past and present, essential to the modern machinery, and "the mirage of China" has added a further *corporeal mystification*. The idea of mass campaigns and mass movements was established during the Maoist years, whose images include huge crowds of people, exuberant and violent, marching in the streets. From a social science point of view, especially if cast from across the Pacific Ocean, the Maoist period must be thought of as one of "mass politics" (e.g., Shue 1988); in turn, the epoch of economic reforms should be seen as a progressive individualization of social spaces (e.g., Davis 2000; Farquhar 2002; Yan 2003). In the 1980s, there existed strong reactions to the Maoist mode of life and knowledge, which had allowed very little individual autonomy or personal freedom. In order to be what one must be in the Maoist society, one would have to wear a collective coat, tailored by the *we*, the masses of the people. There was indeed an existential crisis during the Cultural Revolution (1966–1976) that seemed to have choked the life out of the individual. However, from the late 1990s onward, little has been heard about the Maoist past; instead, a new positivity has developed, whose attention has become fixed on the modern Other.

A new mode of massification—one of *serialization* and *molecularization*—has been made possible by means of statistical surveys and popular opinion polls (cf. Baudrillard 1998). During the Maoist years, the physical gathering of the masses had to be brought to the eyes of each and every person in order to demonstrate the existence of *collective will* as a historical agent. Mass campaigns were the mobilizing movements, since the collective will would have to be demonstrated by the *collection* of individual bodies, visible and physically palpable, for the political struggles. An individual was part of such movements because he or she was forced to join the crowds on the street, shouting slogans together with other faceless comrades while waving their arms or shaking their fists in the air. This was the Maoist massification; it was physical and violent. What is happening *now* is different. Collectivity is no longer, and does not need to be, *visible* in real terms; instead, it serializes and molecularizes individuals into a new kind of mass, making them strangers to their neighbors and even to themselves. During the Maoist years, collectivity meant being gathered together in the street. Today, it is the opposite: collectivity exists only in *virtuality*. Everywhere in the growing urban spaces more and more new apartment buildings, lofty and imposing, have appeared, housing the category of white-collar workers, a middle class that constitutes a new collectivity, although its membership can be verified only through official statistics. These workers are recognized not among themselves but by *a third party* that is objectifying social reality and compartmentalizing people into the categories of a new world. By fitting the definition of "a 5,000 a month" type of person, one is connected to an existence of corporeality, officially identifiable and statistically classified.

By means of such an objectification of self, everyone is massified into a serial or serialized number and, subsequently, into a molecularized pigeon-hole of society. There is no *organic* connection between a person and his or her group; a person is truly living in "the imagined community" of a statistical estimation. This is perhaps not unlike what Sartre described in *Critique of Dialectical Reason* (2004, 256–269): a group of unrelated people getting onto a bus, with different destinies or intentions and of differing backgrounds and experiences, can be viewed from the eye of a third party, if not the Communist Party, as a group or a collectivity, although it can be only a serial relationship without any common individuality. The unity of the group, objectified and objectifiable from a third-party perspective, is a result of their happening to be on the bus; there is no common project or commonality among them other than being in the same place at the same time. This is precisely what is happening today in the newly built high-rise apartment buildings across the vast urban space of the People's Republic: individuals have bought new apartments and moved in as *serialized individuals*; there is no commonality among them except for their physical adjacency and proximity. There is, insofar as the People's Republic is concerned, an emergent *serial structure* of social existence, resembling and reinforced by the serialized individuality of dwelling in a new apartment building. It is a process of massification in molecularizing individual experiences in order to make them serial rather than collective.

Molecularization does not simply mean that everyone now has his or her spacious apartment for privacy; instead, it means the coming of age in statistical or quantitative surveillance of individuals through the diversifying strategies of modern technology. Telephone, television, the Internet, and increasing possibilities of individualistic connectivity have now provided security and justification for the molecularization of personal life. Contrary to the argument that the individual has been given a greater space for privacy and autonomy after the collapse of the Maoist order of things, what is happening today is simply that the masses have come to be governed by a different technology of modernity that involves self-control and self-management. While it is true that today one can connect to others by switching on the computer or picking up the phone, rather than shouting in the street, one must realize that this change in the mode of life and knowledge allows for a different possibility of governance. In this virtual world of connectivity rather than collectivity, as defined in the Maoist sense, one would calculate everything, measuring his or her life against the lives of others. This massification has given birth to a new mode of affinity and association: one does not have to *be* with other people in order to *belong* to their group. The bus, used as a metaphor by Sartre for the unity of serialized individuals, has become a virtual one, statistical and yet real.

An epistemological break seems to have set the Maoist years apart from the present age. The class-classificatory scheme that required every person to be massified in social struggles is no longer present, nor is the mechanism of qualitative differentiations that generated massive violence against class enemies, real or alleged. Today, computation and categorization have produced massification in abstract generalities; it is the statistical figuration and configuration that have placed people into their serialized and molecularized social grids. An individual, being individualized, is no longer considered a person with a reified social worth; he or she has now been reduced to a number, a salary scale, a certain height or weight, a bra size, etc. The urban scene of collective violence has been replaced by the increasing height of urban space, in which various salary groups dwell. A social group that earns a similar salary should possess a "collective consciousness" for the sake of sampling surveys. "Ah, as it says, I should belong to the middle class now," someone exclaimed on the Internet, "although I have not yet got a good car. It is old, and it is not the kind of car that men like me should be driving." This identification with other people by means of a statistical category has paved the way for a corporeal self-understanding. If one would like to argue that all social solidarities are fictional, that of the People's Republic today has become a statistical fiction, as imaginative and lively as any such solidarities could ever have been.

Commenting on the golden years of historical consciousness of the nineteenth century, C. S. Lewis once remarked, "What is new usually wins its way by disguising itself as old."[3] In Lewis's day, the past was not only "a foreign country" but also a place of worship and ancestral austerity that was viewed as holy and sacred. Today, while we are parading into a new age of global corporeality, this remark could be reversed: *What is old usually wins its way by disguising itself as new.* That is, what is "new" or thought of as "new" is often quite old. This is perhaps the signification of the latest trends in the vast province of the People's Republic: old schemes of mentality and sentimentality have come to constitute a *new world* of narcissistic corporeality. The goals and principles of the Maoist years have become "obsolete" in both governmental and scholarly conceptions. Mao's picture is still hanging from the rearview mirror of many taxicabs in Beijing, but, according to the mind of the state, the Maoist past has become a far more remote region than any foreign country in the world. This is a sentimentalized "coming of age" in modernity that is making itself felt as a mirage effect of global transformation in which it is almost impossible to distinguish what is old from what is new and vice versa.

3. Quoted in Hodgen (1964, 17).

An intellectual disjuncture, however, can perhaps illustrate this peculiar *history of sentimentality* experienced by a new leviathan on the global path. In the social science field of the People's Republic, as we have shown, the Weberian spirit, together with the spirit of transnational capitalism, succeeded in winning the sociological battle for comprehending one's self and the world. If a history of sentimentality may thus be written, it is appropriate to bring into view the epistemological contrast between Hegel/Marx and Kant/Weber (Giddens 1971, 195):

> The radical neo-Kantian position which Weber accepts takes as its premise the complete logical separation of factual and normative propositions. In Weber's work, the necessary corollary of this is the postulate of the irreducibility of competing values. It is this epistemological position which Weber takes as separating his perspective most decisively from that of Marx: Marx's work, whatever its undoubted merits, involves the commitment to the 'scientific' ethic of 'ultimate ends', and thus entails the acceptance of a 'total' conception of history. The conception of charisma, and the role which it plays in Weber's work, manifests Weber's conviction that historical development cannot be interpreted in terms of a rational scheme which expresses what is normatively valid. For Weber, science cannot answer the question: 'Which of the warring Gods should we serve?'

Although this contrast may be a bit too sweeping and all-embracing, it is still possible to make a distinction: a history of disjunctive sentimentality can be traced by following the epistemological difference between the neo-Kantian/Weberian spirit and the Hegelian/Marxist dialectic in comprehending history and subject. Although neither of these theoretical positions was indigenous to the world of China, both were used to express an epistemological opposition between the two historical moments in and of the People's Republic. During the Maoist years, Hegel was most probably read only to provide a preliminary philosophical background for a proper reading of Marx's work. Nevertheless, it was a *necessary* background for understanding the idea of dialectical reason, which generated a different vision of the world.

Despite its disturbance to the popular ears today, Hegel's voice continues to tremble behind the loud announcement claiming finally to have discovered the truth of development—*the corporeal truth* of materialistic development—for which the epistemological equivalence of the phenomenal with the statistical or the quantifiable has been made. In such a new "truthful" world, there should be no room to accommodate the Hegelian notion of essence or the unity of being. In the corporeal world of the present age, there are only "difference and repetition," not identity and essence (see, e.g., Deleuze 1994). As Michel Foucault once said, "[W]hether through logic or through epistemology, whether through Marx or through Nietzsche, our entire epoch struggles to disengage itself from Hegel" (quoted in Descombes 1980, 12). It is striking that this intellectual farewell to Hegel, made in Paris at the time when Mao was about to pass away, came to coincide with the embarkation of China upon a path that led to a new mode of life and governance. Few, either within or outside the People's Republic, would be willing to pay a visit to the Hegelian cemetery these days. Nonetheless, it seems useful, from time to time, to bring back the Hegelian spirit as a road lamp so that one can see better the mind of the present age.

> Essence denotes the unity of being, its identity throughout change. Precisely what is this unity or identity? It is not a permanent and fixed substratum, but a process wherein everything copes with its inherent contradictions and unfolds itself as a result. Conceived in this way, identity contains its opposite, difference, and involves a self-differentiation and an ensuing unification. Every existence precipitates itself into negativity and remains what it is only by negating this negativity. It splits up into a diversity of states and relations to other things, which are originally foreign to it, but which become part of its proper self when they are brought under the working influence of its essence. Identity is thus the same as the 'negative totality,' which was shown to be the structure of reality; it is 'the same as Essence.'
>
> Thus conceived, the essence describes the actual process of reality. 'The contemplation of everything that *is* shows, in itself, that in its self-identity it is self-contradictory and self-different, and in its variety or contradiction, self-identical; it is in itself this movement of transition of one of these determinations into the other, just because each in itself is its own opposite.' (Marcuse [1941] 1954, 146)

"'Contradiction is the root of all movement and life,' all reality is self-contradictory. Motion especially, external movement as well as self movement, is nothing but 'existing contradiction'" (Marcuse [1941] 1954, 147). A younger generation growing up on the ruins of the Maoist revolution has failed to notice a similar message that Mao delivered earlier in his famous 1937 essay, "On Contradiction": "The law of contradiction in things, that is, the law of the unity of the opposites, is the basic law of materialistic dialectics" (Mao 2001, 85). By a dim light emanating from the Hegelian lamp, one would perhaps be able to see a distorted refraction of our time in a historical shadow.

All things are contradictory in themselves.

For Hegel, who stood on the hill of a falling or failing philosophy, reality was a negative totalizing *spirituality*, whereas for Marx it was a negative totalizing *materiality* in the sense that historical contradictions in terms of class struggles would inevitably revolutionize the existing mode of production—as a structural totality of productive relations characteristic of each stage of historical development. After the failure of the Maoist revolution, a recoiling drama of theoretical rebound played itself out: the idea of the "negation of negation" as the dialectical movement of history/subject gave way almost completely to the neo-Kantian/Weberian analytical reason, which has become both the effect and the cause of the *re-formation* of the People's Republic into a new leviathan. Contradiction is no longer taken as a precondition for societal or human development; identity is no longer conceived, inherently or necessarily, as a self-differentiation and a self-elopement. Instead, the identity of self or *being in the world* in general has become a corporeal movement in and through the serialized individual, statistically measurable and calculated. If "the real is the rational, the rational is the real," as Hegel proclaimed in *Philosophy of Right*, one might say of today: the corporeal is the rational, the rational is the corporeal. The very essence that sustains the life of such global corporeality is the statistical or econometric datum, which has "falsified," to adopt a Popperian word, the Marxist or Maoist phantom.

Capital, transnational or otherwise, is palpable and tangible, and yet flexible and cunning. The "happy consciousness" of the present age is the happiness of a consciousness that is not aware of its own condition of emergence. This is, of course, not meant to imply that the elephantine world of the People's Republic does not consist of historical contradictions or socio-political conflicts. On the contrary, there are many instances that can demonstrate the existence of such conflicts in the country's drastic developmental advances. However, in view of its mentality and sentimentality, a different mode of reasoning, statistical and corporeal, has met the modern or postmodern pace. Dressed up in a new suit and examining itself in a global looking glass, the People's Republic no longer recognizes the contradictions and conflicts *as such*. A new sentimentality has emerged out of an old set of conceptual schemes. In this "long march," heroic and adventurous, one can see that the power of large numbers, albeit articulated in the technical language of probabilistic theory, has become the master theory of a corporeal world, and that the notion of chance, encompassing ideas such as luck and fate, is *deterministic* in its final use.

For the state of the People's Republic, inferential statistics has become almost a "generative grammar" for making truth claims about development and society, whereas descriptive statistics has come to be used as a forecasting slot machine. A greater lesson from such a journey is that the world will be more globalized as it continues to corporealize. This coupling of corporealization and globalization, in and for the People's Republic, has occurred only because the statistical adventure took place on the ruins of the Maoist revolution. Beneath the observable waves of a sea change, there arrived the neo-Kantian/Weberian social science model, which was supposed to be objective and scientific in its analytical operation. The Hegelian/Marxist vision of history/subject would be considered confusing and self-contradictory, for it would make no sense to the scholar-official mind, which is chiefly concerned with developmental strategies for managing society. "*Economics is not philosophy*," as Zou, the Princeton professor of economics, proclaimed. One could also say that it is nothing but a particular form of global econometrics reified in a specific locale, where a graveyard for both Hegel and Marx, as well many others including Mao himself, was prepared as their historical destiny.

No place is better than the classroom to observe the rise of science as an essential social logic, which in this case has often been discussed in terms of the neo-Kantian/Weberian progression, no matter whether this discussion is truthful to the original articulation or intention. For a younger generation of sociologists and social scientists in general, Hegel's *Phenomenology of Spirit* would not be part of their required reading, nor would Marx's *German Ideology* or *Capital*. Instead, Auguste Comte, Emile Durkheim, Carl Popper, and especially Max Weber—and perhaps also Talcott Parsons, Pierre Bourdieu, and some other newer theorists—make up the core of their *new* reading list. The works of these authors are a fundamental requirement for young sociologists, who, *at the same time*, are taking a two-year course in probability theory and statistics. Hegel and Marx have indeed been buried, but, standing not too far away from their graveyard, we might wonder whether we can have implicit confidence in all the corporealistic assertions made by the neo-positivists about our world. Even if dialectical utopia was indeed a nightmare, unreal and not verifiable by statistical science, can we give up dreaming or transcendental contemplation entirely as a sociological remedy to avoid having another one?

Acknowledgments

I am deeply indebted to those who, on different occasions, have reviewed this manuscript. One does not always know how one's dues should be repaid, as genuine intellectual appreciation is often unidentified. I therefore wish to express my thankfulness to the anonymous reviewers, who have earned by deepest respect and to whom I owe a debt of gratitude. I sincerely hope that my appreciation of your generous support is evident in the efforts that have gone into my writing. This volume could not have been published without your encouragement and suggestions.

I also want to take this opportunity to convey my gratitude to the Department of Anthropology at Berkeley, where colleagues and students have continued to provide me with an enlightening environment of intellectual inspiration. In particular, I wish to thank Laura Nader, Paul Rabinow, and Aihwa Ong, who have shown support in different ways. Dr. Marion Berghahn has played a crucial role in the publication of this study, and I am grateful for her assistance and valuable advice. Shawn Kendrick, my copyeditor, has done a first-rate job in helping me finalize the book.

REFERENCES

Althusser, L. 1970. "From *Capital* to Marx's Philosophy." Pp. 12–69 in Althusser and Balibar 1970.

_____. 1971. *Lenin and Philosophy and Other Essays.* New York: Monthly Review Press.

Althusser, L., and E. Balibar. 1970. *Reading Capital.* Trans. B. Brewster. London: New Left Books.

Aristotle. 1979. *Aristotle's Metaphysics.* Trans. with commentaries and glossary by H. G. Apostle. Grinnell, IA: Peripatetic Press.

Aron, R. 1970. *Main Currents in Sociological Thought.* Vol. 2: *Pareto, Weber, Durkheim.* New York: Penguin.

Baker, H. D. R. 1979. *Chinese Family and Kinship.* London: Macmillan.

Bakhtin, M. M. 1986. "The Problem of Speech Genre." Pp. 65–102 in *Speech Genre and Other Late Essays,* ed. C. Emerson and M. Holquist. Austin: University of Texas Press.

Banister, J. 1987. *China's Changing Population.* Stanford, CA: Stanford University Press.

Barth, F., A. Gingrich, R. Parkin, and S. Silverman. 2005. *One Discipline, Four Ways: British, German, French, and American Anthropology.* Chicago, IL: University of Chicago Press.

Barthes, R. 1973. *Mythologies.* London: Paladin.

_____. 1983. *The Fashion System.* New York: Hill and Wang.

Baudrillard, J. 1983. *Simulations.* New York: Semiotext(e).

_____. 1998. *The Consumer Society: Myths and Structures.* London: Sage.

Berger, P. L., and T. Luckmann. 1967. *The Social Construction of Reality: A Treatise in the Sociology of Knowledge.* New York: Anchor Books.

Berreman, G. 1981. *The Politics of Truth: Essays in Critical Anthropology.* New Delhi: South Asian Publisher.

Boon, J. A. 1982. *Other Tribes, Other Scribes: Symbolic Anthropology in the Comparative Study of Cultures, Histories, Religions, and Texts.* Cambridge: Cambridge University Press.

Braudel, F. 1980. *On History.* Chicago, IL: Chicago University Press.

———. 1981. *The Structures of Everyday Life: Civilization and Capitalism, 15th–18th Century.* Vol. 1. New York: Harper & Row.

Burns, J. P. 1988. *Political Participation in Rural China.* Berkeley: University of California Press.

Burtt, E. A., ed. 1939. *The English Philosophers from Bacon and Mill.* New York: Random House.

Carr, D. 1986. *Time, Narrative, and History: An Essay in the Philosophy of History.* Bloomington: Indiana University Press.

Cassirer, E. 1944. *An Essay on Man: An Introduction to a Philosophy of Human Culture.* New Haven, CT: Yale University Press.

Chan, A., R. Madsen, and J. Unger. 1992. *Chen Village under Mao and Deng.* Berkeley: University of California Press.

Clifford, J. 1986. "Introduction: Partial Truth." Pp. 1–26 in Clifford and Marcus 1986.

———. 1988. *The Predicament of Culture: Twentieth-Century Ethnography, Literature, and Art.* Cambridge, MA: Harvard University Press.

Clifford, J., and G. E. Marcus, eds. 1986. *Writing Culture: The Poetics and Politics of Ethnography.* Berkeley: University of California Press.

Cole, J. 2000. *The Power of Large Numbers: Population, Politics, and Gender in Twentieth-Century France.* Ithaca, NY: Cornell University Press.

Collingwood, R. G. 1960. *The Idea of Nature.* Oxford: Oxford University Press.

———. 1971. *The New Leviathan: Or Man, Society, Civilization and Barbarism.* New York: Thomas Y. Crowell.

Corbett, G. G. 2000. *Number.* Cambridge: Cambridge University Press.

Dangdai Zhongguo de tongji shiye [Government Statistics in Contemporary China]. 1990. Beijing: Chinese Social Science Press.

Davis, D. S. 1995. "Introduction: Urban China." Pp. 1–19 in *Urban Spaces in Contemporary China: The Potential for Autonomy and Community in Post-Mao China,* ed. D. S. Davis, R. Kraus, B. Naughton, and E. J. Perry. Washington, DC: Woodrow Wilson Center.

———, ed. 2000. *The Consumer Revolution in Urban China.* Berkeley: University of California Press.

Dawkins, R. 1989. *The Selfish Gene.* Oxford: Oxford University Press.

Deleuze, G. 1983. *Nietzsche and Philosophy.* Trans. H. Tomlinson. New York: Columbia University Press.

———. 1994. *Difference and Repetition.* Trans. P. Patton. New York: Columbia University Press.

Descombes, V. 1980. *Modern French Philosophy.* Cambridge: Cambridge University Press.

———. 1993. *The Barometer of Modern Reason: On the Philosophies of Current Events.* Oxford: Oxford University Press.

Desrosières, A. 1998. *The Politics of Large Numbers: A History of Statistical Reasoning.* Trans. C. Naish. Cambridge, MA: Harvard University Press.

Dosse, F. 1997. *History of Structuralism*. Vol. 1: *The Rising Sign, 1945–1966*. Minneapolis: University of Minnesota Press.

Duara, P. 1997. *Rescuing History from the Nation: Questioning Narratives of Modern China*. Chicago, IL: University of Chicago Press.

Durkheim, E. 1938. *The Rules of Sociological Method*. New York: Free Press.

———. 1966. *Suicide: A Study in Sociology*. New York: Free Press.

———. 1984. *The Division of Labor in Society*. New York: Free Press.

Eagleton, T. 1994. "Ideology and Its Vicissitudes in Western Marxism." Pp. 179–225 in *Mapping Ideology*, ed. S. Žižek. London: Verso.

Evans-Pritchard, E. E. 1937. *Witchcraft, Oracles, and Magic among the Azande*. Oxford: Clarendon.

Fabian, J. 1983. *Time and the Other: How Anthropology Makes Its Object*. New York: Columbia University Press.

Fang, H. 1997. *"Wu shijian jing" yu shenghuo shijie zhong de "zhenshi": Xicun nongmin tudi gaige shiqi shehui shenghuo de jiyi* ["Non-Event State" and "Truth" in the Life-World: Memories of Social Life of Xicun Peasants during the Period of Land Reform]. Working Paper Series No. 1. Beijing: Research Center for Oral History of Social Life, Beijing University.

Fardon, R., ed. 1990. *Localizing Strategies: Regional Traditions of Ethnographic Writing*. Edinburgh: Scottish Academic Press.

Farquhar, J. 2002. *Appetites: Food and Sex in Post-Socialist China*. Durham, NC: Duke University Press.

Feenberg, A. 1995. *Alternative Modernity: The Technological Turn in Philosophy and Social Theory*. Berkeley: University of California Press.

Fei, X.-T. 1992. *From the Soil: The Foundations of Chinese Society*. Berkeley: University of California Press.

Foucault, M. 1965. *Madness and Civilization: A History of Insanity in the Age of Reason*. New York: Vintage Books.

———. 1970. *The Order of Things: An Archaeology of the Human Sciences*. London: Tavistock.

———. 1977. *Discipline and Punish: The Birth of the Prison*. New York: Pantheon.

———. 1997. *The Politics of Truth*. New York: Semiotext(e).

Freedman, M. 1958. *Lineage Organization in Southeastern China*. London: Athlone.

Fung, Y.-L. 1948. *A Short History of Chinese Philosophy*. New York: Free Press.

Geertz, C. 1988. *Works and Lives: The Anthropologist as Author*. Stanford, CA: Stanford University Press.

———. 2000. *Available Light: Anthropological Reflections on Philosophical Topics*. Princeton, NJ: Princeton University Press.

Gennep, A. Van. 1960. *The Rites of Passage*. Chicago, IL: Chicago University Press.

Giddens, A. 1971. *Capitalism and Modern Social Theory: An Analysis of the Writings of Marx, Durkheim and Max Weber*. Cambridge: Cambridge University Press.

Goody, J., ed. 1968. *Literacy in Traditional Societies*. Cambridge: Cambridge University Press.

———. 1977. *The Domestication of the Savage Mind*. Cambridge: Cambridge University Press.

Gupta, A., and J. Ferguson, eds. 1997. *Anthropological Locations: Boundaries and Grounds of a Field Science.* Berkeley: University of California Press.

Hacking, I. 1975. *The Emergence of Probability.* Cambridge: Cambridge University Press.

————. 1990. *The Taming of Chance.* Cambridge: Cambridge University Press.

Hallpike, C. 1979. *The Foundation of Primitive Thought.* Oxford: Blackwell.

Hegel, G. W. F. 1956. *The Philosophy of History.* New York: Dover Publications.

Hertz, E. 1998. *The Trading Crowd: An Ethnography of the Shanghai Stock Market.* Cambridge: Cambridge University Press.

Hinton, W. 1990. *The Great Reversal: The Privatization of China, 1978–1989.* New York: Monthly Review Press.

Hobbes, T. [1651] 1962. *Leviathan: Or the Matter, Form, and Power of a Commonwealth Ecclesiastical and Civil.* New York: Collier Books.

Hodgen, M. T. 1964. *Early Anthropology in the Sixteenth and Seventeenth Century.* Philadelphia: University of Pennsylvania Press.

Hoffmeister, J., ed. [1936] 1974. *Dokumente zu Hegels Entwicklung.* Stuttgart-Bad Cannstatt: Frommann.

Hsu, F. L. K. 1948. *Under the Ancestors' Shadow: Chinese Culture and Personality.* New York: Columbia University Press.

Huang, R.-Y. 1997. *Wanli shi wu nian* [The Fifteenth Year of Wanli]. Beijing: Sanlian Press.

James, A., J. Hockey, and A. Dawson, eds. 1997. *After Writing Culture: Epistemology and Praxis in Contemporary Anthropology.* London: Routledge.

Kierkegaard, S. 1962. *The Present Age and of the Difference between a Genius and an Apostle.* Trans. Alexander Dru. New York: Harper Torchbooks.

Kornai, J. 1980. *The Economics of Shortage.* Amsterdam: North-Holland.

Laclau, E., and C. Mouffe. 1985. *Hegemony and Socialist Strategy: Towards a Radical Democratic Politics.* London: Verso.

Lee, C.-K. 1998. *Gender and the South China Miracle: Two Worlds of Factory Women.* Berkeley: University of California Press.

Lee, H.-Y. 1978. *The Politics of the Chinese Cultural Revolution: A Case Study.* Berkeley: University of California Press.

Lenzer, G., ed. 1975. *Auguste Comte and Positivism: The Essential Writings.* Chicago, IL: University of Chicago Press.

Levenson, J. R. 1968. *Confucian China and Its Modern Fate: A Trilogy.* Berkeley: University of California Press.

Lévi-Strauss, C. 1966. *The Savage Mind.* Chicago, IL: University of Chicago Press.

————. 1969. *The Raw and the Cooked: Introduction to a Science of Mythology.* Vol. 1. New York: Harper & Row.

Lévy-Bruhl, L. 1975. *The Notebooks on Primitive Mentality.* New York: Harper & Row.

Li, H.-C., and Y.-D. Mo. 1993. *Zhongguo tongji shi* (A History of China's Statistics). Beijing: China Statistics Press.

Little, D. 1989. *Understanding Peasant China: Case Studies in the Philosophy of Social Sciences.* New Haven, CT: Yale University Press.

Liu, X. 2000. *In One's Own Shadow: An Ethnographic Account of the Condition of Post-Reform Rural China.* Berkeley: University of California Press.

_____. 2002. *The Otherness of Self: A Genealogy of the Self in Contemporary China.* Ann Arbor: University of Michigan Press.

Liu, X.-B. 1997. *Chenmo de daduoshu* [The Silent Majority]. Beijing: China Youth Press.

Lobkowicz, N. 1967. *Theory and Practice: History of a Concept from Aristotle to Marx.* Notre Dame, IN: University of Notre Dame Press.

Locke, J. 1959. *An Essay Concerning Human Understanding.* 2 vols. New York: Dover Publications.

Lu, S.-H. 1989. *Shehui tongjixue* [Social Statistics]. Beijing: Peking University Press.

Ma, B.-G. 1994. *Makesi zhuyi jingdian zuojia tongji sixiang yanjiu* [A Study of Statistical Thought of the Marxist Classic Scholars]. Beijing: China Statistics Press.

MacIntyre, A. 1968. *Marxism and Christianity.* Notre Dame, IN: University of Notre Dame Press.

Madsen, R. 1995. *China and the American Dream.* Berkeley: University of California Press.

Mao, T.-T. 2001. *Selected Readings from the Works of Mao Tse-Tung, 1926–1963.* Honolulu: University Press of the Pacific.

Marcus, G. E. 1998. *Ethnography through Thick and Thin.* Princeton, NJ: Princeton University Press.

Marcus, G. E., and M. M. J. Fischer. 1986. *Anthropology as Cultural Critique: An Experimental Moment in the Human Sciences.* Chicago, IL: University of Chicago Press.

Marcuse, H. [1941] 1954. *Reason and Revolution: Hegel and the Rise of Social Theory.* Oxford: Oxford University Press.

Marx, K. 1939. *The German Ideology.* New York: International Publishers.

Mills, C. W. 1959. *The Sociological Imagination.* Oxford: Oxford University Press.

Nora, P. 1989. "Between Memory and History." *Representations* 26 (Spring): 7–25.

Norris, C. 1996. *Reclaiming Truth: Contribution to a Critique of Cultural Relativism.* Durham, NC: Duke University Press.

Ong, A., and S. J. Collier. 2005. *Global Assemblages: Technology, Politics, and Ethics as Anthropological Problems.* Oxford: Blackwell Publishing.

Ong, W. J. 1982. *Orality and Literacy: The Technologizing of the Word.* London: Methuen.

Porter, T. M. 1986. *The Rise of Statistical Thinking, 1820–1900.* Princeton, NJ: Princeton University Press.

Rabinow, P. 1977. *Reflections on Fieldwork in Morocco.* Berkeley: University of California Press.

_____. 1986. "Representations Are Social Facts: Modernity and Post-Modernity in Anthropology." Pp. 234–261 in Clifford and Marcus 1986.

_____. 1996. *Essays on the Anthropology of Reason.* Princeton, NJ: Princeton University Press.

_____. 1999. *French DNA: Trouble in Purgatory.* Chicago, IL: University of Chicago Press.

_____. 2003. *Anthropos Today: Reflections on Modern Equipment.* Princeton, NJ: Princeton University Press.

Rawski, T. G. 2001. "What's Happening to China's GDP Statistics?" *China Economic Review* 12, no. 4: 347–354.

Redding, S. G. 1990. *The Spirit of Chinese Capitalism.* New York: W. De Gruyter.

Riesman, D. 1961. *The Lonely Crowd: A Study of the Changing American Character.* New Haven, CT: Yale University Press.

Russell, B. 1945. *A History of Western Philosophy and Its Connection with Political and Social Circumstances from the Earliest Times to the Present Day.* New York: Simon and Schuster.

Sahlins, M. 1977. *The Use and Abuse of Biology: An Anthropological Critique of Sociobiology.* London: Tavistock.

_____. 1985. *Islands of History.* London: Tavistock.

Sangren, P. S. 1988. "Rhetoric and the Authority of Ethnography: Postmodernism and the Social Reproduction of Texts." *Current Anthropology* 29, no. 3: 415–424.

Sartre, J.-P. 1988. *"What Is Literature?" and Other Essays.* Cambridge, MA: Harvard University Press.

_____. 2004. *Critique of Dialectical Reason.* Ed. and trans. Alan Sheridan-Smith. Vol. 1. London: Verso.

Schram, S. 1989. *The Thought of Mao Tse-Tung.* Cambridge: Cambridge University Press.

Schurmann, F. 1966. *Ideology and Organization in Communist China.* Berkeley: University of California Press.

Schutz, A. 1967. *The Phenomenology of the Social World.* Evanston, IL: Northwestern University Press.

Shue, V. 1980. *Peasant China in Transition: The Dynamics of Development toward Socialism, 1949–1965.* Berkeley: University of California Press.

_____. 1988. *The Reach of the State: Sketches of the Chinese Body Politic.* Stanford, CA: Stanford University Press.

Shuzi Zhongguo: Zhongguo fei baomixing shuzi duben [China in Numbers: A Notebook for Reading China's Statistical Figures]. 2002. Beijing: Guangming Daily Press.

Smith, A. H. [1898] 2001. *Chinese Characteristics.* London: Revell.

Sperber, D. 1985. *On Anthropological Knowledge.* Cambridge: Cambridge University Press.

Stocking, G. W. 1992. *The Ethnographer's Magic and Other Essays in the History of Anthropology.* Madison: University of Wisconsin Press.

Thompson, E. P. 1995. *The Poverty of Theory: Or an Orrery of Errors.* New ed. London: Merlin Press.

Townsend, J. R. 1969. *Political Participation in Communist China.* Berkeley: University of California Press.

Volosinov, V. N. 1973. *Marxism and the Philosophy of Language.* New York: Seminar Press.

Wakeman, F., Jr. 1973. *History and Will: Philosophical Perspectives of Mao Tse-Tung's Thought.* Berkeley: University of California Press.

Walder, A. G. 1986. *Communist Neo-Traditionalism: Work and Authority in Chinese Industry.* Berkeley: University of California Press.

Wang, Q.-H. 1997. *Yaoshi* [The Key]. Beijing: Zuojia.

Weber, M. 1951. *The Religion of China.* New York: Free Press.

_____. 1958. *The Protestant Ethic and the Spirit of Capitalism.* New York: Charles Scribner's Sons.

White, H. V. 1973. *Metahistory: The Historical Imagination in Twentieth-Century Europe.* Baltimore, MD: Johns Hopkins University Press.

Whyte, M. K., and W. L. Parish. 1984. *Urban Life in Contemporary China.* Chicago, IL: University of Chicago Press.

Wilson, B. R., ed. 1970. *Rationality.* Oxford: Blackwell.

Wolf, M. 1985. *Revolution Postponed: Women in Contemporary China.* Stanford, CA: Stanford University Press.

Yan, Y.-X. 2003. *Private Life under Socialism: Love, Intimacy, and Family Change in a Chinese Village, 1949–1999.* Stanford, CA: Stanford University Press.

Yuan, W., R.-E. Ren, and Y.-X. Gao, eds. 2000. *Shidao yong cun: Jinian zhuming tongjixuejia Dai Shiguang jiaoshou* [Always a Master: To the Memory of a Great Statistician, Professor Dai Shiguang]. Beijing: Economic Science Press.

Yue, W. 1994. *Tongji renshilun* [Statistical Epistemology]. Beijing: China Statistics Press.

Zhongguo shehui zhuyi yu tongji shuzi [Chinese Socialism and Statistical Data]. 1991. Beijing: Renmin University Press.

Žižek, S. 1989. *The Sublime Object of Ideology.* London: Verso.

Index

www.ingramcontent.com/pod-product-compliance
Lightning Source LLC
Chambersburg PA
CBHW060037030426
42334CB00019B/2367